When Harry
Hit Sally

When Harry Hit Sally

UNDERSTANDING YOUR CHILD'S BEHAVIOUR

Andrea Clifford-Poston

SIMON &
SCHUSTER

London · New York · Sydney · Toronto

A CBS COMPANY

First published in Great Britain by Simon & Schuster UK Ltd, 2007
A CBS COMPANY

1 3 5 7 9 10 8 6 4 2

Simon & Schuster UK Ltd
Africa House
64–78 Kingsway
London WC2B 6AH

www.simonsays.co.uk

Simon & Schuster Australia
Sydney

A CIP catalogue record for this book
is available from the British Library

ISBN: 978-1-84737-040-2

Typeset by M Rules
Printed and bound in Great Britain by
CPI Mackays

For Sean who hears, even in the silence

and

with three cheers for Murray N. Cox F.R.C.P. (1931–1997)
who was a good thing

Contents

Contents

Contents

Acknowledgements

I have written this book and I take full responsibility for the views expressed in it. However, there is a sense in which I cannot call it 'my own'. It is born of thousands of conversations throughout my life: with family, friends, teachers, lecturers, supervisors, colleagues, students and pupils and, of course, the families with whom I have worked. The field of literature, people in bus queues, on trains, taxi drivers etc., have also made their contributions – the list is endless. I am grateful to them all for enriching my life and helping me to shape my ideas. Nevertheless, there are certain specific contributions to this book which must be acknowledged.

My greatest debt is, of course, to the families who have allowed me to be part of their history for a period. They have kept alive my sense of awe of what it means to be in a family. I have grown with each relationship and they have taught me much.

This is an expanded and updated version of my book *The Secrets of Successful Parenting – Understand What Your Child's Behaviour is Really Telling You*, which was published by How To Books Ltd. in 2001. I am grateful to all the parents and professionals who were kind enough to give me constructive criticism on the first book and to offer ideas for its development. Particular thanks to Ruth Walsh-Sewart.

Adam Phillips, who kindly agreed to write the Foreword, has inspired, supported and encouraged me professionally and personally throughout the writing of this book. At times, the reader may discern his dazzling creativity playing hokey-cokey with the text.

The idea for the book arose from a lecture at Dunnanie School (Bedales Pre-Prep) in Petersfield, Hampshire. I am grateful to Sarah Webster and her staff for their ongoing support and encouragement.

Sarah Adams, Veronica Austin, Cheryl Batt, Morris and Tina Clifford, Sarah Davis, Janice Finnemore, Lin Fitch, Liz George, Mandy Kelly, Barbara Le Ruez, Jenny Marlow, Lorraine Marshall, Elizabeth Roach, Tessa Smith, Nick Weeks, Fiona Windebank and Cary-Ann Young have all made valuable comments on early drafts of the book.

Penny Carter has typed and re-typed the manuscript; she has done so efficiently and professionally, meeting impossible deadlines with calm good humour.

My agent, Stephanie Ebdon (Paterson Marsh), has, as always, held the boat steady as I rocked about in a creative sea. And I am grateful to Kerri Sharp, my editor at Simon & Schuster, for her seemingly boundless enthusiasm and creativity about this project.

Finally, I thank my husband for his continuing struggles to understand my behaviour – although in doing so I realize I thank part of myself.

Foreword

The advantage of living in an 'Age of Experts' is that there is a great deal of useful, specialist knowledge about virtually everything we do. The drawback is that we don't always know where to find it or who we can trust. When it comes to bringing up children – one of the most demanding and essential things we ever do – this can be particularly troubling. Everyone has had their first lesson in child-rearing as a child, with the people who cared enough about them to bring them up. And everyone brings from their own childhood their own theories and strong feelings about what children do and don't need, many of which they are quite unaware of, but have very strong feelings about (i.e., everyone is unconsciously an expert on bringing up children, on how they themselves should have been brought up). And then when people become parents they are literally surrounded by information, as though society is at once keen to be helpful and reassuring about what is always something of a shock, but also perhaps slightly wary of people coming to their own conclusions about what is, after all, something all sorts of people have been doing for a very long time. It is quite possible for a new parent to wonder who their child belongs to: the state with its midwives and paediatricians, child psychologists and teachers; or the family with its always unusual history, and its great internal resource – the previous generation.

What this book shows us is that we don't have to choose – we can use what the best experts tell us, and be surprised by just how much we already know; and we don't have to be intimidated – we can use what we already know to work out what else might be good for us. Andrea Clifford-Poston who, as both a teacher and a child and family therapist is unusually well qualified to speak about these things, has, in other words, written a book that is both immensely (and fascinatingly) informative, and strangely evocative. It brings back memories, whilst stimulating new thoughts. And though it is alive to the very real difficulties of family life, it never forgets that people's pleasure in each other's company is the best reason for them to be together.

Everyone adores their children; that's the easy part. What many people find more difficult is liking them day by day, and finding an enjoyable way to live together with them. What this book does is show us just how practical we can be by not giving up on – by being attentive to – the subtle intelligence of our emotional lives. Children (and therefore adults) are, above all, communicative; their survival, and the quality of their life, depends upon their ways of letting people know what they need. But they depend on the adults to be more than willing to listen to what they have to say (a letter without an address is not a letter). And this means, as Clifford-Poston shows so vividly, being able to bear the child's feelings. This involves a good deal of uncertainty – the child doesn't need its parents to be experts on child-rearing, but just to be as attentive as they can be – and a certain amount of muddling through. Being a parent is not, as this book makes so clear, about getting it right, so much as it is about not fearing getting it wrong.

Perhaps one of the greatest virtues of Clifford-Poston's book is that, despite how much useful basic knowledge it contains, it never loses sight of the fact that every child, like every family, is something of an experiment. It is part of the spirit of her book to see this as worth celebrating. If this is (in the best sense) a self-help book with a sense of wonder, it is because the author knows things, and tells us what she knows, without ever being too knowing. She never makes us feel that to bring up our children well we really need to be her. Now that there is more information than ever before – with children and the whole notion of parenting being studied as never before – we tend to think

that it is only information that we need. In this book the reader will
certainly find the clearest accounts of up-to-date theories of child
development.

But I think there is something else in this book that is more difficult
to describe – more difficult to advertise – and that may be important,
especially in a book about children. And that is, the speaking voice you
can hear in the written words on the page. Listening to this book as
you read – and it is a book literally packed with helpful suggestions
about what to do when – you can hear the spirited affection of the
author's voice. And it is this tone of voice, which leaves us free to agree
and disagree with her, that makes the book so valuable. Between the
questions it asks, and the examples it gives, there is plenty of space for
the reader to think their own thoughts freely about what is, after all, an
endlessly intriguing subject: how children grow up without realizing
what they are doing because someone is looking after them.

Adam Phillips
Formerly Principal Child Psychotherapist,
Charing Cross Hospital, London

Introduction

'Children always know more than they can put into words: that distinguishes them from us adults, who usually put into words so much more than we know.'

(Lusseyran, J.)

'When we came to see you we thought there was a right way [of bringing up children] *... and we were doing it wrong. We expected you to tell us how to do it properly. At first we were angry when you didn't ... then we realized it didn't matter too much if we got it wrong, and then we began to think ... '*

(Father of seven-year-old)

As you, the reader, open this book, I am aware of your expectations of me, the author. This book is born of expectations: parents' expectations of children, parents' expectations of me, children's expectations of parents, and my expectations of parents. What has made you read it? Was it bought purposefully as a result of a troubling child, or idly discovered as you browsed through a shop? Was it recommended by a friend, by a professional who hoped it would reassure, or speak to you in a helpful way? Was it left 'lying around' by someone else, and picked up in a solitary, bored moment? And what are you expecting from it? And what will have to happen for you to feel your expectations have been fulfilled?

This book may differ from other books for parents in that it will focus less on how to control children's behaviour and more on how to understand it – 'the why' of children's behaviour. It is not my intention to provide 'the right way', or instant solutions to difficult child behaviours. What I hope to do is provide an ambiance in which we can think about children's behaviour together. Children have very limited ways of letting us know when they have a problem. If they do not have the language, or if they cannot formulate the problem, then they are likely to use behaviour as a way of communicating with the adults. The problem is, children often choose behaviour which does not accurately illustrate their worry. Then adults construe behaviour as difficult and inappropriate. For example, a four-year-old, hurt and angry by the arrival of a new baby in the family, is mistaken when they think the way to regain their parents' affection is to hit the baby. A vicious circle develops.

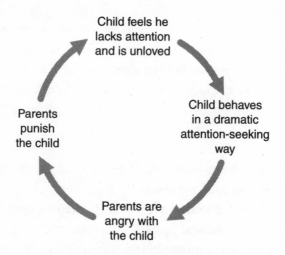

Once parents understand why a child is behaving the way they do, they are able to respond to and manage behaviour in a way that the child feels heard and understood – and consequently under less pressure to repeat inappropriate or undesirable behaviour. Parents are freed to put in place effective boundaries and discipline. The vicious circle can then be broken.

Child feels he lacks attention and is unloved

Child behaves in a dramatic
and attention-seeking way

Parents understand child feels he
lacks attention and is unloved

Parents help child to communicate in a
more appropriate way

Child feels loved

For example, a young mother came to see me distraught at the aggressive and demanding behaviour of her three-year-old son. She explained how he would sometimes stare intently at her after one of his aggressive outbursts, almost waiting to see what effect it had on her. Her five-year-old daughter suffered from cerebral palsy and needed more attention than most children of her age, but she felt she gave both children equal time and attention.

She looked startled when I asked her, *'How would James know when he'd made an impact on you?'*

She was silent for a moment and then her face lit up with relief, *'Well, that's it, that's just what it feels like . . . he's trying to make an impact!'*

James still had a limited vocabulary and he was unable to put into words his worry that his sister preoccupied Mummy's thoughts. He could see the impact she made on his mother.

Most parents desperately want to do their best and are bewildered, confused and hurt when in spite of doing their best, things seem to go 'wrong'. To think of children's behaviour only as 'good or bad', 'appropriate or inappropriate' and therefore only as something to be controlled, is to think of it in two dimensions and ignores what might be going on inside the child. Parents and child are placed at right angles to each other. By adding the third dimension, thinking about the child's behaviour as a communication, I hope this book will provide some understanding in the moments when the obvious may have become obscured, or when supportive relatives and friends are not available. More of this in Chapter 1.

A sound parental instinct?

Donald Winnicott, an eminent paediatrician and child psychoanalyst in the 1950s and 1960s, talked of adults as having 'a sound parental instinct'. What a perplexing suggestion that is! What we call our instincts are often a combination of inclinations, experiments and things we have learned from our own parents. Bringing up a child is a complicated business – a bit of an experiment. This book does not present a plan on how to raise a child, but rather gives suggestions to try which might work. Given time and space to think, most parents can identify with a 'sound instinct' that tells them what to do, i.e., an instant way to respond to their children's behaviour. The problem arises when there may be a mismatch between that 'sound instinct' and the needs of a particular child. Then a parent may begin to feel hopeless, to flounder, to feel they have no 'sound instinct' about parenting – and a strong feeling that 'the books don't work'!

So Donald Winnicott promotes the thought, *'What is the sound instinct of a parent and where does it come from?'*

Knowing and not knowing

'You're twenty-five, you think you know all about life, but, my God, this is something different.'
(Father of a ten-day-old baby)

How and where does one learn to be a parent? Where do 'sound instincts of parents' come from? We presume that we will automatically know how to parent. Our culture abounds with myths about what is 'good for children' and, like all myths, these myths about child-rearing are founded on reality. Children do need sufficient rest, but that does not mean that all children need the same rest! Child-rearing myths may reinforce the idea that parenting is a skill that can be taught, like training for a job or learning the rules of a game. Most people have a personal view of what is 'good for children'. Advice passed on (whether requested or not!) from grandparents to parents, from friends to friends, from professionals to parents, may reinforce the idea that there is only one right way of parenting.

A truculent eleven-year-old, Jack, was brought to see me by his harassed parents because of their difficulty in getting him to bed. They had been more than accommodating and reasonable in negotiating various bedtimes with him, but Jack always made a fuss. They were adamant that Jack had to have a set bedtime quoting a child's needs for adequate rest and sleep.

Maybe children are capable of taking what rest and sleep they need and the demand for a regular bedtime is perhaps more parent-need-based than child-need-based! This may be a good enough reason for having a set bedtime, but in Jack's case it was self-defeating. His parents agreed to a new regime whereby Jack would be allowed to stay up as late as he liked – although, after 8.30p.m., he had to be in a different room from his parents – on the condition that he was down for breakfast at 7.30a.m. It was pointed out to him firmly that should he be later than 7.30a.m., then that evening he would have to go to bed at a time chosen by his parents.

For the first three nights Jack stayed up well past his abilities, but always managed to be down for breakfast at 7.30a.m. Eventually he settled into a regular bedtime, coincidentally not much wide of the mark his parents would have set. By freeing themselves from a 'cultural myth', Jack's parents were able to remove the battle from one area of his management. They were freed to think more creatively about how to handle other difficulties of his early adolescence.

Maybe a sound parental instinct is less a question of information about children and more to do with an indefinable 'something else'. So what are you expecting from this book, to have more information about children or more faith in your ability to parent . . . or what?

So where do we learn to parent?

As children grow up in a family, they are learning how to be an adult, how to acquire adult skills, how to become a man, how to become a woman. We are all familiar with how small children will try to imitate their parents in order to be like them. I remember a three-year-old trying to 'help' his father to clear an outside drain. Returning to his mother in the kitchen, he was clearly rather fraught and het-up.

'Has Daddy cleared it?'

'No,' replied the little boy, *'it's still blocked. Blast it!'*

A mother found her four-year-old son sitting on his father's loo with a newspaper upside down on his lap. He fixed her with a steely gaze and said: *'Will you leave me in peace.'*

So in a family children are also learning how to parent. We learn to learn from our parents and we pick up a lot of other things along the way. What our parents did is absorbed over a number of years until it becomes an instinctive way of behaving.

Most people will have a desire to do some things differently from their parents, equally many people are surprised to find themselves doing it in the same way. It is distressing for parents, particularly for parents where there is a real desire not to, when they find themselves making the same or similar mistakes as their own parents. A child may feel humiliated at the parents' attempts to 'do the right thing', be it a contrived or theoretical attempt at creative play on the sitting room floor or anxiously attending all school functions. Our expectation is that we will be as good as parents as our own parents, better than our own parents, but also that we will make the same mistakes.

If you are a single parent

In the past there has been a strong emphasis on the idea that it was essential for a child to have both parents living together. Now we are beginning to think about the advantages as well as the disadvantages of having a single parent. Family structures are changing; there are lone parent families, adoptive families, same-sex parents, older parents, etc. (I am wondering as I write this book what kind of parents it will be useful for, and am hoping that I have found a philosophy appropriate for everyone.) It can be argued that in this fluid time for families, books on parenting are more important – and also more difficult to write – than they have ever been. There are now so many concepts of a family. There are so many people trying to make it work in so many different forms, races and cultures. And the relative success of so many of these families is comforting. In Chapters 9 and 10 I will explore in detail some of the most relevant issues around and advantages in single parenting.

A soft option?

While I was putting the finishing touches to this introduction I happened to see a snatch of a television programme on the pros and cons of smacking children. The audience discussion was dominated by a pro-smacker who argued forcibly that *'children push boundaries'* and a smack is often *'the only language they understand'.* He saw any other form of discipline as a *'soft option'* and the child *'turning you into the servant'.* It was interesting in that calling a smack 'a language' this parent was able to construe adult behaviour as a communication. Children's behaviour, on the other hand, was simply divided into 'good' or 'bad' and had to be controlled accordingly.

What is a soft option in child-rearing? Certainly not understanding children's behaviour as a communication. Children need clear, firm boundaries throughout their childhood to feel secure and in order to develop a sense of self, as a unique individual, separate from other people. A good boundary is strong, but flexible. Boundaries help to keep us safe and help us not to behave in ways which may bring us sadness and regret. Boundaries are also there to be crossed when it is appropriate. If you are clear as an adult about your own boundaries and how to maintain them, then you will find it easy to give your child boundaries. Of course children will 'push the boundaries' – that is how they learn exactly where a boundary lies. A smack will show a child a boundary, i.e., how far he can go, but it may do little for developing mutual respect. In my experience, smacking a child simply makes a child angry – and eventually that anger will be played out in one way or another. We will explore the implications of smacking more in Chapter 4.

Thinking about your child's behaviour as a communication, and trying to match your response is no 'soft option'. You are communicating to your child that you are trying to understand what they feel and that you can help them find a better way of expressing themselves. By communicating their feelings in an appropriate manner, children are not only respecting other people, but they also stand a much better chance of getting their needs met! It is hard work for you as a parent. It is very different from a 'soft option' where boundaries may depend very much on the parent's mood in the moment. When tired, stressed, angry, unwell or even just feeling indulgent, many parents will admit to 'giving in' rather than maintaining a boundary. As an isolated incident in family life, this should cause no problem, but as a way of life for a child, it can be disconcerting. The child who cannot rely on secure boundaries is likely to feel insecure and chaotic.

'For now sits expectation in the air . . .'

It is no coincidence that a pregnant couple are described as 'expectant'. Parents are expectant in a number of ways. In the first chapter I want to discuss these expectations, beginning with what the baby isn't! In further chapters I will discuss specific ordinary problems of childhood, sibling rivalry, schooling difficulties, lying and stealing, bullying, how these behaviours may be understood as a communication, and when parents should begin to regard these behaviours as 'extraordinary' and perhaps seek professional help. In the final chapters we will reflect upon the impact of divorce on children and some of the ordinary and extraordinary problems facing mothers who work outside the home.

Andrea Clifford-Poston
18th September 2006

CHAPTER 1

Great Expectations

– How Children Change Our Lives –

'Children are born into a world of expectations, and parents and children spend the rest of their lives trying to both extricate themselves from and to satisfy each other's inventions.'
(Andrea Clifford-Poston)

You did not choose your parents. You took what you got and made the best of it. But the fact that you did not choose them probably did not prevent you from having a wide range of expectations of them as you grew up. When these expectations were met, they were the best parents in the world. When they were not met, it is possible you were reduced to anger and sadness, feeling you had drawn the short straw of the most insensitive and unreceptive parents ever.

At the same time, your parents will have been expressing their joys and disappointments about you. You will have learned very quickly how to please and how to anger them. Whilst your expectations of them may have seemed quite reasonable, you probably found their expectations of you at best unreasonable and, at worst, controlling and crushing.

The best-laid plans

*'Nobody tells you . . . nobody warns you what it will be like. We
did talk about it, we did make plans . . . resolutions. We said we
must make time for each other, we must share this and that, but no
one prepares you . . . for the emotions. At antenatal classes it is all
practical, changing nappies and the like . . . no one prepares you
for the shock, for the feelings.'*

(New mother)

It is difficult for anyone to prepare anyone else for the truth of having
children. Perhaps in previous generations there was no preparation.
People simply had babies and got on with it, doing very much as their
parents had done. Nowadays, many couples think about and plan their
lives with their future children. However, there is often an unconscious
expectation that the baby will fit in with their plans. Whilst you are
planning to adapt to your baby, there may be a 'not thought about'
assumption that the baby will also adapt to you.

*'In the books it says do this and that, and the baby will do the other,
but my baby hasn't read the book.'*

(Debbie, 32, new mother)

So why did you want, and what did you expect, when you took on this
job of parenting – a twenty-four-hour-a-day, seven-day-a-week job –
for life – and seemingly without pay?

Consider this:
- Why did you want a child?
- Did your partner have different reasons for wanting a child?
- How much did your parents want you to have children?
- Of course, you may have had an innate urge to procreate, but that
  biological fact accepted, what were the other concerns and reasons,
  thought about and not thought about, you experienced in deciding
  to have a child?

Social expectations

'We couldn't conceive of not having a family'

How influenced were you by family expectations that you would have a child? Even in an age when couples are delaying decisions about marriage and starting a family, days of house-husbands, of 'sharing the care', there seems to be a prevalent expectation that couples will have children. Couples choosing not to can be thought at best a little cold and, at worst, selfish or unnatural. Although it may be a reducing tendency, a woman in particular, who has not had children, may be expected to express some sadness or sorrow at that fact.

'You will just die out . . .' – continuing the line

> 'My parents thought [my son] would be just like me. My father even said, "There'll be another little George running about."'
> *(New father)*

> 'My parents kept on about it . . . they made us feel guilty . . . that we should be starting a family.'
> *(Parents of six-year-old)*

A four-year-old, on hearing a relative had broken off an engagement, cried, '*But you will just die out! You've got to get married. You've got to have babies, or you'll just die out.*'

Sometimes in families there may be a general assumption that the lineage must be continued, or else! This assumption may be based on practical reasons, for example there may be a family business which it is hoped will be continued into the next generation. At other times it is much less obvious, perhaps being linked to a general human deep-seated fear of 'dying out'? Is our mortality, and indeed our parents' mortality, made less painful if we have children to 'carry on' after us?

'Don't do it for us to have grandchildren . . .' – on pleasing Mum and Dad

Pressure from grandparents for grandchildren can leave a couple feeling that they have only been an adequate or good-enough son or daughter if they have provided a continuation of the line. Sometimes parental pressure is overt, for example, *'I want to have my grandchildren while I'm young enough to enjoy them. When are you two going to get on with it?'*

More complex is the message from the hopeful grandparent who says, *'Oh, don't have children for us, we've had ours, don't have them for us to have grandchildren.'* This is a mixed message. In effect, such grandparents could be heard to be saying to their children, *'We have done something, and what does it mean that you haven't?'* In saying, *'Don't have them for us'* they are stating to the couple that they not only want grandchildren, but that they are missing something by not having any. By technically giving the couple permission not to have children, they are implying that it is something they should do!

Creative fulfilment

But many couples can resist the pressures of older generations. At some point in many relationships there comes a time when a couple will feel a desire to create something together, something good, that belongs to them, i.e., creative fulfilment.

On the whole, a healthy child validates feelings of virility, wholeness and wellbeing in the parents. A healthy, thriving baby may be seen as an outward, visible symbol of a couple's creative and happy relationship – if you like, a neon-sign stating 'all is well here'. And we must remember that our capacity to nurture a child is a message to our own parents. It may be a validating message of 'look how well you have taught me' or even 'this is how you should have done it'. We will talk more about this later in the chapter.

> Childbirth is not only about a baby being born. Parents repro-
> duce themselves when they bring a child into the world. This
> fact may be pleasing to some parents – and threatening to
> others. In times of stress, parents may feel that a child has
> inherited *the worst of both of us*.

Not just expecting a baby

Even when a pregnancy is unplanned or unexpected, many parents will report a sense of pride and joy at the idea of their personal continuity. During pregnancy, parents may dream and talk endlessly of their expectations for their coming child – a perfect baby who will live out their hopes and dreams.

A parent might say, *'I wanted a little girl, to dress her up, make her look pretty'* – such a wish takes little account of the fact that the expected little girl may turn out to be a tomboy who will wear nothing but jeans and sweatshirts. The young couple who plan to return to the paternal grandparents' home in Yorkshire for the coming birth in case the baby is a boy, and therefore eligible to play cricket for the county, are taking little account of the fact that they may give birth to a male ballet dancer.

> *'If it's a boy . . . will he be a pig? Will he be a chauvinist?'*
> *(Expectant couple overheard in a restaurant)*

Of course, during pregnancy, you could have only imagined, and therefore 'unreal', expectations of your child. When you first saw your baby, you could not help but modify some of that thinking; a blatant example would be if you were convinced you were expecting a girl and then had a boy. However, at an unconscious level, it is likely that many of your hopes and expectations were still present.

I am always surprised in talking with other professionals about a child who is experiencing difficulties, when I hear the comment, *'The parents have such unreal expectations.'* I can only respond, *'Of course.'*

> At some point, all parents have to come to terms with the fantasy perfect baby and the reality of the one they have produced: an independent personality with their own desires, drives and ambitions.

Delight and disillusionment

A young mother who was enduring weeks of sleepless nights said, in a moment of poignant sadness, '*At the antenatal classes they had a doll. When they bathed it and changed it, they laid it down and its eyes closed . . . I thought babies were like that.*'

Consider this:

- What were the three main expectations you each had of being a parent?
- Did you both have the same expectations, or different?
- How have your expectations changed after having a baby?

Mr and Mrs J were describing how they expected to feel many things in the first few months of parenting, but they had not expected to feel disappointed: '*Exhausted, yes, but not disappointed.*' After the birth of the child, in amongst all the joy, some parents may experience a vague sense of disappointment. This may be obvious disappointment, like the baby not being the desired sex, or it may be unconscious – with people having feelings that they can't quite identify. For there is a sense in which no one can ever have the child they want. Perhaps even from childhood people have fantasies about what their child will be like. Parents have to deal with the disparity between their idealized child and the child they have, however much, of course, they may love that child.

Gains and losses

It is highly likely that during your pregnancy many of your thoughts were focused on what was coming and what was to be gained by having a baby. It is likely that you paid scant attention to what you might lose. I am interested that when asked this question, most parents seem to give the same answer: that a wife loses her freedom, and a husband loses his wife.

The impact of a new baby on a couple's relationship can be tremendous. What the eminent paediatrician Donald Winnicott called your 'primary preoccupation' is likely to be the baby, not each other. You may both begin to experience a sense of disappointment at the loss of focus on each other. During pregnancy you were probably advised, and fully intended, to work hard to make time to be alone together as a couple after the baby's arrival. However, as one mother said: *'We wanted to be alone, we wanted to have time together, but no one prepared me for the overwhelming feelings for the baby that kick in after the birth . . . It was just very hard to think of leaving her even for a few hours.'*

Maybe there are no solutions to this dilemma only ways of living with it. It is so important to keep sharing feelings on the impact of your relationship.

Consider this:
- What did you lose when you gained a baby?
- How did you think a child would change your relationship with each other?
- How did you think a child would change your family and other social relationships?

The first task of parenting
Childhood is a time of conflict. As a child grows there is inevitable conflict, in some families more than others, between the child growing into the kind of man or woman they want to be, and growing into the man or woman that the parents may want. As you begin to think less about your dreams and expectations and more about the very real child that you have in front of you, you are beginning to negotiate one of the first stages of parenting. This first conflict may be seen as representational of all the stages of childhood which are potentially conflictual. There may always be conflict between what the child wants to be and how you may want them to behave.

> Maybe parents do not survive child-rearing by solving the
> problems of childhood, but more by tolerating the conflicts.

In a way, parenting is an act of faith. It is the child's responsibility to
develop; they will learn to walk, to talk, to read, to write, to socialize.
It is the parents' job to have faith that this will happen in time, though
it may be at a different rate to the boy next door, or a female cousin
two years younger, etc.

You do not have to make your children grow up, you just have to
provide 'good enough conditions' for the child to thrive and make their
way. The key to providing 'good enough conditions' may be the ability to think about what the child's behaviour may be communicating
and, most importantly, to whom.

Consider this:
- What are the three most important things your parents gave
  you?
- How do they differ from the three most important things you
  would like to give your children?

Surviving the experts
Did you notice how as soon as you became a parent you seemed to be
surrounded by experts on parenting? Grandparents, childcare books,
television programmes, professionals such as health visitors and doc-
tors, all help to make up a long list of people who seem to know best
about your child. Other new mothers play their part. Whilst such
friends, at times, may be of enormous support, they can also be subject
to endless conversations of 'topping'. For example:

'She had us up three nights last week.'

*'Three nights? You're lucky. We haven't had a full night's sleep for ten
days!'*

Why do these 'experts' cause parents stress during those first early
months? The answer has to lie partly in all parents' very natural desire

to 'get it right'. It must also be linked with another expectation of parenting: that there is 'a right way' to parent and that there are simple answers to childhood problems which can be applied to all children all of the time.

Consider this:

- Once parents feel free to think about their child's behaviour as a communication, then they have less need of 'experts'.
- Maybe the key to surviving parenthood is developing the ability to tolerate everyone else knowing best, whilst accepting that you as the parent are fundamentally at sea.
- The feeling of being at sea may be an essential part of understanding your child because it takes time to get to know a child.

> Parents have said to me, *'If we were getting it right, if we were good parents, we wouldn't have to come and see you.'* Feeling you're getting it wrong as a parent may be an indication that there is a living, growing, developing relationship between you and your child, rather than a kind of textbook, two-dimensional, 'child does this, parent does that' attitude. If you and your child are unafraid to surprise each other, then the relationship is alive and developing.

I appreciate that the feeling of being 'at sea' in managing a child can lead parents to feel helpless and that they have no 'sound parental instinct'. In such times, it may be useful to follow the advice given to me as a quite definitely below-average student on a sailing course. I remember the skipper saying to me in a moment of exasperation, *'If you don't know what to do, put your rudder in the middle, and think.'*

Of course, it is while 'at sea' that parents most need each other's support, and single parents need the support of people around them. This period of trying to survive the experts may be complicated by the shattering of another dream – that a baby brings a couple close together.

'A baby brings a couple closer together?'

It is likely that during pregnancy you expected that the coming child would bring you closer together, would unite you into being a family. As a single parent, you may have hoped that having a baby would strengthen your bonds with your existing family. Of course, in the long run this may hopefully be true, but what raising a child also does is highlight the differences between parents.

In parenting your children, you are forced, to some extent, to relive your own childhood. Memories will come flooding back to you as you bring up your children, e.g., it may be difficult to buy your child their first bicycle, without remembering receiving or not receiving your own first bicycle, and this will trigger happy or painful memories.

> When you came together to create a family, you brought with you your own experiences of family life. Your histories may have much in common, but they may also have much that is very different.

For example, I was asked to see six-year-old Howard and his four-year-old sister, Gemma, who were running rings around their fraught parents. At our first meeting the parents listed a catalogue of disasters in disciplining the children; they couldn't get them to bed, let alone to sleep; they couldn't get them to sit at the table for a meal; and they couldn't stop Howard hurting his sister, or stop her from biting him. I wondered aloud what was making it so difficult for them to manage the children. Each blamed the other for being 'too soft' and giving into the children for a quiet life.

Both the mother and father had been raised by authoritarian parents and were anxious to bring their own children up in a less rigid manner; on that they were agreed. However, fundamental differences emerged between them in their own childhoods. The father's father had been more gentle than his mother, who had done most of the disciplining, so he came to parenting expecting, consciously or unconsciously, that the mother would do most of the 'firm handling' of the children. The mother, on the other hand, had a mother of the *'wait 'til your father gets home'* variety and had come to parenting expecting the father to be the disciplinarian. Neither parent was conscious of their expectations; they had just assumed that this was how it would be and so the matter had never been discussed.

As I have already said, we learn to parent primarily from our parents and we also learn a lot as we go along from siblings, other people's parents, teachers, etc. Whilst it is likely that there may be common ground in these experiences, it is likely that there will also be huge differences. There may be much in your childhood that you felt your parents got right and you would want to do likewise with your own children. And although you may swear to do some things very differently from the way your parents did, like most people you will find yourself doing it in the same way. The natural instinct to do it the same way is so strong that it is almost impossible to ignore.

I was asked to see Paul, aged nine, because of his difficult and negative behaviour. During my conversations with his parents, it emerged that the father's father had placed a heavy emphasis on good manners and appropriate social behaviour. The father was anxious to reassure me that, apart from demanding a reasonable standard, these were areas in which he did not pressurize Paul. Only the most outrageous breaches of etiquette were corrected. In a family session, when I asked Paul what he felt his father most admired about him he replied:

'When I do well at school.'

'Anything else?'

Silence. Paul shook his head. His father was surprised to realize that he was carrying on his own father's model of parenting, but in a different area. Paul was left feeling the same way as his father had as a child: that he was only loved and accepted if he achieved in certain areas.

Raising a child will make you realize the different ideas you both have about parenting, and such potential conflicts between you have to be overcome. The degree to which you can handle conflict will form the basis of your ability to deal with disputes over your children, and possibly with professionals, when your child enters the outside world.

A united front?

Some parents think they must always be united and smooth differences over. It can be argued that the advantage of having two parents is that you get two points of view. Parents who feel they must present the same view may make children feel that there is only one right way to do things.

Because you hold different views it does not mean that one of you is right and the other is wrong. It doesn't mean that one is a good person and the other is a bad person. It means no more nor less than that you have different views.

Ten-year-old Jimmy lived with his mother and step-father, regularly visiting his father who lived in America. His mother and step-father took a rather liberal and relaxed attitude towards Jimmy, believing that he would eventually find his own way in the world and that pressurizing him into academic or, indeed, any other kind of success was not appropriate. His father, on the other hand, was very anxious that Jimmy should do as well as possible at school, and go on to university before perhaps joining his business.

As Jimmy began to approach adolescence, he found it increasingly difficult to cope with these two contrasting views. The matter was not helped by his parents' inability to respect each other's way of living. Jimmy's father would constantly criticize his mother for not being more rigorous about, for example, Jimmy completing his homework, and his mother would be critical of his father for placing so much pressure on him.

> What matters to children is the way in which you present your conflicts and differences, rather than the fact that you have conflicting views. Saying something like, *'I would let you, but Daddy won't . . .'* may not be the most helpful approach.

The conflict became much more manageable for Jimmy when both parents were helped to present their differing approaches to life as alternatives of equal value, rather than as an 'either or' choice.

A helpful way to present a difference of opinion may be something like: *'Mummy and I don't agree about this, but we have talked about it and on this occasion we're going to do things Mummy's way. It doesn't mean we will always do it Mummy's way, but that's what we've decided to do this time.'*

What does being a family mean?

There must be as many ways of being a family as there are families.

'Everyone has to do what everyone else wants . . . it's not fair. Nobody does what they *want.'*

(A seven-year-old)

'It's being snugly – I mean like watching Star Trek. *My dad makes room on the floor cushions.'*

(A six-year-old)

Giving them what I never had

Of course you want your children to have the things that you enjoyed and also the things that you never had, be they opportunities, possessions or leisure activities. But it can be difficult when your child does not seem to appreciate these things as much as you feel you would have appreciated them as a child.

Family life can be most disappointing for parents where there is an overriding desire to live through their children. By this I mean that children will follow the career, recreational activities, etc., that the parent longed for as a child but was never able to have. This desire may be expressed with rather controlling views of how the child should be and should lead his life, even to the extent of a future career.

I remember talking with some very disappointed parents whose eleven-year-old daughter had just failed to gain entrance into the school of their choice. She was about to begin school in a much less academic environment than the parents would have desired. It had long been their hope that their daughter would eventually take over the family business, and her lack of academic achievement was making this a less and less likely option.

Mother: *'If she doesn't go into the business, she could do secretarial training or something, she needn't be a hairdresser.'*

Me: *'She might want to be a hairdresser.'*

Mother: *'She doesn't need to be . . .'*

Me: *'She might want to be . . .'*

Mother: *'Oh, my God!'*

The problem here is that people don't always know what they want. Many parents have not realized they had an unlived life until they had a child. For example, what if you find yourself in the position where your son desperately wants to go into the army and you desperately don't want him to enlist? In thinking about why you don't want him to enlist, you may realize that you have always wanted to join the army, or that you never wanted to join the army, you disliked your father being in the army, and so on. Recreational activities can be another source of disappointment. Your child may not inherit your love of tennis and prefer to spend long hours playing computer games or skateboarding.

Can your family tolerate such differences, differences of every kind, or is the philosophy 'sameness is togetherness'? There can be a fantasy that if everybody likes doing the same thing, then the family is closer than if they are free to follow their individual likes and dislikes.

Perhaps this is, in some sense, a legacy from images of the family that were projected by the media in the 1950s. This portrayed the mother and father having very distinct and different roles, the children modelling themselves on the parent of the same sex, and everyone doing things together. In some ways, it may have been a true picture, perhaps families did spend more time together before the advent of such things as individual televisions in individual bedrooms. But it may have left a legacy that there is something wrong with a family that operates more independently. A family where members have different interests, but take an active interest in each other's pursuits, can be just as close.

> Your expectation of what your family will be like will be coloured by your own experience of family life as a child. You are likely to have two levels of expectation. A conscious or thought-about level, the kind of family you planned to create. And an unconscious, not-thought-about, level, that is the way your parents did it.

Doing it better than our parents

'Help! I sound more and more like my dad' is a common fear for many people. You are likely to be most distressed as a parent when you find yourself making the same or similar mistakes in child-rearing that you feel your parents made. This will be particularly disturbing if you have a real desire to be a different kind of parent. Perhaps a part of your not-thought-about reason for having a child was to show your parents how to do it properly.

> It is a truth of life that we can only pass on emotionally to our children what we ourselves have inherited from our parents.

If you experienced a loving and warm relationship with your parents, then you will instinctively pass this on to your children. If your relationship with your parents was less happy and constructive, then you may have to think more carefully about the way in which you parent your children.

For example, how did your parents handle your temper tantrums? If your parents took the attitude that such behaviour warranted removing you from the room, and leaving you alone until you had 'calmed down' or 'were going to be reasonable' then it will be difficult for you instinctively to respond to your child's outbursts of behaviour in a different way and without the child feeling that it isn't contrived. Children are very quick to pick up when you are 'parenting from theory' and may feel humiliated at your attempts to 'do the right thing'.

> *'I was late collecting her. I was frantic. I kept imagining she'll be thinking I'm not coming. She'll be lost, the last to be collected. She'll feel so alone . . . When I got there she was fine, sitting on a chair looking at a book. She's different to me.'*
> *(A parent talking about her nursery school child)*

Follow your instincts

One parent said to me: *'I don't know how to be a father . . . not to a ten-year-old . . . my father had left by then. What do fathers do with ten-year-old boys?'* When such occasions arise, you may find that you are not able to follow your own instincts, to do 'what comes naturally'. When I asked this father what he would like to do with his ten-year-old, he replied, *'Teach him golf.'* He had been unable to follow up this natural desire with his son, because it had evoked painful memories of watching the boy next door going off to play golf with his father, after his own father had left the family home.

It is difficult to give your children the good experiences you missed out on in childhood without raising the pain of the fact that you missed out. You may not want to remember that pain, or to think about it, and may try to block it out. But it's difficult to block out one thought without unintentionally blocking out other thoughts.

The romance of childhood

The desire to do it differently from our parents may also be linked to another expectation in pregnancy: to keep in touch with our own childhood in an unconscious hope that maybe those idyllic times have not really passed . . . or, conversely, that an unhappy childhood can one day be seen differently.

> You will relive your own childhood through the experience of parenting, but you cannot change it. You can use the trials and tribulations of your own childhood as a key to understanding your child's behaviour. In this way, what was painful in the past may be positive in the present.

We are all familiar with the father who buys his son a train set with which the child never plays, but with which the father seems preoccupied. Likewise the mother who encourages her daughter to have friends round to play in a delightful and welcoming atmosphere cannot eradicate the experience of her own mother who refused or made it difficult for her to have such experiences. Of course it's essential to keep in touch with the child within, by which I mean the ability to be spontaneous, to play freely in any given moment, to be vulnerable and to forgive readily – maybe this is the essence of all good parenting.

Consider this:

- When you are really struggling to understand your child, it may be helpful to reflect upon what you were like at the same age. What sort of child were you at the same age as your child is now? How was it for you?
- Such reflections may lead you to more understanding of and wisdom about your child than any book can offer. Thinking about yourself at the same age, what helps and what didn't, may be of crucial importance.

And what if you are a single parent?

It will be obvious now that this chapter is written with two parents in mind, and this can be misleading. Whilst all children originate within a couple, you may be reading this as a single parent, either by choice or because of death or divorce. Support systems for lone parents are crucial.

To some extent all that is written about the relationship between mother and father will be relevant to the lone parent and your support system. The friend, relative or childminder who shares the care of your child and is seen to be openly supportive of you may very well come into the kinds of conflicts with the child that often occur between parents.

Perhaps this book places emphasis on 'the couple' because there is still an expectation in society of a couple raising children. Now the expectations may not be so much that the parents are living together, but that they are both active in the upbringing of the child, both physically and emotionally. This perhaps raises another expectation relevant to the chapter: What are the couple's expectations of what the child will do for the couple?

It is very common in acrimonious divorce cases for aggression between the parents to be worked out over issues concerning the child, such as access or money. Such parents may often be very surprised when it is pointed out to them that they seem to have an expectation that they can use the child to carry on an unfinished argument or hostility. We will explore this further in Chapter 8.

As we mentioned earlier, it is equally very common to hear of a couple having a baby 'to save a relationship', be it a married couple or not. The expectation is that somehow having a child will cement the relationship, without the couple having to try to resolve their difficulties. Many couples believe that there is some magic that could transform their relationship and it's not unusual for children to be seen as that redemptive feature. Consequently, such children may be a bitter disappointment to both parents if the relationship does then break up.

The child may also feel they have a heavy burden to carry in life. I remember a ten-year-old girl who was worrying both her teachers and parents with her general lack of confidence and feelings of failure. After several family sessions, she said: *'Well, I have failed, haven't I? I have failed!'* What emerged was that unconsciously she realized she had been a marriage-saving baby and, aware of her parents' current unhappiness, felt she had failed in the purpose of her being.

A similar problem can arise when a mother decides to have a baby *'because I want a change'*, almost seeing motherhood as a change of career. If motherhood is disappointing, it is not easy to hand in one's notice!

Disappointment and envy . . . the child-free couple
The child-free couple may be a source of envy to parents, for whom in the hurly-burly of feeding, nappy changing and broken nights, the joys of children may have temporarily been masked. I remember vividly one young mother expressing hostility towards her children. When I reflected that she didn't seem able to enjoy children very much at the moment, she responded: *'I'm too exhausted to enjoy them, I'm too exhausted not to like them, and I'm just exhausted.'*

Consider this:
- Is there a sense that the child-free couple are seen to be living the unlived lives of couples with children? Their relative freedom to pursue their own interests, seemingly to come and go as they please, and relatively uncluttered homes may provoke the thought in parents that if *'we'd known what we were doing, we wouldn't have done it.'*
- The child-free couple may provoke thoughts and anxieties about children that parents would prefer not to think, let alone express.

A bitterly disappointed father, who found it very difficult to make a relationship with his daughter, whose looks, personality, and developing interests were a far extreme from what he would have hoped and wanted, burst into tears one day and said: *'If I hadn't had her, I wouldn't want her, but I have got her so I love her.'*

Another mother describing how her very troubled six-year-old had laid down in a shop and had a massive temper tantrum told of her exhaustion and helplessness at coping with this very difficult child: *'I wanted to think, Christ, I can't stand that bloody little monster any longer, but I didn't.'*

'We thought it would be fun'
Surely one of your greatest expectations in planning a baby was that it would be fun! Your expectation was that the coming baby would be a source of joy, not only to you but to the outside world. When you are most worried about your children's behaviour, when things seem to have gone wrong or got into a muddle, don't ask yourself, *'What have*

we done wrong?' or *'What is wrong with our child?'* but rather, *'What is happening to prevent us all from enjoying each other?'*

In the coming chapters I would like to discuss some of the ordinary problems of childhood, to highlight signals children may give to parents that things have got into a muddle. These ordinary problems are no longer developmental stages but have become 'extra-ordinary problems' in an attempt by the child to communicate an anxiety to the adult.

Summary

- Children are born into a world of expectations, and parents and children spend the rest of their lives trying to extricate themselves from and trying to satisfy each other's inventions.
- We learn to parent from our parents and we pick up of lots of things from other people as we go along.
- Childhood is necessarily a time of conflict. Maybe parents do not survive child-rearing by solving the problems of childhood, but more by tolerating the conflicts.
- It is normal to feel a sense of disappointment as well as elation after the birth of a baby.
- A baby may bring you closer together as a couple, but parenting will also highlight your different expectations of family life.
- 'Feeling at sea' about your child's behaviour may be an essential part of understanding that behaviour.
- Memories of your own childhood will come flooding back to you as you bring up your children. Being aware of this helps you be open to what your child is communicating, rather than being disappointed that they aren't following your script.
- Because you hold different views as parents, it does not mean that one of you is right and the other is wrong. It doesn't mean that one is a good person and the other is a bad person, it means no more, no less, than you have different views. What matters to your child is not that you have conflicting views, but how you present those views to them.
- If sameness is always togetherness, can your family tolerate differences of every kind, personality, interests, expectations, etc?
- In parenting, we can only pass on what our parents have given to us.

CHAPTER 2

The First Great Refusals . . .

– Why They Don't Eat and Sleep –

'She won't eat . . . she won't sleep. I'm at my wits' end.'
(Mother of three-year-old)

Eating and sleeping are the fundamental organizers of our lives. We need to sleep and we need to eat in order to function as human beings. So we should not be surprised when children use eating and sleeping to communicate their most important worries and disturbances. We can think of difficulties in feeding and sleeping as a basic language between children and parents. That said, most children have issues with sleeping and eating at some point in their development and we need to remember that these disruptions are an ordinary problem of childhood. It is also true that children will eat and sleep as and when they are tired or hungry; they will not starve themselves of either, except in cases of extreme disturbance. We only need to worry about sleeping and eating problems if they persist or if they dominate a child's life. What we are going to think about in this chapter are some of the ordinary eating and sleeping difficulties arising in childhood and how to recognize when these have become extraordinary and parents should seek professional help.

Feeding difficulties

'I don't know . . . I just feel I'm not a proper mother . . . I should be able to breastfeed enough.'

(Mother of eight-week-old baby)

Nothing worries parents – especially it would seem mothers – more than feeding problems. And, of course, when your child is difficult about food you remember how you felt about food as a child and how you felt about your early relationship with your mother. The new mother quoted above was voicing what many mothers feel: that if their child has a problem eating then there is either something wrong with them as a parent or something seriously wrong with the child. This mother had just been advised by her health visitor to top up breastfeeds with a bottle as her baby seemed to need more nourishment.

On one hand this was a practical and helpful suggestion, which the mother could acknowledge, but, on the other, it made her feel inadequate as a mother and constantly question whether she was giving her baby enough. We can wonder if she would have had the same reaction if the health visitor had advised an extra bath or nappy change.

> There is something about feeding problems parents cannot help take personally.

Seventeen-month-old Guy's parents came to see me because he had begun to refuse food. They were older parents who had waited until they were financially secure before having Guy; his mother had given up a successful job to care for him full time. Both parents were worried that Guy was now playing with food, refusing to be fed, pushing the spoon away, and often tipping his plate onto the floor. Guy's mother was feeling puzzled and rejected: *'It's good organic food. I cook and purée it myself . . . there's nothing wrong with it.'* But Guy's father's real worry emerged towards the end of our meeting: *'He's being awfully rude. I don't want him to grow up into a thug.'*

One of the most powerful, and troubling, aspects of all feeding difficulties is the way that once a child stops eating,
parents become very preoccupied with their child's appetite.

Feeding is, of course, a very intimate experience and a process about
much more than taking in food; it is a time for intimate contact, both
physically and emotionally. Maybe it is interesting here to reflect on
how much adults socialize around food; having people to dinner, meeting for lunch or coffee, or a drink in the pub. Preparing food for other
people is a way of showing both affection and respect; refusing food
can be a child's way of creating an environment in which their needs
have to be heard and thought about.

Consider this:
- Feeding difficulties seem to be a child's way of saying, '*I need you to
  think about me more. There is something I just can't take in.*'
- Eating is also about what we can take in and digest emotionally as
  well as physically.

When five-year-old India began school she lost a third of her body
weight in the first term. Each morning she would begin to feel car sick
on the way to school and once at the gates would vomit violently.
Interestingly, she was never car sick on any other journey. Six months
earlier her mother had given birth to her twin brothers and India had
seemed delighted and remarkably undisturbed by their arrival.
However, as time went by we began to think of her as not having been
able to digest their arrival and certainly not able to digest going to
school leaving Mummy at home with the twins. Once India felt her
worries were understood, she very quickly settled down at school.
However, it was interesting that we met again six years later when she
was re-referred back to me with mild bulimia – a problem which had
begun just as she had changed from the junior to the secondary
school.

Parenting, food and feeding are inextricably bound together. Children like India who discover early on the powerful effect not eating can have on a parent may unconsciously decide to use this as a way of communicating difficulties throughout their life. Indeed, many adults find they have difficulty in eating at times of stress or unhappiness.

Feeding is different from disciplining

Good eating habits are about knowing when you are hungry (as opposed to empty in other ways, be it emotionally or physically) and knowing how much to eat and what to eat to satisfy your needs. If you use food as a reward, e.g., *'You can have some sweets for being a good girl'*, or as a punishment, e.g., *'You're not having sweets because you've been naughty'*, then you run the risk of your child growing up confusing bodily and emotional needs. Many adult yo-yo dieters will admit that they experience food as a reward: *'I lost 4lb this week so I deserve a treat'*, or as a comforter: *'I didn't lose anything this week, I felt so miserable I had a Mars Bar to cheer me up'*. Ideally children should get the message that they can have food because they are hungry or because it is available, not because they have or have not behaved in any particular way.

Since five-year-old Finlay's father had left home suddenly he had become increasingly difficult to manage at mealtimes. He was picky about food and would loll about at the table, frequently rubbing his hands over his face sighing, fidgeting and knocking things over and, above all, eating with his fingers. All this infuriated his mother who was anxious he should have good table manners. She reported a distressing time when he had refused to use his knife and fork, in spite of repeated requests to do so: *'I smacked his hand hard . . . but he did it again . . . and so I smacked his hand again . . . and he did it again and then he suddenly lost control and started shouting and screaming at me that I had sent his daddy away.'*

This is an example of how discipline and eating can get into a muddle. Finlay was using eating to communicate a great number of preoccupations: he was fighting his mother over table manners as a way of expressing his distress and anger at his father's departure. He knew how highly his mother valued table manners and so he knew that his behaviour was bound to make an impact on her, i.e., he knew she would listen to the bad table manners when he thought she wasn't listening to his distress in other ways.

Good and bad foods?

Most parents will want to encourage their children to eat a healthy diet. The risk is that we live in a society preoccupied with image and appearance; children as young as four and five are becoming acutely fashion and weight conscious, often construing 'being thin' as necessarily 'being healthy'. And we live in a world of good and bad foods. Seven-year-old Aiden's mother had a major row with the head teacher at her children's school. At home she kept him and his brothers on a health-conscious diet – crisps and sweets were replaced with nuts and yoghurt-coated raisins. As a small child Aiden had been cooperative, but he was now demanding more usual snacks to take to school as he 'felt different'. His mother responded by trying to get the teachers to ban unhealthy foods in school. The headmistress took the line that labelling foods as 'good' or 'bad' may cause children to feel guilty about what they were eating. She felt it was better to encourage an overall healthy diet, with hopefully only small amounts of junk food included.

> The risk of you stressing the importance of good or healthy food is that your child may respond by rebelling against them. It is no coincidence that *forbidden fruits taste sweet'*.

Consider this:
- The media's preoccupation with a healthy diet is consciously or unconsciously feeding (!) the idea that it is possible to be a perfect parent.
- Most parents want to do the best for their child; the issue nowadays is whether or not they feel free to do so.
- It may be best to try to describe food in the home avoiding the words 'good', 'bad' and 'diet'.

The idea of the healthy diet suggests implicitly that it is possible to engineer a socially happy child. The implication is that if you get the environment and the conditions right, then the child will automatically thrive. Of course, it is true that good environmental conditions help children to thrive but, more importantly, parenting is more about getting to know your child's individual needs rather than trying to live up to an idea of perfection as promoted by the media.

The impact of family attitudes to food

> 'Whenever I was upset, my mum said, "Eat something, you'll feel better if you eat something." I don't want Trisha to grow up thinking over-eating is a good comfort.'
>
> (Nine-year-old Trisha's mother)

Trisha wanted to go on a diet. While she was not slim, she was certainly not chubby, let alone fat, so what was this request from a nine-year-old all about? Trisha herself certainly didn't seem to understand why she needed to diet. She was not being bullied or teased, she had a solid group of friends, and seemed a happy enough girl. But she was quite adamant that she needed to diet. And we know her request is not as extraordinary as we may want to think for a girl of her age today.

In March 2007, Maurice Chittenden reported in the *Times* how a group of parents was beginning to protest against *'the toy industry practices they claim are "sexualizing" young children'*. Among the toys they were most concerned about were a *'Peek-a-Boo pole-dancing kit'* and *'My Scene Bling Bling Spa'* in which a doll *'hangs out at the coolest bar in town'*.

Modern culture seems to focus entirely on sexuality. We are led to believe that the secret of a successful and happy life is to have a beautiful, sexy body. Not only that, the media dictates what is sexy and beautiful and also how this can be achieved instantly by the use of cosmetics, spas and surgery.

We know from current research that children are being influenced by these advertisements. Research by Hill and Pallin shows that girls as young as eight are drawn to dieting to improve their self worth, and that nine-year-olds associate a fat body shape with being 'stupid and unpopular' and a thin one with being 'popular, intelligent and kind'. The overall effect is that children are being made to feel uncomfortable about their bodies and appearance. The research also showed that girls are strongly influenced in their wish to diet by their mother's attitude to her body shape and what she eats.

Trisha's parents seemed to have a rather superior attitude to food. Her mother enjoyed cooking and provided a healthy, well-balanced diet for Trisha and her two younger sisters, but the parents themselves seemed to pick at small amounts. *'Well, one doesn't really need these large meals,'* said her mother. *'We often just have a sandwich.'* There was a clear attitude in the home of 'eat to live' and for no other reason, even though this was a family who always ate together around the table.

The parents' history with food was interesting. Trisha's mother had been the eldest of three girls and was overweight and teased as a child; she put this down to her mother's 'force feeding': *'Our plates were always overflowing and we were allowed to snack whenever we wanted.'* Trisha's father had been sent to boarding school aged seven and what gradually emerged was that, while he was happy and settled in the early days, he had found mealtimes in school unbearable because they were the times when he had been acutely aware of missing his family: *'I used to dread going in* [to the dining room] *. . . I was terrified I'd cry . . . it was all so noisy . . . so busy . . . so different from home.'*

We can see how both these parents had been unaware of the emotions triggered by food and the sense their children made of them. Trisha seemed to believe that to be a happy woman you mustn't eat too much. Her mother was amazed to realize that perhaps she saw little difference in enjoying food and being gluttonous. On the other hand, Trisha's chubby younger sister seemed to live with the slight doubt that there would always be enough food around and 'stuffed herself' at every meal.

Consider this:

- How you feel about food is going to influence your child's attitude to food.

- You will always give more than one message: the ones you want to give and the ones you give without intending!

The child who refuses to eat

Many parents will claim their child 'refuses to eat'. Usually, when we delve deeper, we find that their child refuses to eat food presented to them at mealtimes. Very few children refuse to eat anything, and we will address this problem later in this chapter in the section on Eating Disorders. For the time being, let us return to the seventeen-month-old Guy and his parents. Was Guy refusing to eat as his parents construed him or was he simply being a seventeen-month-old beginning to practise the first steps towards independence? At this stage, babies have very limited ways of showing, *I can do it my way*. He could also have been reminding his parents how exciting and interesting it is to be a new person in the world and discover new things. While his mother saw a carefully prepared bowl of organic food purée, Guy saw colour, taste, texture, all waiting to be explored. If you like, his mother could be understood as thinking, *'Eat this up'*, and he was thinking, *'Now what can I do with all this?'*

Parenting is not orderly. Guy's parents had carefully planned his arrival in their lives; they had read every parenting book and watched every TV programme on childcare. The emerging problem was that Guy hadn't. They described him as an easy baby and said this was their first problem.

Managing the child who doesn't eat

- First of all, we had to help Guy's mother not to take his rejection of her food personally as there was nothing wrong with it. Guy was simply trying to establish some independence. (Yes, in this sense, he *was* rejecting her but that is a lifelong process!)
- She needed reassurance that he would eat enough and was unlikely to fail to thrive.
- She needed to understand there was no link between Guy's eating and her being a perfect mother! Indeed, his non-compliance probably meant he felt secure enough to challenge his routine.
- She tried to take less trouble over Guy's food. While she stuck to a

healthy diet, she avoided the risk of feeling resentful and rejected at the amount of time and effort she had spent on preparation. (Child psychologist Penelope Leach points out that bread, cheese and an apple is a perfectly balanced meal, which takes thirty seconds to prepare!)

- We tried to reduce the sense of conflict at mealtimes. She allowed Guy to play with his food and eat with his fingers, and helped him to learn to spoon-feed himself as non-intrusively as possible. She allowed longer for mealtimes so they were less stressful and she tried describing out loud what was happening: *'Yes, you're pushing the food round your tray',* which moved the focus to her relationship with Guy rather than the mess. She was delighted to report a month later that he had *'A real sense of mischief'.*

- Guy's parents also realized that even at seventeen months their baby was telling them that some day he would be independent of them. They began to think once more about their relationship as a couple as well as parents.

There was an interesting follow-up to Guy's story when I saw his parents a year later. By now Guy was a boisterous and lively two-and-a-half-year-old. His father described his healthy appetite and said, *'Yes, now he's a real trencherman . . . loves his food.'* The father then volunteered that he had always equated a good, healthy appetite with being manly. He did not want a son who was *'faddy'* or *'pecked at his food!'*

The picky child

Andrew, aged two, was driving his parents to distraction with his food fads. For the previous three months he had turned down more and more food choices until he was now living on a diet of bread, peanut butter, banana and yoghurt, with the occasional concession to something different. His health-conscious parents were highly anxious about the impact of this diet on his development and even survival. They had tried praise and encouragement and offering bribes and rewards for eating what was placed in front of him. They had even tried refusing to give him any other food than the meal offered but, as they said, *'He has a stronger will than us.'* Nothing seemed to work.

As children grow up they need choices. Even small choices – fish fingers or eggs for lunch? – can make a child feel they have some power in their lives. And choices help us to develop both a sense of identity (I am me and I like eggs) and a sense of privacy. Young children may feel secure believing, *'Mummy and Daddy know everything about me.'* As the child grows they need more sense of a private life, and privacy involves the right to a personal taste and appetite. Very rarely, perhaps as a guest in someone else's home, does an adult have to eat what is put in front of them; many children are expected to do this on a daily basis.

Consider this:
- Would you rather go hungry than eat something you really did not like?
- Is your child a 'faddy' eater or is it that they are simply experimenting with choice and finding out that they may prefer different foods to the remainder of the family?

Managing faddiness in young children
Even before I met Andrew's mother I could feel her stress levels on the telephone. It was easy to surmise that there was a risk she was transmitting that anxiety to Andrew at mealtimes and, as a consequence, meals were getting off to a bad start. Like Guy's mother, Andrew's parents had to first and foremost try to relax about his faddiness as a simple developmental stage.

- Accept that you cannot make a child of any age eat.
- Try to present a faddy toddler with some play food. By this I do not mean junk food, but rather food that they can relate to and so which will appeal to them. For example, a sandwich may be more exciting if it is cut into a smiley face or a sun with rays. One four-year-old pushed sausage and mash around his plate sulkily for weeks until his father one day served up a mashed potato castle with a sausage soldier and a gravy moat.
- Toddlers do not understand the philosophy of, *'No dessert until you've eaten your main course!'* Try to avoid bribes and rewards to

eat what you want them to eat. The likelihood is that your toddler will construe the main course as what *you* value most and so the treat or dessert becomes even more what he desires.

• Andrew's parents decided to offer him only the food they knew he would eat in as calm and nonchalant a way as possible. This was not an easy task, but as everyone relaxed at mealtimes, they began to introduce one new food at a time without insisting that Andrew ate it.

• Be patient: Penny Leach reports some toddlers need to have new foods presented to them twenty or thirty times before they will put them in their mouth.

Food fads in older children

The toddler's need to use food fads as a way of finding out how they are a separate and unique individual in the family may well return in the middle years of childhood. From nine years old, children are beginning to take a greater interest in the world outside home. They are beginning to experiment with all sorts of ideas and ways of living. And they will express these in myriad ways. They may become intensely concerned about animal welfare and try to make their contribution by becoming vegetarian. They may become passionate about 'superfoods' and insist on eating a restricted diet, eliminating any food they consider to be unhealthy. One ten-year-old tried to eat only pomegranate seeds and smoked fish because he had read they would 'improve brain power'.

Like so many aspects of daily life, food fads for this age group may become a way in which they feel they can assert their views and autonomy. You may need to hold in mind that when they insist they can't eat meat, they may also be challenging you to try and make them.

Managing the older faddy child

• Try to remember older children's food fads are less likely to be about their preferences than about a power struggle.

• As with toddlers, how are you going to make them eat something they don't want to eat?

- You can allow an older child reasonable choice at mealtimes. But remember children are learning to make choices
- Sometimes nonchalantly stating your views can both avoid an argument and reinforce your case: '*I think you should eat it, but I can't make you so I'll have to let you not eat it.*'
- Respecting your tween's taste in food is just the beginning. As one father said, '*I could never understand her putting sugar on fried eggs when she was nine but at nineteen I can't stand her taste in boyfriends!*'

The child who will eat only one thing

It is extraordinary how common it is for children, especially small children, to insist on eating only one thing; it is also extraordinary how healthy they manage to stay on a diet of nothing except, for example, bread and butter with sugar sprinkled on the top! If a picky child is worrying and irritating, then the child who will only eat one thing may drive their parents to distraction, particularly as this is a stage that may go on for as long as a couple of years. Of course, we can understand such a parent's concern but it is also interesting to reflect on the fact that babies start out by eating only one thing – milk.

> The single food fad is an extension of the picky eater. We can think of such a child as trying to return to the mother they had in infancy, that is, a mother who is closely attuned to the child's needs.

In Chapter 1 we talked about Donald Winnicott's thoughts on 'maternal preoccupation' where, in the first few weeks and months of life, the mother is totally focused on the baby and their needs. Babies have very few ways of communicating their needs and so you, as a parent, have to be constantly alert to discern what it is a baby may need at any given moment. As children grow up they develop more ways of asking for what they need and so, in one sense, parents can be less vigilant. Sometimes faddiness or insisting on only eating one thing is the child's way of asking, '*Do you still understand me? Do you still realize what I do and don't want?*'

It is difficult to tolerate your child only eating one thing without becoming excessively anxious about their health. However, providing your child is not losing weight or failing to thrive, it may be better to place your emphasis on extra love and attention rather than on what they may or may not be eating. And, as with all childhood behaviour worries, it may be worth asking yourself, *'If I wasn't worried about his eating, what would I be worrying about?'*

When does pickiness become an eating disorder?

> *'How do I know my very picky ten-year-old is not becoming anorexic?'*
>
> (Worried mother)

There is a big difference between a child who is 'picky' and a child with an eating disorder. When food becomes fraught with symbols, a child may find themselves impelled not to eat. They are unable to eat because for them food has too many meanings attached to it. Eating disorders are a complex communication between a parent and child who may be trying to deal with a number of issues all at once.

Consider this:
- They may feel angry or powerless.
- They may be overanxious about becoming adolescent. The idea of coping with both their own sexual desires and sexual attention from others may be overwhelming.
- They may feel excessively driven to succeed academically. We have thought before about how children may develop the idea that they are only lovable if they are succeeding. The child with an eating disorder may have developed unreal expectations of themselves.

How to recognize an eating disorder
We used to think of eating disorders as almost exclusively confined to teenage girls. However, these are becoming more prevalent in both boys and girls at a younger age. Children may swing from refusing to

eat (anorexia) to binge eating and vomiting (bulimia). We know many children are becoming preoccupied with their weight and body shape, but this does not necessarily mean they are developing an eating disorder. However, parents should be concerned if their child seems excessively or exclusively concerned about their weight. You should also take seriously the child who finds excuses not to eat what is provided *all* the time, or who tries to avoid mealtimes by claiming they are unwell or not hungry or even doing their homework. Equally of concern is the child who always seems hungry or is overeating but at the same time is losing weight. When 'pickiness' turns into a consistent refusal to eat very much, especially if this is focused on fats, sugars or carbohydrates, then you should begin to consider whether or not your child is developing an eating disorder.

Managing eating disorders

- Don't presume your child knows why they have an eating disorder. They will need your help to understand just how confusing food can be for them.
- It is natural to praise your child's appearance and indeed they need to know you admire their looks. However, you may need to shift your emphasis for the child who has an eating disorder. Try to comment on and praise aspects of their personality and behaviour. This can be very casual in conversation, for example: *'I thought it was very kind of you to do so and so etc.'*
- It may help your child to have you talk about the aspects of your looks you disliked and struggled with when you were their age. A child may feel less isolated if they realize we all feel dissatisfied with our own appearance in some way.
- How much does your own diet model a healthy way of eating? Eating together as a family will give you an opportunity to assess what your child is eating and also let them see what you eat and your attitude to food.
- Now may be a time for you to reassess how much freedom and choice you are giving your child. Could they have good reason for feeling angry and powerless?

- Talk to your child about how you felt when entering adolescence and going on first dates.
- Seek professional help when you or your child seems too worried or unhappy. Your doctor or health visitor would be a good first port of call.

You can't win them all

Eating difficulties are always idiosyncratic. They are indeed a matter of taste! We can all sympathize with the young mother who described trying to cope at mealtimes with an eighteen-month-old refusing food in a bid for independence, a three-year-old who would only eat marmite toast spread with banana, and a five-year-old whose pickiness at mealtimes depended entirely on, *'who she went to tea with yesterday and what they gave her to eat!'* The interesting issue in this family was that mealtimes seemed to be the only battleground; give or take the odd tantrum the rest of the family life seemed to trundle along quite smoothly. So it was interesting to look at why the children may have been choosing food as a way to communicate.

Sleeping problems

We begin our lives sleeping most of the time and we are asleep for approximately a third of our adult lives. We talk of needing 'a good sleep', an indication of both the pleasures and healing qualities of sleep. Shakespeare referred to sleep as, *'The season of all natures'* and *'knitting up the ravelled sleave* [sic] *of care'*. And yet most adults and children have difficulty sleeping at one or indeed many times in their lives. You are likely to feel quite dreadful after a broken night's sleep, particularly if you have been disturbed during the deeper stage of sleep, known as 'dream sleep'. Children, on the other hand, can be very cheerful and bouncy after a broken night's sleep because they tend to wake naturally at the top of each of their sleep cycles, maybe as much as five times a night, though they may not realize they are doing so. So in one sense, sleep disturbance is more of a problem for a parent than a child. In this section we are going to think about some of the emotional aspects of sleep, how a child may construe both being sent to bed and going to sleep, and the various emotional functions of sleep.

What is a sleeping problem?

In a survey of pre-school children, Naomi Richman found that difficulty in settling at bedtime and frequent waking during the night was a problem with over half of one- to two-year-olds and almost a third of three-year-olds. Studies also show that having a child who is a poor sleeper can cause significant stress to parents. Dorand and Mindell monitored parental depression and marital satisfaction and found both to improve when their children's sleep problems were resolved. Richman defined a sleep problem as:

- A child has difficulty in sleeping a full night for more than three months.
- A child is waking five or more nights during the week.
- A child is waking three or four times a night.
- When a child is awake for more than twenty minutes at a time during the night.
- When a child persists in going into the parents' bed to sleep.

On being alone

Four-year-old Aubrey found it difficult to go to sleep and would call out for his parents several times during the evening. He woke five or six times a night, coming into his parents' bed and demanding to sleep with them. In a family meeting, his mother was trying to get to the root of the problem: *'I don't know why you can't go to sleep . . . Mummy and Daddy are just downstairs,'* she said.

There was a pause as Aubrey struggled for words: *'Yes, but Mummy and Daddy have two and I'm just one . . . I don't like it by my own self.'*

For children, going to sleep means being away from their parents and not knowing what their parents are doing. Going to bed and sleep can be an intensely lonely experience and there is no more poignant image than that of a lonely child. Many adults like to have a rather romantic notion of childhood as a carefree time of innocence; indeed, it is not uncommon for *not a care in the world* to be an observation made on a sleeping child. Some adults may have had this rosy experience of childhood; they may indeed remember being put to bed as a most intimate, cosy and happy time. Others may maintain this image of childhood as a defence against the pain they suffered as a child, a sort of 'this was the childhood I would have liked' approach, and sometimes the need of adults to protect children from their pain blinds them to obvious needs in child development.

> Children need to be lonely in the sense that they need to experience being alone, to experience solitude. It is easy for us to underestimate how demanding children find adults! Children, like adults, can only have certain experiences by themselves.

Throughout this book, I am highlighting a child's need for 'attachment', i.e., the need for a close and intimate relationship with at least one adult carer during the first years of life. But children also need time and space to practise independence. From the moment of birth parents and children are negotiating separation, for children need to learn what Winnicott calls 'the capacity to be alone'.

He highlighted how children can only develop their individual identity fully if they can feel comfortable being alone as well as with other people. Psychotherapist Robert Hobson developed the idea of aloneness and togetherness being independent by highlighting how the word 'alone' carries overtones and undertones of 'all-one'.

Consider this:
- What does the phrase 'falling asleep' mean to you?
- Why is it called 'falling asleep'? Where are we falling to?

Sleeping and death
When children go to sleep to some extent they are entrusting themselves to their own body rather than to those of their parents. And this can cause anxiety because we all lose vigilance when we sleep. Five

years after her husband's death, an elderly widow was explaining how she rarely slept for a full night: *'I wake up constantly, I'm not distressed. . . just watchful.'*

Everybody has mixed feelings about states of unconsciousness. Sleeping and death seem inextricably linked in our unconscious minds. The very language we use to describe death highlights this fact: *'Falling asleep . . . Not dead but sleeping . . . Resting . . .'*

And just as we begin our lives sleeping most of the time, so it is often the manner of our dying. We talk of drifting off to sleep and we also talk of someone drifting into death. Many parents will admit to checking several times when their child, especially a baby, is asleep to *'see if they are breathing'*.

We say to children, *'Close your eyes and go to sleep'*, and we also talk of, *'Keeping a watchful eye'* on children. In a child's mind, closing your eyes may mean that the watchful eye is also closed and so they may feel very vulnerable when asleep (as indeed we all are!) for if Mummy or Daddy are not there, who is protecting them? In my early days as a primary school teacher the mother of Grace, a five-year-old West Indian girl in my class, died suddenly and unexpectedly of a heart attack. Grace was understandably inconsolable. She was devoted to her father and grandmother who now cared for her full time, and as time went by she seemed to be both grieving well and coping well, apart from the fact that every evening she produced the most dramatic tantrums and would refuse to go to bed. Her family were deeply committed Evangelical Christians. They had assured her, *'Jesus had taken Mummy for an angel'*, and that God was looking after Mummy and her in her grief. Christmas was approaching and two things happened which helped the adults to understand Grace's sleeping problems. Firstly, she painted a typical five-year-old's picture of a house and garden, but instead of a sun shining there were watery grey dots of rain. She then painted two large black circles over the entire picture.

She told me this was, *'A scary painting . . . the family is trying to hide from the rain'*, but she offered no explanation of the black circles until I commented,

'Those are big black circles . . . '

'Yes,' she said, *'*[they're] *the eyes of God. God sees everything . . .* [then very loudly] *everything you do.'*

The second incident arose out of the casting of the nativity play – always a highly emotionally charged event in a Year 1 classroom! The class and I were listing the characters we would need for the play and inevitably somebody called out, *'Angels! I want to be an angel.'* At this point Grace became hysterical sobbing, *'I don't want to be an angel.'*

We all came to understand how Grace was terrified of dying in her sleep, a common enough issue for this age group, but her father's and grandmother's well-intentioned metaphors had heightened rather than allayed her fears. If Jesus could take Mummy for an angel, could he not also take her just as suddenly? Instead of feeling protected by an all-seeing God, she seemed to feel intruded upon.

Bedtime is an ending. It marks both the end of the day we have known and the dawning of the unknown day ahead. For bereaved children, any ending can remind them of their loss, but small children may also worry about exactly *what* is ending at the end of the day. For example, when Grace's grandmother told her at bedtime, *'Put your toys away'* she meant, *'Put your toys away until morning.'* Unconsciously, Grace feared she was saying, *'Put your toys away forever.'*

Sleeping and separation anxiety

*'I feel awful about it . . . I begin to count the time to bedtime . . .
and it's not their fault they are just being children.'*
(Mother of three)

Winnicott wrote that there is no such thing as a baby, only a mother and baby in a relationship. Babies begin their lives as close to their mother as it is possible to be, i.e., inside her, and during the first years of life parents keep their children close to them. So, difficulties in going to sleep are rarely only a child's problem. In her book *Through the Night*, psychotherapist Dilys Dawes highlights how many sleeping problems are due to what Dr John Bowlby called 'separation anxiety', i.e., how anxious or not a parent and child are about being apart.

We talk of 'putting a child down to sleep'. Many parents will report both a mixture of relief and sadness when they put their children to bed at the end of the day. Something we all know, but that is rarely talked about, is that at times all parents hate their children as well as love them. We have been thinking about the links between sleeping and death and maybe this young mother was voicing the unconscious fear of many parents who find it difficult to put their baby down at night, i.e., the fear that at times they may feel like getting rid of the baby completely. And, of course, children have the same fear in reverse.

A four-year-old boy had a recurring nightmare that, *'A big crocodile came with a big, big mouth and eat my mummy up.'* We talked about how boys of four sometimes feel very angry with their mummies and he eventually chipped in, *'Yes, they might wish they'd get eaten up but I don't!'*

Will Mummy be there when I wake up?

Learning to separate means being able to both trust the unknown world away from our parents and being confident they will be there when we return. Child psychoanalyst Melanie Klein describes this as our discovery that we have good parents inside us, looking after us wherever we go. For most children this is a natural process which goes relatively smoothly, but some children will take longer than others, and other children's life experience will give them cause to doubt as to whether this can be true or not.

Five-year-old Ross had moved house when he was three, and shortly afterwards his parents had separated and the family dog had died. Ross found it impossible to sleep at night without waking up to go and see his mother. He didn't complain he was scared or of having a bad dream, or that he couldn't sleep, he would simply say, *'I comed to see you.'* Ross was anxiously checking that he hadn't lost his mother during the night as he had lost his previous home, his father and pet dog.

The good fairy and the bad witch parent

Some children have a sleep problem not because they fear their parents might not be there in the morning, but more that they may magically change in the night. Klein explained how babies form the idea they have two mothers; there is the 'good mother' who responds to their crying when they are hungry or distressed, and there is the 'bad mother' who does not. She explains how gradually the baby comes to realize that they do not have a perfect mother, but rather one who sometimes gets it right and sometimes doesn't.

Six-year-old Chara could not settle to sleep at night because she was afraid of having her *scary dream*; a dream in which she was playing in the garden with the fairy queen. She throws a ball to the fairy queen but it goes past her over the hedge to the neighbour's garden. Chara realizes she can reach the ball by crawling under the hedge, which she does but, when she returns to play, the fairy queen has turned into a bad and angry witch.

Chara's parents had high standards and Chara had a deep-rooted worry that she was only loved if she was 'a good girl'. She thought she was 'a naughty girl' for crawling under the hedge into next door's garden and was afraid, unconsciously, that her good, fairy mother may have turned into an angry witch mother to punish her. Her parents had not intended she should get this message, but it had slotted into Chara's fears of a good and bad mother.

What does separation mean to you?

Sleep, like our appetite, is sensitive to stress. Not sleeping is our way of registering our present circumstances and, in one sense, it would be odd to always have a good night's sleep. However, it is not only children who may worry about being separated from their parents; parents also worry about being separated from their children. And of course this is a natural part of the need of parents to protect their children. It is only a cause for concern when the degree of the parents' anxiety is inappropriate to the child's age and stage of development. For example, a six-year-old and an eight-year-old out on a family trip wanted to join the crowd climbing the steps to the top of a castle, *'To see all the world'*.

'*Oh, no,*' said their mother. '*What would I do if you fell from up there?*'

How you feel about leaving your child, even for the night, is going to affect how well they sleep.

Consider this:

- How well did you sleep as a child?
- If well, why do you think that was?
- If badly, what would have helped you to sleep?

Eighteen-month-old Kevin had been a disturbed sleeper from birth. His mother explained how his birth had been traumatic in that her labour went so fast she was only just about on the delivery table when he arrived. Added to that, he had breathing difficulties at birth and there was a degree of panic in the delivery room. She remembered asking repeatedly, '*Is he alright?*' and feeling that the reassuring, '*Yes*' belied the paediatrician's busyness with her baby in another corner of the room. She described how anxious she felt and how she hated her baby being removed to the nursery at night: '*He was always crying when they brought him back for a feed.*' Unlike the other mothers on the ward, she refused the staff's offer to babysit on her last night in hospital so she and her husband could have an evening out. '*I just didn't want to leave him, I know it's silly, but I just didn't want to be that far away from him . . . I didn't trust anyone else to look after him.*'

We began to think about Kevin's mother's own experience of separation. She had busy professional parents who did not return home until late in the evening, so she was often put to bed by the au pair without seeing them. She remembered bedtime as a rather hurried, perfunctory affair. Once she was in bed the au pair was off duty and she felt her bath and story were always achieved as fast as possible: '*I never felt she really wanted to read to me.*' She remembered being left alone '*in the big, dark bedroom*' listening for her parents' return and she recalls frequently thinking as a child, '*this room is too big for one little girl.*'

There is no experience like parenting for evoking childhood memories. Because of her own experience, Kevin's mother felt it was, *'like sending him to Coventry'* when she put him to bed. If we combine these unhappy memories of childhood with all the natural anxieties about Kevin at birth, it is easy to understand how his mother could have been transmitting to Kevin that bedtime and sleep were experiences to cause him to be anxious. It had not occurred to Kevin's mother that because of her own experiences of bedtime she knew exactly what Kevin needed to have a good sleep, i.e., all the experiences she didn't have of a quiet, relaxed time, as described by one little girl as *'all comfy and snoozy'.*

The importance of dreams

Dreaming is very important. Freud said that dreams were the 'Guardian of sleep'. When we dream we file away the experiences of the day so they do not clutter the beginning of the next day. When we don't sleep, we risk not processing the day and so may begin the coming morning already overloaded. Children use dreams to contain their feelings about the day. In this sense, dreams help children (and adults) to sleep. However, when we are asleep and dreaming we are closest to our inner-most fears and this can be especially frightening for children whose feelings are relatively strong, raw and primitive. So when a child says they can't go to sleep because they have 'bad dreams' it may be that they are telling you that they are afraid of their deep feelings.

To leave them to cry or not?

> *'I was ecstatic when she was born . . . and then I heard her cry and my heart sank, because I knew I was destined to answer that cry for the rest of my life.'*
>
> *(Mother of a three-year-old)*

Crying is the most common and powerful way babies and children let their parents know they are in need. A young mother came to see me with her eleven-month-old daughter and asked the perennial question, *'Should I leave her to cry?'* Her own mother had left when she was six months old and she was brought up by her father, with extended family helping out. Her father had been prone to violent and abusive outbursts and she was still rather afraid of him. She told me how she had been to stay with him recently and he had insisted she left the baby to cry herself to sleep at night. She had found this unbearable and felt overwhelming sadness and distress every time it happened: *'I just knew it wasn't the right thing.'* She then told me of an incident which had surprised her greatly on the last day of her visit. Her baby hated having her hair washed and used to kick and scream violently when it happened. As she was struggling to wash her daughter's hair, her father rushed into the bathroom and told her to stop. He was clearly upset rather than angry and was pleading with her to *'leave it, she can't bear it.'* She recalled how she continued with the hair wash to the end, not because she felt it was the right thing to do, but because, *'I wanted to show him she was my baby and I knew she always did this.'* But she was astounded at 'the tenderness' of her father's concern.

> Wondering, *'Should I leave my baby to cry?'* cannot help but remind you how you felt about being left to cry.

We don't know what was going on for this grandfather, but we can guess that both his tough insistence on 'leaving her to cry' and his emotional reaction to hearing his granddaughter cry were responses to memories of his own unhappy childhood.

Consider this:
- Babies cry for all sorts of reasons and responding appropriately to their cries is bound to be a matter of trial and error.
- If a baby is wet or hungry of course then they need to be picked up.
- It may also be appropriate to pick up a baby who is feeling temporarily lonely, anxious or just in need of reassurance.

But Dilys Dawes suggests that being put to bed is 'an interesting conversation' between parents and their child. The parent may feel they are being kind to put the baby to bed to sleep; the baby may be of a different opinion. They may feel a little abandoned and feel the need to protest. Dawes points out how parents who pick up a baby in such a state of mind may be unconsciously blackmailing the baby to believe their version, i.e., they are being kind. She stresses the importance of parents being: *'sensitive . . . to the real needs that he may be expressing. Allowing a baby to be separate includes allowing the baby to be angry and to express this anger.'*

It is painful and evocative to hear a cry. The upside of worrying how to respond to your baby's crying is that you are hearing and listening, and therein lies the answer on how to manage, to pick up or to ignore. For gradually you will get to know your baby and hear the different tones and qualities of their cry, so you will slowly begin to recognize intuitively whether or not they need the attention of being picked up.

To sleep in your bed or not?

Parents and children spend a huge amount of time together. The younger and more dependent your children, the more likely you will want to keep them close to you and this raises the question of whether or not bedtime and sleep are a natural or enforced time for separation. In some cultures, it is the norm for parents and children to share a bed until the child naturally moves into their own room around the age of three or four years old. However, *'letting them into our bed'* can be a constant topic of debate (and argument) in indigenous Caucasian British families. Sometimes both parents will feel happy to have their baby sleeping with them on the basis that it is natural, and the baby is less likely to wake and be restless because of their closeness to their parents' bodies, and if they do wake they are easier to settle because they have not had to wait for a parent to come to them. Other parents take the view that, as one mother put it, *'I like my nights'* i.e., they need to have time away from the baby and would rather have to cope with having to get out of bed at night than have the baby sleeping in bed with them. The same issue arises with toddlers and the older child who wakes in the night fearful and distressed. Some parents will happily take them into their bed on the basis that everyone gets back to sleep quickly. Others feel their child must learn to sleep alone and may also feel that they cannot sleep satisfactorily with a small child in their bed.

Of course, most difficult is when parents have differing views on these matters!

Most children love sleeping in their parents' bed. It may or may not be true that if allowed to sleep in their parents' bed from babyhood, children will naturally make the move to their own bed in the late toddler years. But in my clinical experience, children protest strongly when parents decide it is time for them to move.

Consider this:

- What are you hoping to achieve for your child if you let them sleep in your bed?
- Whose needs are being met if you let them sleep in your bed?

We have already thought about how part of growing up is learning to meet our own needs. The risk of immediately allowing a wakeful child into your bed is that they will not learn, or will be slower to learn, other ways of dealing with their anxiety. I was surprised by a conversation recently with a three-year-old who was telling me she had bad dreams about monsters and: *'I get scared and I go into Mummy and she says, "Go back into your own bed."'* I was surprised at the firm tone of voice the little girl used in repeating what her mother had said and asked, *'And how does that make you feel?'*

'Lovely,' she said, *''cos my own bed is all warm and snoozy.'* This little girl wanted to be in her own bed and simply needed the reassurance she was safe in her own bed.

There are all sorts of reasons why a child may want to sleep in their parents' bed, and why a parent might want to keep their child in bed with them. A young mother whose husband was adamant their baby should sleep in an adjacent room volunteered that when he was away on business trips she always took the baby into bed with her 'for company'. A six-year-old boy whose father worked away from home during the week slept in his own room quite happily on weeknights. However, at weekends he would regularly wander into his parents' room in the night demanding entrance to their bed, *''cos I'm scared'.* We gradually came to understand his competition with his father over who was the man of the house! Pleased as he was to see his father at the weekend, he felt unconsciously that he intruded on his weekday intimacy with him and his mother.

We also need to remember that by sleeping in your bed children may provide an unconscious way of negotiating difficulties between you two as parents. When three-year-old Isabelle insisted on constantly sleeping in her parents' bed, her mother described her as, *'a great contraceptive'*. Unconsciously, she was glad to have Isabelle providing her with a reason for not having sex with her husband.

Conversely, it is not uncommon for parents in times of stress or unhappiness to sleep with quite big children in their bed. A seven-year-old boy had moved into his mother's bed for comfort for them both following the sudden death of his father. Aged eleven, he was still sleeping in her bed and neither of them seemed to feel the need to address the issue. In this case it wasn't necessary as the boy himself gradually moved back into his own bed before his twelfth birthday.

Sleep problems in older children

In times of stress or unhappiness other children may experience difficulties in going to bed, getting to sleep or waking in the night. We are all familiar with the child who is restless and unsettled before an exam or other important event. However, by seven years of age most children are sleeping through the night, and if they are regularly waking we should be concerned, even if the child himself does not seem stressed. We should also take seriously any sudden change in a child's sleep pattern that persists. A ten-year-old girl suddenly became afraid of going upstairs alone and would go to enormous lengths to persuade one or other parent to accompany her. She became skilled in prevarication when it came to bedtime and, although she didn't ask her parents to stay in her bedroom with her, she would try and persuade them to be 'busy upstairs' once she was in bed. An eight-year-old boy developed a similar problem, but he would try to get his mother to lie with him on the bed until he fell asleep and would also frequently go into his parents' room during the night saying he couldn't sleep.

In unravelling these stories, it was interesting to discover that both children shared the same anxiety. They both felt that they had temporarily become slightly distanced emotionally from their parents. The girl's father had recently had a promotion at work, which involved him being away from home frequently and often at very short notice. This had caused considerable tension between her parents and she was left feeling that neither of them was keeping a keen eye on her. In the boy's case, his grandmother had been seriously ill in hospital and come to live with the family so she could be cared for until she was well enough to return home. His mother admitted that she had been finding it very difficult to juggle a full-time job, running the home and caring for her mother with giving the children very much individual attention. Her son felt that he could not, in his words, 'Catch hold of Mummy', as she was always rushing from one place to the next.

Difficulties in sleeping well may also be an indication of a secret worry such as being bullied. Older children need time, space and individual attention to be encouraged to discover and talk about why they can't sleep.

Managing sleep problems in older children

- It is, of course, impossible to make any child go to sleep, but it is possible with older children to suggest that they have to be in their bedroom by a certain time, i.e., you will only be available to them in case of an emergency. You will remember the story of Jack in the introduction.
- It may be best not to comply with a child's wish that you stay with them while they go to sleep. The risk here is that it reinforces the message that there is something they need to be protected from in going to sleep. It might be best to offer to check on them every fifteen minutes or so. Or you could try the tactics of one wily father who offered his eight-year-old £5 if he could stay awake all night. The child was furious that he fell asleep 'When I was trying to stay awake'.
- All children need routine at bedtime and need to be given plenty of notice that bedtime is approaching. A slow build-up to this routine may be essential for even quite grown-up children.

Who has problems?

One of the functions of children's sleep is to give parents time alone together. If your child is persistently not sleeping, it could be worth asking yourself if it suits you to have the child around rather than to be alone. Could there be any reason why you two would not want to be left alone together in the evenings?

Managing sleep in younger children

The North Downs Community Health (NHS) uses a management programme introduced by Dr Olwen Wilson. She argues that we associate the last sequence of events at bedtime with going to sleep. *'As adults we put out the milk bottles and the cat, turn off the TV and begin to yawn as we climb the stairs.'* She highlights how if we were at a party or out to dinner, our usual bedtime may come and go without our noticing. Children also associate the last bedtime sequence with sleep. So when they wake in the night, they feel the need for this sequence to help them to settle again. Wilson points out that on her sleep management programme, the task is not to stop the child waking, but to recognize that the child does wake and has sleep-associated habits. In order for the child to be able to get back to sleep, their sleep association needs to be one which does not need the parent to be in the room with them. The last thing the child sees and hears before they drift off to sleep should be the same thing they see each time they rouse in the night. Children need help to recognize what they see when they wake in the night as the same things they saw when they went to bed: *'The bed or the cot, the room, the teddy, familiar pictures on the wall in the dim light – but no bottle, no Mummy or Daddy, no TV, no back soothing,'* says Wilson.

The key to Wilson's programme is helping parents to provide support, but not attention, when the child wakes. Parents are advised to follow the normal bedtime routine, then at the very end kiss the child goodnight and promise to come back in a minute for another kiss. Wilson advises that they should actually return in seconds: *'They should move just a little, then back to give another kiss, then a little more, then another kiss, then occupy themselves – for example, by putting away some clothes in the drawer – and give another kiss. Then out and back for another kiss and so on.'* The idea is that the child understands the routine to be head on pillow, then a goodnight kiss, no more chatter, no more cuddles, no more stories, plays or drinks; just kisses until the child is asleep. Wilson warns that this may take up to 300 kisses and three hours the first night, but it should be slightly less the second night, then less again on the third and fourth nights. The fifth night may be as bad as the first, but once you have passed this test night, by the sixth and seventh nights the new routine is usually secured.

Summary

- Eating and sleeping are the fundamental organizers of our lives and so we should not be surprised that children will use eating and sleeping as ways of communicating their most important worries and disturbances.
- We also need to remember that eating and sleeping disruptions are an ordinary problem of childhood; most children have issues with eating and sleeping at some point in their development. We only need to worry about sleeping and eating problems if they persist or if they dominate a child's life.
- There is something about feeding problems parents cannot help take personally.
- One of the most powerful and troubling aspects of all feeding difficulties is the way that once a child stops eating parents become very preoccupied with their child's appetite.
- Feeding difficulties seem to be a child's way of saying, *'I need you to think about me more. There is something I just can't take in.'*
- Eating is about what we can take in and digest emotionally as well as physically.
- Parenting, food and feeding are inextricably bound together.
- Feeding is different from disciplining! If you use food as a reward or

a punishment then you run the risk of your child growing up confusing bodily and emotional needs.

• Try not to over-focus on 'good' or 'bad' foods as your child may take this as an invitation to rebel against them.

• The media's preoccupation with healthy diet is consciously or unconsciously feeding (!) the idea that it is possible to be a perfect parent.

• Most people want to do the best for their child; the issue nowadays is whether or not they feel free to do so. The idea of the healthy diet suggests implicitly that it is possible to engineer a socially happy child.

• It may be best to try and describe food in the home avoiding the words 'good', 'bad' and 'diet'.

• How you feel about food is going to influence your child's attitude to it.

• Is your child a faddy eater or is it they are simply experimenting with choice and finding out whether they prefer different foods to the remainder of the family?

• Food faddiness may be an older child's way of trying to establish that they are individual, distinct and different from the rest of the family.

• The single food fad is an extension of picky eater. We can think of such a child as trying to return to the mother they had in infancy, i.e., a mother who is closely attuned to the child's needs.

• Eating disorders are different to 'pickiness' and are a result of a child feeling food has too many associations for them. These may centre on issues around power and control and emerging sexuality.

• Children need to be lonely in the sense that they need to experience being alone to experience solitude.

• When children go to sleep to some extent they are trusting themselves to their own body rather than to that of their parents. And this can cause anxiety because we all lose vigilance when we sleep.

• Sleeping and death seem inextricably linked in our unconscious mind.

- Some children have a sleep problem because they fear their parents might magically change in the night.
- It is not only children who worry about being separated from their parents; parents also worry about being separated from their children.
- Wondering, *'Should I leave my baby to cry?'* cannot help but remind you of how you felt when you were left to cry.
- What are you hoping to achieve if you let your child sleep in your bed, and whose needs are being met?
- We need to remember that by sleeping in your bed children may provide an unconscious way of negotiating difficulties between you as parents.
- Difficulties in sleeping may well be an indication of a secret worry, such as being bullied, in older children.

CHAPTER 3

The Stealing of Crowns

– Sibling Rivalry –

'. . . Sneaping frost That bites the first born infant of the spring . . .'
(Shakespeare)

It seemed a good idea at the time – to have more children! By the time you were pregnant for the second time, many of the expectations discussed in the first chapter would have been tried and tested. Now a further expectation comes into view – that your children will love each other and take a harmonious pleasure in each other's company. While you were probably expecting the traditional sibling spats, you maybe did not anticipate the constant hostilities that frequently seem present as one child tries to make another's life a misery.

A further expectation . . . 'someone to play with'

'We didn't want him to be an only child; we wanted him to have someone to play with.'
(Father of two children)

'We were only children; if we died she'd have nobody.'
(Mother of two children)

The most common reason given when I ask parents what made them decide to have a second child – (usually out of my sense of awe at how they have managed the first) – is that they wanted their children to be companions for each other. A small and wistful seven-year-old once observed quietly in a family session when such a comment was made, *'But you didn't ask me if I wanted a sister to play with!'*

You may feel disappointed and dismayed when your children seem to fight and argue excessively. It is also likely that you worry you are doing something wrong – the fantasy being that this doesn't happen in other families. It is ironic how, in times of anxiety, we can suddenly be aware of exacerbating factors all around. A friend, recovering from major surgery, said he was surprised at the increase in the number of wheelchair users in his home town. Of course, the likelihood is that there was no such increase, but being in a wheelchair himself made him more aware of others in the same position. Equally, it seems that when parents are most worried and anxious about their own children's sibling rivalry, they feel surrounded by other families where total harmony seems to reign all the time.

Consider this:

- Would any child really choose to have a younger sibling? We can wonder what, from a child's point of view, they gain by having a sibling.
- Why did you decide to have a second or third child?
- Did you have different reasons for having different children?

> We need to hold in mind that the idea that siblings should get on may be much more that of the parents rather than of the children!

It is rather like having a dinner party, where you invite a group of people who don't know each other but have things in common, in the hope that they will 'get on'. Sometimes they do, sometimes they don't;

there is no guarantee because other factors, aside from having common interests and a friendship with you, come into play – and so it is in families.

> Maybe what matters is not whether or not your children are rivalrous of each other, but your ability to acknowledge such rivalry as an ordinary problem of childhood. Helping your child to negotiate rivalry is as ordinary a task as helping him to learn to walk.

Is sibling rivalry inevitable?
No, but it is a natural phenomenon. The balance of relationships within a family will change with exits and entrances. Dr Penelope Leach describes vividly how the only way an adult can understand what it is like for a child to have a sibling is for you, the mother or father, to think of your partner coming home and saying, *'Darling, you're such a wonderful partner, I'm going to get another just like you, and she/he is going to come and live with us.'*

> Remember, sibling rivalry is first and foremost a grievance against you, the parents, for having another baby.

If parents are sensitive to the feelings of existing children, and respond with understanding, rivalry may be kept to a minimum. On the other hand, it may not!

Is there a good age to get a sibling?
This is one of those questions that is easy to talk around and almost impossible to answer. And as even the best-laid family plans can go awry, it is almost not worth worrying about. What can be more useful is to understand the developmental stage your child is at when a new baby arrives and how that may colour their response to you.

- Children under 18 months are still babies themselves and as they are pre-verbal they can only show you how they feel by their behaviour.
- From two years old, toddlers will understand much of your explanation about the coming baby, but will still rely on behaviour to communicate how they feel. This may range from aggression towards you and/or the baby to regression to baby ways themselves.
- By five-plus years, children will have established their special place within the family and, at an unconscious level, may well feel that they have escaped having a younger sibling. However, they will have more sense of who they are and will have consolidated their relationship with you. They are also more able to understand advantages of being a little more grown up.
- It can be argued that the older the child when a sibling arrives, the less likelihood there is of intense sibling rivalry. The older child is likely to have established his identity and own life, and is, therefore, less threatened by the new arrival. Teenagers will certainly be more focused on their life outside the home. But as with other human predicaments, there are no guarantees.

'Why can't I have the money? You give Tom money.'
'Tom is only four years old.'
(Angry exchange between a seventeen-year-old boy and his father)

- And, of course, it is never wise to ask your existing children if you should add to the family. Firstly, it is an almost impossible question for the child to answer and, secondly, what do you do if they say no? Your first child is used to your sole attention and if they are still a toddler, may have a sense that they rule the world. And why not? Their every need is met, usually, on request, leading them to believe that they are in charge of you, rather than vice versa. Older children will be used to their special place in the family – the baby, the only girl, the eldest son, etc. – and are unlikely to relish the idea of their position being changed by the arrival of a new baby.

'We did everything right. We talked to him about the baby, we let
him feel her kicking inside, etc . . . the baby bought him a present,
we have gone on giving him special time . . . but he is so jealous.'
(Desperate parents of a five-year-old)

'He stole my crown, he stole my crown!' Eight-year-old Sam explodes and
sums up the dismay he felt as a three-year-old on the arrival of his
younger brother. He not only had to share the attention of his adoring
parents and grandparents but, in his view, was usurped by him as the
king of the family kingdom.

For a child under five, the arrival of a new baby in the family
can raise a worrying question: 'Why did Mummy and Daddy
want another baby, when they'd already got one?'

Two of the most common conclusions children come to are:

• Mummy and Daddy forgot that they had already got a baby.
• I did something wrong or I wasn't good enough and that's why they
  got another baby.

Six-year-old Tim

Tim was six years old when his parents sought my help about his
demanding and worrying behaviour. He was difficult to settle at
night, never wanting to go to bed, and once he'd been put to bed, he
would call or come downstairs at regular intervals. He rarely slept a
full night, and would frequently wander into his parents' room
demanding entrance to their bed during the night. During the day
he was always 'on the go', constantly restless, both at home and at
school. His parents described how, even if he was watching TV, he
would be fidgeting next to them on the settee. He frequently had
minor and relatively superficial accidents, such as falling off his
dining room chair, for which he would seek an inordinate amount
of attention. He would sob, wail and demand endless cuddles and

reassurance, even when his parents were sure that the accident couldn't have 'hurt'. Much of this behaviour had begun when his mother was pregnant and it had deteriorated further after his sister was born.

I asked Tim's parents how his restlessness made them feel. They were frank in their irritation with him: *It's impossible to even watch TV when he's around, he's always in the way . . . he's always on our mind.'*

Throughout this book we are thinking about how children have very limited ways of telling adults when they have a problem. If they haven't the language then they are likely to fall back on behaviour as a way of communicating. In Tim's case, his restless behaviour was construed as a problem in the family. But maybe, for Tim, this problem was actually a solution. Maybe Tim felt he had to work very hard to stay in his parents' minds.

In a family session, Tim said he thought his parents had got the baby, *'in the night, when I wasn't there'.* Tim seemed to be worried that his parents had got another baby because they'd forgotten they'd already got one. He was worried he had somehow fallen out of his parents' mind, and could do so again if he did not constantly remind them he was around.

Tim's parents understand . . .

When you are worried about your child's behaviour, it is always worthwhile thinking about how the behaviour makes you feel. Tim's parents' irritation with him – and their feeling that he was *always on our minds'* – was a crucial clue to Tim's worries. Tim was making his parents feel his worry, i.e., you mustn't forget me. Anyone who has held a crying baby knows that babies communicate by projecting feelings. By this I mean babies make the adults feel what they are feeling. The interesting thing about 'problem behaviour' is that so often the behaviour is a problem to the adults; to the child, it may be a solution to a real worry or puzzle. Once Tim's parents were able to think of his behaviour as a communication, they found it much easier to manage. His reluctance to go to bed and disrupted nights were understood as his fear of leaving his parents alone together. He knew that if he left them alone they might make another baby.

. . . and helped Tim to understand

- Tim needed to be helped to talk about his fears and anxieties. He seemed relieved when his parents gave him open and honest explanations about why they had had another baby. He was reassured that he had not been, and could not be, forgotten by them. His parents explained that, although at times they might be thinking about other people and things, they both had a space in their minds labelled 'Tim', and that space was always there, and so they could never forget him.

- Through his behaviour Tim was communicating that he felt babies got the better deal in the family. His parents began to think about what was in it for Tim to be the elder child in the family. What rewards did he get for being the eldest? They realized that whereas it may have been appropriate to treat a three-year-old and a five-year-old in approximately the same way as regards bedtimes, etc., now that Tim was eight years old he needed some privileges for being the eldest.

- Rewards, such as being able to stay up a little later, being given pocket money, etc., helped him to establish his own particular place and identity within the family. Tim's destructive behaviour began to decrease.

- A slow build-up to bedtime enabled him to go to bed without too much protest. About forty-five minutes before bedtime his parents would say, *'Tim, soon it will be time for bed, what do you need to do before you go to bed?'* Twenty minutes later they would remind him that he had twenty minutes more and a similar reminder was given at ten minutes. (*'Ten minutes* more 'always seems longer and has a more positive connotation than *'Ten minutes* left'.)

- If he did wake during the night, his parents would reassure him that he was not forgotten, and return him to his own bed. Tim became generally more relaxed and less frenetic because his anxieties had been communicated and heard.

Five-year-old Sophie

Sophie was a naughty little girl who took every opportunity to disobey, make mischief or spoil a family event or outing with a massive temper tantrum in public. Any attempt at disciplining her was met with massive sulks and an outburst of, *'I know you don't love me.'* Her parents were at their wits' end when they came to see me.

Sophie had a younger brother, born when she was nearly three years old. Her parents remembered bewilderedly how, in the couple of months before her brother's birth, Sophie had frequently asked, *'Am I a good girl? Am I a good girl?'*

Sophie's mother talked at length of her deliberate naughtiness: *'It's as though she wants to be told off.'* Maybe Sophie did, maybe she felt she'd done something wrong, or there was something wrong with her, and that's why her parents had decided to have another baby. When children are persistently and deliberately naughty, it can sometimes be their way of trying to find out what is wrong with them. The hope is that if they find out the 'big wrong' and are punished for it, then all will be well – and in Sophie's case, the baby would be returned from whence it came! Her mother remembered rather movingly an occasion when she had been trying to read Sophie a story, but was frequently interrupted by her baby brother crying. *'Mummy, can't we put the baby in a cupboard and just get him out when we want him?'* Sophie asked.

Sophie's parents understand . . .

What did Sophie need to help her regain her confidence in the fact that she was loved and lovable? How do you give a small child the message that she is loved simply because she is who she is? Sophie needed to be spoiled:

- To have special time and treats with her parents.
- To be surprised by them with sudden hugs or inexpensive little gifts or treats for no reason – not because it was her birthday, or she'd been 'a good girl', or achieved something, but simply because she existed.
- To have her parents verbalize that they enjoyed her company. It can

be very helpful to such a child for parents to say, *'I am enjoying playing this game (shopping, driving to school, etc.) with you'* as an event is happening. In this way Sophie was reassured of her parents' pleasure in her.

The importance of spoiling

It can be a daunting task for parents to try to spoil a child who seems to be behaving inappropriately; won't it encourage the child to persist with unacceptable behaviour? There is a difference between indulging and spoiling. Allowing a child to be in control is a terrifying experience for the child. Children need and want the adults to be in charge. Giving a child special time and attention, in however small a way, when he is troubled can give the message, *'We love you because you are you, even when you are being this version of yourself we find difficult.'*

> *'Things are much improved, spoiling her really seems to be helping.
> . . but I'm running out of money.'*
> *(Father of nine-year-old)*

Spoiling doesn't necessarily mean the giving of material gifts. While these may be useful at times, parents are usually resourceful in finding ways of spoiling a child without breaking the bank! Such spoiling should go hand in hand with firm, but kind, discipline. It may be acceptable to be jealous of your brother, but it is not acceptable to communicate this by hitting him.

Seven-year-old David

David was referred to me because of his difficulty in making friends. I was assured by his parents of his close and loving relationship with his five-year-old sister, whom he was said to adore. His parents wondered if his closeness with his sister was preventing him from making friends – was it that he simply didn't need other children? They recounted how he was recently invited to spend the night at a friend's house. He had become highly distressed at bedtime as to whether his sister, Rowena, *'was alright'*, declaring he was missing her so much that he wanted to go home and he could not be persuaded to stay. I was also told of his terror of *'monsters and things that go bump in the night'*; he would often have nightmares that a monster had come into the bedroom to hurt him.

Magic thinking

Children easily confuse wishing something would happen and making it happen; a sense of magical thinking, akin to the adult experience of not wanting to say something out loud for fear of making it true. Why could David not relax and enjoy the company of his friends, whom he knew very well, without being so anxious about his sister's wellbeing? Perhaps his closeness to his sister was a communication of how much he'd wished she'd go away. His desire that something would happen to her had so overwhelmed him that he felt she was only safe if he was around to protect her. Separated from him, he was afraid that his wishes to harm would do just that.

At some point, many children will wish their siblings dead; or at least that they will go away. It is also quite ordinary for children to wish their parents dead, or at least exiled for a while. Accepted as a normal human phenomenon, this should cause no problem. But sometimes such a wish, and the fear it may come true, can overwhelm a small child.

Inside and outside monsters

Children can easily be overwhelmed by strong, powerful feelings and need to find a way of communicating this to adults. David tried to describe 'the monster bit of himself' that wished to hurt his sister, and possibly his parents for having her, by his fear of the monsters entering his bedroom to cause him harm. He may have at least two reasons for doing so:

- David could make sense of his overwhelming feelings by describing them as monsters.
- By personalizing his feelings he was able to put them outside himself, i.e., it wasn't him who felt aggressive and destructive, but the monsters in the bedroom.

Terrified – or big and bossy?

David tried to overcome his fear of harming his sister by trying to protect her with a pseudo-devotion and concern. Other children may attempt to master their destructive thoughts by becoming dominant and controlling. They are trying very hard to communicate that they are big, strong and powerful, whereas in reality they are often hoping the adults will realize how helpless and powerless they feel in the face of their own aggression.

I remember a seemingly rather pompous, self-opinionated adult client who had always maintained he had a close relationship and a deep affection for a brother born when he was eight years old. I was suspicious. One day he told me how he remembered his brother being brought home and his mother saying, *'This is your baby brother, and you love him very much.'* We came to understand how he had spent his life trying to feel what his mother had told him he felt, but at the same time, developing his superior manner in an attempt to dominate his aggression towards, and his rivalry with, his baby brother.

David's parents understand . . .

David needed:

- Permission to feel angry and jealous. He had to realize that while he didn't have to like his sister, he did have to respect her.
- David's parents talked to him about 'magic thinking' and explained that nothing bad was going to happen to his sister because he wants to hurt her. There is only magic in fairy tales.
- David needed to understand that his 'monster feelings' were ordinary. The family as a whole shared angry 'monster' feelings. Everyone talked about what made them very angry, and how they felt when they were angry. Again, it was stressed to David that 'monsters' only exist in fairy tales, but acknowledged that perhaps sometimes he felt like a monster and that was frightening – like a monster coming into his bedroom.

Ten-year-old James

> *'I remember when I was four, sitting in the sand pit on a sunny day*
> *and thinking, "isn't this happy" – and Stephanie got born – every-*
> *thing was alright until Stephanie got born.'*

A pale, tense ten-year-old James was trying to *'explain my life to you'.*
Clearly a bright child, he had always found it difficult to settle at his
boarding school, making few close friends. He had initially made
good academic progress, but over the three terms prior to his referral,
his grades had consistently declined. He had been a weekly boarder
since the age of eight and had become increasingly reluctant to return
to school on Monday mornings. His parents explained it had never
been their plan for him to board, but from the age of seven he had
pleaded to do so and they had eventually reluctantly agreed. He persuaded them he missed being with his friends, and that he would love
'sleeping in dorms', and at boarding school *'you can play sport in the*
evening'.

'*He really hates his sister; he makes her life a misery.'* James's parents
were worried and bewildered. Concerned as they were about his
unhappiness, and lack of success at school, they said, *'Top of our list*
of worries is the way he bullies his sister.' I heard how he had always had
difficulty accepting her arrival and over the years he had constantly
hit, teased, bullied and provoked her. James's parents were at their
wits' end: *'We've run the gamut of our list of what to do. We've tried*
understanding, we've tried punishing, and nothing seems to make any
difference.' James's mother was particularly upset, explaining, *'I fre-*
quently lose it with him, and give him a kick up the pants. I can't stand
the way he treats her.' She confessed she often looked forward to his
return to school on Mondays: *'Life is so much more peaceful without*
him.'

James's parents understand . . .

Why did James want to board? James's parents and I thought about his
request to go to boarding school. Was it, as he said, because he *'missed*

being with his friends, wanted to sleep in dorms and play sport in the evenings' – all conscious or 'thought about' reasons for James, or was there another unconscious, or 'not thought about' reason?

> If problems hunt in pairs then so do feelings. For adults and children alike, loving and hating are always present together.

There is much truth in the old joke 'she's my best friend, and I hate her'. It is likely that your children are ambivalent about each other. You will have observed how they can fight like cat and dog one minute and be the best of friends the next. We began to understand that James had really wanted his sister to go away. Invariably, such a child gets into an enormous muddle for at least two reasons:

- James also had genuine feelings of affection for his sister. Children are as good as lovers as they are haters. He wanted to hurt her, but he also didn't want to hurt her.
- Like most children, James's aggression was overwhelming for him and he feared that if he did harm his sister, then he would lose his parents' love. He found himself in a 'no-win situation' and when he hit his sister, it was a hollow triumph.

When James asked to be sent to boarding school he was maybe setting his parents a test to which they gave the wrong answer! Unconsciously, he wanted to protect his parents and sister from his aggression. He felt that the only way to do this was to send himself away from the family. At the same time, he was afraid that maybe the same thoughts had crossed his parents' minds. And so he asks, *'Can I go to boarding school?'* hoping his parents will say, *'Oh, no, of course not, we love you far too much, we'd miss you far too much, we couldn't even think of you being away at boarding school.'* When he was allowed to board, it confirmed his worst fears that he was not wanted within the family because *'I hit my sister.'*

Managing children like James

- First and foremost James needed to be reassured that he was not the only brother to feel like this about his sister. His parents opened up the topic gently by saying things like, *'Lots of boys aged ten find it very difficult to have a sister and they may have lots of secret feelings about her.'* It doesn't matter if your child denies they are like that or sloughs you off; what matters is that you have opened up the topic for conversation.

- James needed to be reminded that it was his parents he was really angry with for having his sister, not his sister for her latest transgression against him. His parents consciously *'redirected his flack'* by explaining this to James when he complained about his sister.

- Children like James need to know and understand that everybody gets angry and that everybody finds it difficult to manage their anger at times. Once again, James was helped by his parents talking about their feelings and relationships with their own siblings.

- Gradually James's mother began to realize that *'Whingeing about his sister'* was James's way of trying to get her attention. Whilst we were all agreed that there was nothing wrong in wanting or needing attention, this was an unhelpful and destructive way for James to try to get his needs met. His parents decided to try to get James and his sister to sort out their difficulties themselves. When James came moaning about his sister or when his sister ran screaming that James had hit her, their mother would say gently, *'Well, what do you want me to do about it?'* When the usual replies of, *'Tell him'* or *'Stop her'* came, she would encourage the siblings to try and sort things out for themselves without resorting to violence. Initially the parents would keep a watchful eye on the dispute from a distance and seemingly ignore it, but the change in the children's behaviour was interesting. Not only did James become less aggressive but his sister also became more assertive in standing up for herself.

Managing older children's rivalry – 'The little ones get more attention'

Jonathan was six years old when I overheard him whispering to his three-year-old brother early one morning, *'Billy, when you were asleep last night, I got up and had ice cream with Mummy and Daddy.'* If you have a rivalrous elder child, it is likely that two aspects of their behaviour will irk you most:

• You will be angry when they hurt the younger, more vulnerable child.
• You will be angry when they gloat over their siblings.

This may be especially true if you have tried hard to give them some special treat or privilege in an attempt to alleviate their jealousy, only to have them rush off and immediately *'Rub his sibling's nose in it'.*

> Maybe gloating needs to be kept in proportion. You may regard it as an unpleasant character trait, but is it not one of the rewards of being the older child, to triumph over the younger one?

That said, no sibling should ever be allowed to bully another one. And there is a difference between gloating and contempt. It may be a healthy, developmental stage for a younger (or even less talented) child to negotiate their sibling's 'gloating', but continuous contempt is undermining of their self-esteem. There are ways in which you can manage this rivalry:

• Your older children may find it useful if you help them to think about how children of different ages need different kinds of attention. Help your eldest to think about exactly how the younger ones get more attention; they are likely to say they get help with dressing, washing and feeding. Agree with them and acknowledge that this is a lot of attention, but that it is two-year-old attention. Ask if they want two-year-old attention or do they want age-appropriate, six-year-old attention?

- Make a list with them of what would be special six-year-old attention: for example, staying up later, having pocket money, getting special treats a two-year-old can't have, etc. In this way, an older child may gain a sense that they are as much in their parents' mind as the younger, more actively, demanding ones.

- Explain that it is alright not to like or even to hate a sibling, but that it is not alright to disrespect or abuse them verbally or physically.

- You can encourage your child to air their feelings about their sibling by helping them to find names for their feelings. For example, they may be feeling angry, but maybe they also feel a bit sad about something.

- When children are jealous it doesn't always cross their mind that they may also be enviable. Asking your child what they think they have that their sibling might like sometimes helps them to get the relationship into perspective.

The family baby – how do you feel when you make a mess of it?

An eleven-year-old was watching her fourteen-year-old sister try on a particularly becoming bikini. Her sensitive mother, noticing her envy, said to her, *'When you're fourteen, you can have a bikini like Amanda's.'*

'No,' the younger girl replied, *'when I'm fourteen, I'll have that bikini. All I ever get is what Amanda has finished with.'*

Ten-year-old Jane was exploding with rage as she recounted an argument with her twelve-year-old brother, over who should sit where in the car. *'Tim said he should always sit in the front of the car because he's older than me.'* I said to him, *'You're always going to be older than me, so at that rate I'm never going to sit in the front.'*

One of your tasks as a parent is to help your child to come to terms with their incompetence. To small children, the skills and abilities of adults can seem almost magical. I remember a school friend telling me how as a child she thought that grown-up life would be so easy because *'adults know and can do everything'.* It is hard to feel incompetent. At best, most adults have an ambivalent attitude towards their own incompetence, at worst it can make them feel angry and frustrated. It is sometimes difficult to remember that making mistakes is an important part of learning.

Can we relate to the young mother who, when having her in-laws to Sunday lunch for the first time, forgot to bake the Yorkshire puddings – *'Oh, I didn't worry,'* she said. *'I served them up as profiteroles for tea!'* How we feel about our incompetence may depend on how it is described. For example, is a child shy, or do they have their own particular way of getting to know people? No wonder our incompetence makes us angry – it reminds us all the time that we are not omnipotent; we cannot do and know everything.

'It's not fair, Paul can stay up late . . .' – the oldest get everything

It is likely that your youngest child is not only envious of your skills, but also those of his older brothers and sisters. Just as older siblings may misconstrue age-appropriate attention given to the family baby as a demonstration of favoured affection, so younger children may perceive the skills and privileges of an older sibling as favouritism. The younger child may feel that everything he wanted to do, the older one has done first, and set the family standard.

Don't pretend the older children are not more skilled . . .

Faced with the younger child's explosions at the advantages of the older one, his cries of 'it's not fair' and his very obvious distress and rage, you may have fallen into something of a muddle in handling the children. It is not uncommon for parents to describe handling a younger sibling's envy by keeping the privileges or advantages of the older child a secret or by allowing the younger child to do the same as the older child – for example, by merging bedtimes in an attempt to blur the differences. Such solutions can, on the whole, only lead to resentment and confusion:

- The older child may feel rightly robbed of the privileges and rewards of being the older child and also of the ability, already discussed, to triumph over his younger sibling.
- The younger child may be led to a sense of hollow victory. He may have won the right to go to bed at the same time as the older child, but his envy of the older child's skills will remain.

Pretending children are the same age, or have the same skills and abilities, will not make them the same age, and will not give them the same skills and abilities. This is as true for age-related differences as it is when one child is more talented intellectually, creatively or physically than another in the family regardless of their age.

Helping the family baby with rivalry

- Explain to the family baby that you understand how disappointing it is for them to have to wait to grow up, but also highlight all the exciting things they can do while they are waiting to grow up. They need to know that you understand their frustration and disappointment.
- Reward them for being the youngest in the family. This may involve making a double effort to ensure that they do not always wear hand-me-down clothing, etc., even if such clothing appears to be virtually brand new.
- Talk about how you felt about your own position in your family as a child. This can be useful both if your position marries up with the position of the child having difficulties or not. Just hearing how Mummy and Daddy felt when they were the same age can bring enormous relief to a worried child. A little boy, riddled with jealousy of his older brother's ability to go and play football for the school on Saturdays, took enormous pleasure in his father's story of how, when he was small, he used to hide his older brother's football boots just as he was going out to play in a match.

Do you provoke jealousy?

'Can you do magic?' asked eleven-year-old Sam.
'It sounds as though you'd like to do magic,' I replied.
'Yes, I'd turn the blues into pinks,' said Sam.

Sam was the eldest of three children, with two much praised and adored younger sisters. From the time he was seven, his parents grew more and more anxious as Sam took every opportunity to *'dress up in chiffon and scarves',* and generally pursue what, at the time, might have been described as 'girlish activities'. Anxiety about his sexuality was running high when his parents finally came to see me – he was eleven years old.

Sam's behaviour was not communicating his sexual orientation, but it was about his sexuality. He thought that girls got a better deal in the family than boys, and presumed that his father's delight in his younger sisters was due to the fact of their sex, the fact they were girls. He began to worry that he was 'the wrong sex'. Sam was trying to behave like a girl because he thought that would bring him closer to his parents.

Consider this:

- How you handle your child's sibling rivalry is going to depend very much on your experience of sibling rivalry in your family of origin.
- You will be influenced by how your parents handled your feelings of rivalry but also you may find yourself identifying with the sibling who has the same position in the family as you had as a child, e.g., if you were a bullied younger sibling you may find yourself more sympathetic towards your youngest child.
- Equally, if you were a jealous older sibling you may feel you can relate more readily to the predicament of your elder child.

Seven-year-old Martha
Let us not forget the only child, who is not necessarily free from sibling rivalry. I was asked to see Martha, aged seven, who had become

extremely irritating to her teachers. She always seemed to be asking for unnecessary additional help. One teacher quoted a particularly irritating habit of her asking, *'Shall I turn over?'* when she reached the end of a page in her exercise book. The teachers were sympathetic towards her, in a way understanding that her behaviour could be a sign that she needed attention, but somehow 'needing attention' was being construed as a fault, rather than a genuine need.

Martha was an only child, born ten years into her parents' marriage. Both parents had busy careers involving not only long hours, but also a good deal of social entertaining. From Martha's point of view, it felt that her parents were *'always having fun at work and play'.* She grew up feeling jealous of her parents' relationship; as they were always going out together it felt to her that they would rather have each other than her. Of course it is true that there are times when all parents take greater pleasure in each other's company than their children, but Martha's worry was that this was generally true for her parents.

Martha's parents understand . . .

We tried to understand the meaning of Martha's attention-seeking behaviour. *'Oh, she's just trying to get attention',* is a phrase you have probably used many times about your own children. Adding the word 'just' tends to give the impression that children should not try to get attention, as though there is something wrong with having needs and trying to get those needs met. Attention-seeking behaviour so often indicates that a child is trying to get attached, i.e., close to someone. Martha wanted to feel close to her parents and to feel that they enjoy having her around. So we began to understand her 'attention-seeking' behaviour with her teachers as her trying to work out, *'Am I wanted and accepted by the adults?'* The problem was, her behaviour was so irritating to her teachers that she ran the risk of being given the very answer she so feared. Martha's behaviour left her feeling that while her teachers may remember her, they maybe didn't like her very much.

How Martha's parents and teachers helped her

- Martha's parents made a particular effort to have some special family treats with her each week and to tell her how much they enjoyed having her around. However, there are times when parents do want to enjoy being alone together. Martha's parents sometimes had to explain to her, *'Mummy and Daddy are having time alone together now. It's disappointing for you, but someday you will have a boyfriend/husband to go out to dinner with and to sleep with.'*
- Once Martha's teachers understood her need to be close, they found her behaviour much less irritating.
- They were able to help Martha to feel close in positive ways, such as sitting her at the front of the class and giving her special responsibility in the classroom.

'I can never get it right'

There will be times when you will feel as exasperated with your children's sibling rivalry as the mother who said, *'If I bring home two kit-kats, and let Penny choose before her brother, she'll say she chose the worst one.'* But your child may also feel they can't get it right. We could understand Penny feeling she couldn't get it right, because what she wants is what her brother has got, a different sex.

Will they grow out of it?

Most people have had the experience, at work or socially, of having inexplicably strong hostile or confused feelings towards another person which they do not understand and find difficult to manage. An adult client found it impossible to tolerate her landlady, often adding to her list of complaints, *'and that ginger hair!'* One day she realized how the landlady reminded her of her powerful, ginger-haired older sister, in whose care she was often left as a child.

> Sibling rivalry is rarely completely negotiated and the confusion and fears surrounding it are seen in adult life.

An ordinary condition

Envy and rivalry seem to be natural facts of the human condition. Adults come across it frequently in their workplace, and it is therefore not surprising that it is an issue children are likely to find in their 'workplace' – the home. If you can foster an attitude that love, affection and attention are not a cake, from which a slice is taken for one child, therefore leaving less to be shared between the others, but more like sun which shines and makes us feel warm, regardless of how many other people are sitting on the beach, then your children's sibling rivalry may stay in perspective. However, both parents and professionals will agree, that either we have to believe that some children are born more envious than others, or that at the moment we do not properly understand children with the most severe difficulties around sibling rivalry.

It's okay to hate your sibling

Perhaps the issue has never been summed up better than the eight-year-old, who described meeting her baby sister in the hospital, *'I ran over to the crib intending that I would love her all my life, but when I looked in the crib, I was jealous.'*

There is no magic solution to sibling rivalry because it is not soluble. It can be more or less well handled, but it is an issue which continues throughout our lives and which to some extent has to be endured as well as negotiated. That said, those of you reading this with pre-school children may take comfort from the fact that often children work out their sibling rivalry once they begin school. Their peers and teachers take on the role of family and parents, and issues within the family can be re-enacted and managed in a completely different way.

Accept that your children may not like each other. In so far as you can, foster an atmosphere of mutual respect rather than affection. Problems are most likely to arise if you make your children feel guilty or naughty for having ambivalent feelings about their siblings.

And beware of the dog!

As I finished writing this chapter, a friend reported, with a mixture of amusement and horror, that her six-year-old had *'sibling rivalry with the dog'*. This only child had longed for a pet but quickly became hostile and aggressive towards the dog as she perceived it taking her parents' attention from her as they trained it. *'Now we have to say, "good dog" and "good girl",'* laughed her mother. Sibling rivalry is not confined to brothers and sisters; a child may feel threatened not only by a pet, but your work, your hobbies or anything they perceive is important to you!

Summary

- Sibling rivalry is first and foremost a grievance against you, the parents, for having another child.
- It is the expectations of parents – not their children – that siblings will get on together!
- For adults and children alike, loving and hating are always present together.
- Small children may wonder on the arrival of a new baby, *'Why did Mummy and Daddy want a baby, when they'd already got one? Was it because there is something wrong with me or did I do something wrong?'*
- Most children are ambivalent about their siblings. Whatever position a child has in the family, he needs to feel that there are rewards for being in that place.
- Don't try and blur differences between your children, and allow for both triumph and disappointment.
- Only children may feel jealous of their parents' relationship.
- Sometimes parents can, without thinking, provoke jealousy.

CHAPTER 4

Rules, Regulations and Remonstrations

– Getting Them To Do As They're Told –

'Young women especially have invested in being nice people, and it is only when you have children that you realize you are not a nice person at all, but generally a selfish bully.'

(Fay Weldon)

Naughtiness is very much a matter of the way a child's behaviour is construed by adults. Six-year-old Sandy and her family were leaving her grandparents' house after a rather fraught visit on a cold and wet day. Sandy was told to, *'Jump into the car quickly'*. She did so promptly but, instead of getting into her car seat, began to tidy up the books and toys on the rear window ledge. As her mother stood in the rain holding her baby sister, her grandmother declared, *'That child can never do as she's told at once.'*

'Well,' her father replied gently, *'she thinks she is helping,'* and, leaning into the car, he said, *'Good job, Sandy, and can you now get right into your seat.'* Sandy promptly obeyed, saying proudly, *'Now Mummy has a nice tidy place to sit.'*

We can think of numerous other situations where a child may seem to be 'going their own way', when actually they think they are trying to please the adults. Is the excited five-year-old who rushes to greet much-loved visitors as they arrive and at the last moment thumps them, rude and uncontrolled? Or is he simply overwhelmed by his excited feelings and momentarily just forgot how to show people he is delighted to see them?

In these situations, the adults' response is crucial. Sandy's grandmother would have told her in a no-nonsense way to do as she was told and get into her seat at once. We can think of a range of responses from Sandy: she may have complied but felt misunderstood and even disliked; she may have argued and tried to explain which would have probably escalated the situation; she may have burst into tears which would have elicited a range of responses from her parents. Everybody is misunderstood and misconstrued from time to time in their lives but when a child is persistently misconstrued they are likely not only to become angry, but also to lose their sense of who they are as a person because what is real to them doesn't seem to be real to other people.

Consider this:
- If your child is naughty, what does it say about your child?
- If your child is naughty, what does it say about you?

We learn to parent from our parents

> *'What really influences you . . . what really makes you think about telling the kids off is how you felt as a child when you were told off. . . I just don't want to give them those awful feelings.'*
> (Mother of three)

In Chapter 1, we looked at how we learn to parent from our parents and pick up a lot of other skills as we go along. If what your parents did felt good and helpful you are likely to want to repeat it with your own children. You probably won't even think about it, you will react instinctively in the same way. The difficulties may arise when you want to do things differently from your parents. The risk here is that you are then left parenting from theory. You know exactly what you don't want to do, but may feel unsure about what you should do because you have no instinctive internal model to draw on. This is how conflicts may arise between parents over discipline and boundaries. If your parents managed temper tantrums by sending you to your room on a 'time out' principle, and your partner's parents managed temper tantrums by cuddling them until they calmed down, you as a parental couple may be coming from very different positions when it comes to managing your own child's temper tantrums.

Again in Chapter 1, we looked at how parents have to survive the conflicts parenting will inevitably throw up between them. However, at this point it is worth mentioning that the advantage of having two parents is that you get two points of view. Marcia's parents were discussing whether or not at aged eight she was old enough to walk to the village shop alone. Her mother felt it was too much of a risk. Her father felt she was a sensible girl and the time had come to give her more independence. *'Who's right?'* they asked anxiously. Well, of course, they were both right. Marcia needed to be protected, but also needed to be encouraged into the world. What her parents had to do was work out how they were going to do this now she was growing up.

'I suppose she could take a mobile phone,' said her mother reluctantly.

'Why?' replied her father. *'It's a five-minute walk; you can practically see her all the way from the garden.'*

Children need discipline

Both parents and children know that children need discipline as much as they need freedom and choice. By discipline I mean clear and consistent rules and boundaries At this point we need to remember that parents always give children two messages: the first is the conscious message, the thought-about message, which is what we say to children. Then there is the unconscious message, the not-thought-about message, which may be about what we really feel, but not what we want to feel! In a family session, an eleven-year-old and her mother were discussing why she had been the only girl in her year not to go on a school trip to the circus. Her vegetarian mother was passionate about animal welfare: *'I told her I didn't mind her going, she could go if she wanted to and all her friends were going.'* The eleven-year-old quickly interrupted, *'But I knew you didn't really want me to go . . . I just knew it!'*

This story also illustrates how parents and children differ. You are an adult with the ability to make adult decisions and choices, be they good or bad. Your child on the other hand is still developing the ability to make these choices. The boundaries you set, and the way in which you set them, will help your child to make the best choices. We need to remember that a genuine choice is always a genuine risk.

Why they need to disobey

As they grow up, children become increasingly aware of how adults and children are different. They begin to put their own first boundary in place by gradually separating from you. We can see this in a range of child behaviours, most often associated with physical care. As babies, we are very dependent on our parents' bodies for feeding, dressing, washing, etc. We can think of measuring how grown up and independent a child is by observing how separate they are from their parents' bodies. So the two-year-old who refuses help with dressing, even though they stand no chance of doing up their buttons, and the nine-year-old who locks the bathroom door, are both establishing a natural boundary.

Children are born into an unequal world where they have virtually no power and the adults have a great deal of power, or at least children's power is different from adult's power. In the process of growing up, children want to please their parents but they also want to have some of their power. Remember, a little defiance is no bad thing! A degree of defiance may be difficult for parents, but for a child it is essential. Children need to push and pull their own world in order to develop their independent personalities, but they need to do so within the security of firm boundaries.

Of course, most parents know the importance of secure boundaries, so why is it so difficult to say no?

Why is saying no so difficult?

'I hate saying no to her . . . she just looks so disappointed . . . I can't bear it.'

(Mother of three-year-old)

Parents should not be surprised if they find saying no difficult, because it *is* difficult. When we say no, we are reminded of the feelings we have when we cannot have what we want. Add to that the fact that we have to face the child's feelings of protest, anger, disappointment or persistence, and it is easy to understand why saying no is hard even when we know it is in the child's best interests.

Saying no can make us feel as though we are bullying, being aggressive, or even just spoiling someone else's fun. Why else is it so difficult to turn down unwanted invitations? Parents may feel they are deliberately denying their child for no valid reason, even though they are not. But perhaps most of all, saying no is difficult because it is likely to provoke an argument.

> Saying no creates distance between people. When you say no to your children you risk them hating you.

Being told no may particularly enrage small children who are still under the illusion that you think what they think and want what they want. I remember watching a fraught mother for half an hour as she insisted her sobbing four-year-old slept in his own bed not hers. Through his screams he eventually choked out, *'Look, Mummy, I've got an idea. You say, "Come in my bed" and . . .!'* It was as difficult for that mother to persist in saying no in the face of such naïve innocence as it was for a mother faced with a persistent three-year-old who eventually cupped her face in his hands as he said, *'Oh, Mummy, please say "I suppose so" . . .'* But, of course, by saying no you are helping your children to learn not only that there are boundaries between you and them, but also how to put boundaries around themselves and other people. Saying no helps children to learn:

- Who we can say no to.
- When we can say no.
- Why to say no.
- When we can stop saying no.

Why children need discipline

In this chapter we are presuming that rules and boundaries have a purpose and, of course, they do. If you want to play football, you need to know and understand the rules and if you want to excel at football, then you have to abide by the rules. Family life is not entirely like a game of football. I have said elsewhere that it is more akin to imaginative play, but it is true that if your children are going to have a good life then they need to understand some of the rules about human beings being together. Discipline is an adult's response to a child's behaviour, and so it is worth spending some time thinking about the purpose of the rules you want to put into place. The first question must be: 'How will you know this rule has been a success?'

- *'It will make my life as a parent easier.'*
- *'It will stop my child behaving that way again.'*
- *'It will offer my child a different way of behaving in the same circumstances.'*
- *'It will keep my child safe.'*
- *'My child will understand the consequences of their behaviour.'*

These are valid answers. The crucial questions in discipline matters are:

- Do I want to prevent my child from doing something?
- Do I want to guide my child into a certain way of behaving?
- What or whom do I hope to change?

Rules are always a prohibition and a temptation at the same time.

It is interesting to think about the times parents want to introduce a new rule. Sometimes a child may have surprised them with behaviour they had never anticipated. But parents can also be motivated by more nebulous reasons. They may try to ensure that the family feels close and secure by having rules, such as nobody going to bed angry with someone else, or that everyone eats together at mealtimes. In such rule-making, parents may be hoping the rule will act as a kind of spell to hold the family together which, of course, may or may not work.

Discipline helps to keep us safe

Most parents will feel that rules and discipline will keep a child safe. We want children to be safe from other people. Knowing the boundary between you and others also helps prevent you from behaving in a way you may put yourself at risk.

When children learn to respect their parents' wishes, they also learn that they have the right to have their feelings and wishes respected. So we can think that the advantage of rules and boundaries is that they help children to develop a sense of privacy – their own and other people's – and of respect for themselves and others.

The problem with rules and discipline

Privacy is an interesting state. Most people enjoy a sense of privacy and we may feel that a degree of privacy is essential for a good life. But the consequence of our privacy is that we may feel lonely. Rules and discipline highlight the differences between children and families in that what is allowed in one family may not be allowed in another. In this sense, boundaries may make children feel cut off from each other.

And if privacy is complex, so is the notion of boundaries. Children and parents will experience boundaries and rules in different ways. Let's think about bedtime: you will feel that setting a reasonable bedtime for your child is an act of love, ensuring they get enough sleep and rest. They may experience bedtime as a frustration because they are not allowed to be with you. And, of course, older children are likely to experience any rules as an attempt to sabotage their fun.

Getting them to do as they're told

> 'I've learned that people will forget what is said, people will forget what you did, but people will never forget how you made them feel.'
> (Maya Angelou)

Maybe what matters is not so much the rules and boundaries you choose to enforce as the way you choose to enforce them. For a child, discipline is a mirror. Do you want your child to see themselves as someone who is lovable but fallible and will be supported to change their behaviour? Or do you think they should see themselves as someone who should be ashamed and who is unlovable when they disobey you? Let's consider two obvious real-life examples.

Eight-year-old Martin and his family had guests to lunch. Martin made a reasonably valiant attempt at trying to cut up his food. When he was unsuccessful, he picked up his chicken and began to eat it with his fingers. His father reprimanded him severely and sent him to finish his meal alone in the playroom.

Eight-year-old Hannah and her parents also had friends to lunch. Hannah had the same difficulty in trying to break her fruit salad in to a child's bite size. She eventually gave up and speared an orange segment with her fork and then lowered her head to try and bite the orange off the fork in several mouthfuls. Her mother noticed but made no comment to Hannah. Smiling at her guests she muttered, *sotto voce*, *'I'm sorry, Hannah has a lot to learn about social eating.'* Later, she was seen showing Hannah in the kitchen how to break an orange slice and reminding her that she could also ask for a knife.

How you choose to discipline your child will be influenced by many factors and not in the least by the habits you have developed in parenting. Family life can be hectic and stressful. You may find, like many parents, that you are beginning to react to your child's behaviour with an automatic response, whether or not it works in the short or long run. Consciously or unconsciously these habits are going to be influenced by how your parents disciplined you. You may be repeating your parents' pattern of discipline or you may be trying to find a different way of parenting – a solution to your parents' parenting. We are now going to think about some automatic responses to children and what they may be, consciously or unconsciously, solving for parents.

Some common automatic responses to behaviour:
- Insisting, *'Because I say so'.*
- Setting very few rules or none.
- Being a martyr.
- Believing your child will learn by their own experience.
- Shouting all the time.

'Because I say so'

Maybe your idea of discipline is based on the understanding that parents should expect obedience all the time. You may feel that if your child does not obey you it is because they are wilful, naughty and rude and they disrespect you. All in all, you may well experience the parent/child relationship as one of a battle which only you or they can win.

It is true that children of all ages need simple, clear rules stated in a kind and firm manner and so a consistent approach gives your child the message. *'Like it or not, this is how it is and always will be.'* Your child will know exactly where the boundaries are and what you will and will not tolerate.

When your two-year-old refuses to do as they are told they are not only asserting their independence, they are also using defiance as a way of finding out how resolute you are and what you really believe in. If you are rigid in demanding obedience, you may undermine your child's confidence. They may feel powerless to challenge you and, in consequence, may not learn how to assert themselves as they grow up.

They may also feel that relationships are always based on one person having power and the other feeling helpless. As adults, they may always be timid and meek or, conversely, they may make relationships in which they behave in an obstreperous way. They do so believing that it is important to always be in control in a relationship.

Consider this:
- When you say, *'Because I say so'*, what are you hoping will be achieved?
- Sometimes saying, *'Because I say so'* can be a solution to feeling

anxious. You may worry about losing control as a parent, or your child being out of control.

- What does being out of control mean to you?

When you set few or no rules

Some parents do not believe in setting fixed rules for their children. They veer towards a more egalitarian view of parenting where they prefer to discuss issues as and when they arise with their child. As such a parent you may view parenting as a kind of friendship between you and your child. In any conflict with other authority figures, such as teachers, you are likely to find yourself supporting your child to the extent of being openly critical of other adults.

Setting too few or no rules may be a solution to being afraid of being too punitive. You may have been harshly or unnecessarily disciplined as a child yourself and worry that if you try to enforce rules you will give your child the same experience. Children with egalitarian parents may be the envy of their friends! However, one of the tasks of growing up is to begin to have a sense of what it is like to rely on yourself. Learning to be autonomous can be confusing and frightening, and too much freedom too soon may leave a child floundering. If you don't provide sufficient rules and boundaries your child may feel they are the same as the adults. They may feel very grown up on the surface but underneath they know they lack the resources of an adult. Some children may respond by struggling to develop coping skills but feel confused by their responsibilities. Others may feel the lack of rules indicates that their parents do not care enough about them. After all, it is easy for a child to misunderstand being allowed to choose whether or not they do things as their parents 'not caring what they do'.

Being a martyr

- Parenting is a difficult and, at times, stressful task, and so it is not surprising that at times most parents will resort to trying to make their children feel guilty. You may raise your eyes heavenward in a resigned air of sad disappointment and enduring patience in the face of your child's latest crime or misdemeanour. More often than not you may simply be trying to appeal to your child's better nature, but the martyred parent may be consciously and deliberately trying to control and discipline a child through guilt. Being a martyred parent can be a solution to being anxious about being over-angry or aggressive with your child.

- The disadvantage of the martyred parent is that it can leave children feeling confused. It may feel to your child that although you rarely get angry with them they can never be sure how to please you.

Martyred parents tend to try to discipline children with appeals to do things *'for my sake'*. A twelve-year-old recounted a story to me of an incident that had happened when she was five years old. She was playing with her favourite paint box when her mother entered the room carrying her three-year-old brother. Her mother asked her if her little brother could play with her paints. My patient remembered how strongly she had not wanted to let her brother use the paint box because *'he used to mess it up'*. When she declined her mother's request her mother hugged her little brother more closely and said, *'Oh, please, let him have it, for my sake.'* My patient could clearly remember, even at such a young age, thinking, *'Well, he's got her, I'll have the paint box'*, and refused to let her brother paint. She recalled her sense of loss and abandonment as her mother then left the room carrying her brother. She felt confused by her mother's behaviour. In a way she would find it easier to bear if her mother had been angry with her. She could then have retaliated with explaining how unfair it felt to her to have to share her paint box. Instead she was left feeling guilty by her mother's obvious hurt and disappointment in her behaviour.

The 'you will learn by experience' parent
Six-year-old George was refusing to put his coat on before a winter walk with family friends. His mother shrugged her shoulders. *'Oh, he'll find out, he'll be freezing.'* Sure enough George did become very cold on the walk, but his mother said, *'This is the only way he'll learn.'*

Of course it may be true that children learn from their own mistakes. However, as I have said before, small children need their parents' help to make the best choices and, as in George's case, sometimes they need their parents to insist they make the best choice. Older children who may be struggling with a bid for independence need to have the experience of knowing that their parents stand firm alongside them. If you are constantly parenting by letting your children learn from their own mistakes then there is a sense in which you are abandoning your parental responsibilities. You are also likely to be giving your child the message that unless they do it your way they will forsake your support and guidance. You may be doing so for the following reasons.

- It may be that you started out with a very clear set of rules but were flummoxed when your child was not cooperative and you did not know how to enforce them.
- It may be that you dislike confrontation and tend to be parenting by a rather mechanical 'this is what my parents did' way, or you may be trying very hard to parent from a strong theoretical stance.

Either way, you may feel de-skilled as a parent if your child does not respond to you the way you responded to your parents or if the theory doesn't work. You will feel de-skilled because you have no instinctive, internal parenting model to fall back on as a resource to give you an alternative course of action.

We can argue that it does children no harm to learn on occasions that they have exhausted their parents' resources. This, in a sense, is a clear boundary. However, this is very different from a child feeling that if they don't abide by their parents' discipline then they will be abandoned by them.

When you shout all the time
It's easy to lose track of what ridiculous things we can say to children in the heat of the moment:
    'Can I watch TV?'

'TV? TV? I'll give you TV.'

What does that mean to a child? When you find yourself constantly shouting at your child you may wonder if you have forgotten how to talk to them.

> *'I try to be patient with them . . . but sometimes I end up shouting and then I just shout at them for the rest of the day . . . there's got to be a better way . . . I just feel so awful about it.'*
>
> *(Mother of three children)*

As much as we may dislike it, shouting seems to be part of parenting. However, persistent shouting at your child may leave you frustrated and disappointed in yourself as a parent, especially if you are shouting as a response to feeling powerless to find a way to make your child do as they are told. Of course you may have good reason to shout at your child frequently, but shouting can quickly become an automatic response (even though it is not the best way to deal with things) and this is where you may find yourself losing control of the situation before you have even had a chance to think.

You probably shout at your child because you are frustrated, but what message does that pass to your child? Learning how to deal with frustration is a vital part of growing up, and your child needs to experience frustration as a way of moving from one thing onto the next. The risk of shouting at your child too much is that they may grow up thinking that shouting is the only way to manage frustration.

- The problem with shouting at children is that they learn not to take your shouting seriously. As one eight-year-old boy said, *'Oh, my mum got in a bate about it . . . but I knew she'd calm down . . . and then I could do it.'*
- Shouting at children often invites them to shout back. If you find yourself in a shouting match with your child, try to stop by saying, *'Look, you're shouting, I'm shouting and we're both unhappy. Let's take a big breath and we'll both stop shouting and start again.'*

Baby boundaries – is it possible to spoil a baby?

In a word, no. I was sitting with a young mother when she heard her baby begin to cry in the next room. She waited a second or two and, as the cries escalated, went to see the baby. She returned with the four-week-old infant in her arms, and said, 'My mum says I'll spoil her doing this. She's not wet or hungry but, poor little thing, you're lonely, aren't you?'

The idea that a baby can be spoilt is rooted in the thought that if babies always receive attention when they cry they will continue to seek attention. As one mother put it, *'They just play you up'.* This notion not only completely misunderstands what it is to be a baby, it also gives an extraordinary picture of childcare, as though children should not want to seek their parents' attention and parents should not want to give their children attention.

Winnicott said there was no such thing as a baby, only a mother and baby in a relationship. By this he meant babies have no sense of who they are, no capacity to think about what they want or need. In a sense, they are simply a bundle of physical sensations such as hunger, which they cannot understand let alone name. They cry to communicate these needs to their carers. And what happens in 'good enough' parenting is that by responding appropriately, i.e., feeding when a baby is hungry, the parent gives shape and meaning to that experience, so the baby comes to identify the feeling of 'hunger' as different and separate from other feelings. As the mother at the beginning of this section shows us, this shaping and giving meaning does not only relate to physical needs. This young mother was able to recognize that babies have emotional needs as well. Responding to a baby's cry is very much a matter of trial and error and it is interesting how our first response is often to check both ends, i.e., are they wet or hungry? It is easy for a new parent to feel de-skilled or despondent if a baby goes on crying in spite of being physically satisfied, but this young mother teaches us a crucial lesson about the importance of parents 'containing' their baby's distress. We do not know if this baby was 'feeling lonely', but we do know that by her mother responding to her by trying to give some meaning to her distress, she will feel alive and connected to meaningful relationships.

But, of course, growing up means learning to comfort ourselves, meet our own needs, and know how to include other people in doing so. We can say that it is possible to spoil a baby by not helping them to develop the skills to meet their own needs. Babies learn to do this through routine in childcare, by which I do not mean a rigid timetable unrelated to how the baby may be feeling, e.g., feeding every four hours whether the baby is hungry or not. Rather I mean a flexible, planned routine where the baby may learn to extend and delay their needs to fit in with family life. A routine helps a baby to sequence and so to consequence and in this way they begin to make sense of the world.

So, I am not saying that every time babies cry they should be picked up. I am saying that leaving babies to cry excessively is distressing for them and potentially emotionally harmful. By trial and error you will learn to what extent to respond to your baby's crying – be it a brief, gentle reassuring pat or picking them up. You will learn by experience how to wait and see if they can settle and comfort themselves or whether or not they need your help.

Babies do not understand your anger
Anyone who has held a crying baby will know that babies communicate by projecting feelings, i.e., they make the adult feel what they are feeling. When we cannot comfort a baby we feel helpless and anxious, and also frustrated and angry. The value of feeling angry is for you the parent, as it allows you to let off steam. But babies and young toddlers cannot understand anger, and being unable to make the links between their behaviour and your reaction will make them feel distressed, rejected and confused.

At a family gathering, the seventeen-month-old grandson was the focus of attention. Suddenly, he accidentally knocked his juice off the table onto the carpet. Several adults leapt to their feet to help and he was eventually settled down with another drink. After a couple of minutes, he thoughtfully, carefully and deliberately poured this drink onto the carpet . . . and appeared bewildered by the angry commotion that ensued.

Small toddlers are both curious about and puzzled by the world around them. This child was not 'being naughty' or 'provoking the adults'; he was trying to understand what had happened. As adults we know all too well the ramifications of juice on the carpet. All he knew was that something had happened which had made the adults very excited. Children re-enact or play out situations in order to try and make sense of them. What he needed was not anger or punishment but a firm, kind, simple explanation, for example letting him feel the wet carpet.

The terrible twos: myth or reality?

Above all, toddlers want to explore their parents' love. They want to please you, not to make you feel good but because your pleasure in them validates them, helps them to feel secure and motivates them to grow up and acquire adult skills to be like you. They want to explore sameness and differences, how you and they are alike in your needs and desires. So why have two-year-olds got their reputation for being hard to manage? In order to answer this question, we need to think about the life tasks and nature of a two-year-old.

Toddlers have begun to realize what you always knew: that they are an independent person from you with their own thoughts, feelings, desires and needs. They are beginning to grasp and understand their own power. They are curious and impulsive, keen to explore and examine the world and yet still unaware of the risks and dangers involved in doing so. They feel big and strong and capable and also frustrated and distressed when they come face to face with their own limitations. They will often try to cover up their mistakes and lack of skill by pretending, *'I meant to',* as one little girl declared as she fell over a step in the road. They may experience the ordinary demands of everyday life, for example tidying up toys, as restrictive, frustrating and even bewildering. They are still at a stage of not necessarily being able to link their behaviour with your anger because what they are doing is trying to work out the limits of your love. So, if you do get angry with them they are likely to respond by:

- Feeling you don't like them, this will be one of those inevitable moments when they feel they have lost your approval. They will not understand that it is their behaviour, not them, of which you are disapproving.
- Repeating what you've just said: *'Don't do that', 'Stop it', 'No'*. They are doing so not to be cheeky or insolent but to try to understand what is going on between you and them.
- Turning their anger onto another child or a toy or making another child or a toy do something. A two-year-old in a nursery group was reprimanded for walking around eating a biscuit and made to sit on a chair by his nursery nurse. Within a few minutes, he had crossed the room to another child and pushed him onto a chair. This was not a toddler bullying; he was trying to regain the sense of power he had lost when he was made to do something by an adult.

Toddlers are adept at drawing you into infantile confrontations and making you behave at their level. Edward was refusing to put his toys away at bedtime:

'Put them away at once,' said his mother. *'I'm not telling you again.'*

'I'm not,' replied Edward.

'If you don't put them away at once, I'm going to take all your toys away and put them in the attic.'

'Then I'll get them out again,' replied an even more angry Edward.

'Then I'll put them on the roof where you can't get them,' retorted his fraught mother.

This is a human enough interchange, but it was unproductive and could only end in tears. You may have to accept that, despite your good intentions, there will be times when your toddler will bring out the toddler in you.

Managing toddlers

How you manage these situations is going to depend very much on your attitude to the terrible twos. If you approach this developmental stage as a battle to be won then a battle is what you are likely to get. And while you may win in one sense because you are bigger and stronger, you will both end up exhausted and unhappy. Parents are almost bound to get angry with toddlers from time to time because toddlers themselves are often angry and frustrated and they will set out to make you feel what they feel. But on the whole they want to please you, and so you can aim to capitalize on that when disciplining your toddler. This may not only smooth the toddler years, it will stand you in good stead in later years!

- Remember that difficulties will arise when your toddler does not realize that what pleases them will not necessarily please you. He may, for example, enjoy decorating the dining room wall with mashed potato or posting toast into the DVD player!
- When you want to insist on your child doing something, you could try the 'eyeball to eyeball' approach of looking them firmly in the eye and saying calmly, *'What will please me now is . . . '* and keep repeating this until they get the message.
- Try to avoid negatives: for example, there is a difference in saying *'No'* when a toddler picks up something they shouldn't, and saying *'Down, please'*, which is a clear instruction of what you want them to do to please you. Equally, *'Don't drop it'* plants the thought that they may do so, while *'Hold tight'* encourages a positive skill.

Temper tantrums

Two-year-old Jonty was the middle of three children. His older sister was at school and he had enjoyed a period of time alone with his mother until his younger sister was born six months earlier. Jonty's mother sought my advice about his temper tantrums. They seemed to occur most frequently around teatime, always a busy time in a family, when he would become more and more defiant and difficult, culminating in a tantrum. His mother explained how the crescendo would often be reached when she was answering the phone or at a crucial point in cooking the meal. *'How do I discipline him,'* she asked, *'when he doesn't understand?'*

The more we thought about it, the more we could understand from Jonty's point of view. He was bewildered by the arrival of the new baby and the loss of his mother's attention. He had an opportunity to re-enact this experience and try and understand each day when he again lost his mother's attention at a busy time. He was clearly furious with his mother, and each day eventually became overtaken by his rage.

> Toddlers in a temper tantrum need 'time in' not 'time out'. Why? Because when toddlers throw a tantrum they are overwhelmed by their feelings of frustration and anger and they are terrified. They may not be able to hear what you are saying, let alone decide whether or not what you are saying is reasonable.

Time out teaches toddlers their behaviour is not acceptable to their mother, but it does not help them to understand and simply leaves them feeling disliked. Such a situation may also help a child to grow up believing that there is something bad about being angry, rather than the problem being with the way they are expressing their anger.

Try to stay with your child. Calmly explain that while they are so angry they need you with them. At the same time make it clear that you are not going to talk to them until they stop screaming. This is, however, very hard to do. In the hurly-burly of family life you are left with the question of who is going to look after the other children, etc., while you are sitting with the child in a tantrum? Also, nothing makes an adult feel more hopeless than dealing with a tantrum because there is absolutely nothing you can do until the child decides to stop.

The middle years of childhood

> *'She's become so rebellious since she went to secondary school.'*
> *(Mother of eleven-year-old)*

As your child grows up, pleasing you is going to begin to take second place to pleasing themselves and their peers. Once children enter the world of school and, later, out-of-school activities and clubs, they begin to compare their home life and culture with that of their friends. They are exposed to a whole range of customs and manners that give them a choice about the kind of person they can become. We will think more about this in Chapter 7, but the point I want to make for now is that if your child has learned in the early years that you are someone who has clear and firm ideas about how you expect them to behave, and mean what you say and say what you mean but don't withdraw your love when your child has made a mistake, then you have built a solid foundation for the more complex years to come. There is no magic way of setting rules and boundaries for this age group, but there are more or less helpful ways of parenting.

For example, let's think about a nine-year-old waiting with her friend for her mother to give them a lift to ballet class. The mother asks them to clear the table and load the dishwasher. They don't do it, even after being reminded twice. What are the parenting choices available to this mother?

- She can send the friend home.
- She can cancel her daughter's pocket money.
- She can refuse to let her daughter see her friend again for a week.

These may all be pertinent sanctions, but none help her daughter to understand why she was expected to clear the table. It would be more helpful for her mother to stay calm and explain clearly that these jobs have to be done and that if she leaves them for her mother to do they will miss the beginning of the ballet class.

- Try to avoid ultimatums. A degree of conflict is inevitable in parenting but ultimatums hype up the tension and also leave neither you nor your child room for manoeuvre. Rather than saying, *'If you do this, I will do that'*, it may be more helpful to say something like, *'I won't allow this because if this happens that will happen, and I will make sure it happens.'*
- Think about exactly what message you want to give and also remember you will be giving more messages than you intend. What

exactly do you want your child to do or not do? Be clear, concise and specific: for example, *'Tidy your room'* is far too vague and can be readily interpreted as, *'I just have to make my bed.'* Saying, *'Tidy your room by making your bed, putting your clothes away and bring down any dirty mugs'*, gives your child a clear task to complete.

- This age group responds well to being given choices. Sometimes children do just have to be told what to do, but a lot of the time there is room for manoeuvre. It is also a matter of how you phrase choices, so saying something like, *'If you want to watch that television programme then you have to do your homework and have supper first'* may be construed by the child as giving them an option to be defiant. However, phrasing it as, *'As you want to watch that television programme, when are you going to fit in supper and homework?'* In this way, the child hears that they are going to be allowed to watch the television programme, but they have other tasks to do as well.
- Try to avoid empty threats. I remember one father wringing his hands in desperation over his eight-year-old son's behaviour as he told me, despairingly, *'He had three final warnings!'* You can't have three final warnings. Why should your child presume that the third warning was any more final than the first? So the message is, be careful what you threaten because you are going to have to follow it through.
- Yelling from another room never works!
- Rows with this age group can often be diffused by humour on your part. This may range from using a fashionable word or phrase from their culture, for example, saying something like, *'If you keep on I'm going to have a cadenza'*, or shrugging your shoulders at their rants and say, *'Whatever!'* can sometimes temporarily divert them away from the focus of their rage to telling you just how *'sad'* you are to be trying to imitate their language. Or humorously confirming accusations can sometimes have the same effect, i.e., saying something like, *'Yes, you're right . . . and I feel really sorry for you . . . you have really drawn the short straw because we are the worst parents in the world and what's more you are stuck with us for life!'*
- You need to know at what point you are immovable and you also need to be prepared to not know, in the sense that as your children

get older you will inevitably have a sense of feeling your way around rules and boundaries.

Room to manoeuvre

We have been thinking about how children of all ages will pitch their behaviour against yours, and there is nothing more exhausting than pursuing methods of discipline that simply don't work. If you find that you are tirelessly repeating yourself, then it may be time to find some energy in a different way of management. This may give both you and your child a new way of looking at the problem. As psychotherapist Adam Phillips says: *'A repertoire might be more useful than a conviction, especially if one keeps in mind that there are many kinds of good life.'* (And, of course, nothing works *all* the time.)

At the beginning of this chapter we were thinking about how saying no can create distance between people. As parents, you may have to accept that in putting rules and boundaries into place your child is going to hate you at times.

The problem of punishment

While it is true that sometimes parents will give instant punishment as a response to their child's behaviour, many parents think seriously about what punishments are and are not appropriate for their child. You may find yourself doing both. The risk of instant punishments is that they may be excessive or harsh. Once you have 'gone over the top' it is difficult to retrieve the situation. Instant punishments are a response to your child but they may well ignore your child's needs.

More considered punishments may respond more appropriately to your needs for clear boundaries. However, they share with instant punishments the risk that you and your child will get into a power struggle. In such a fight your child may well feel they are always the injured party. This may lead them to try and reassert themselves by becoming more defiant. You may then find punishment becomes your only response to your child's behaviour and constantly punishing a child simply doesn't work.

When you find yourself in a cycle of defiance and punishment with your child then it is worth trying to understand what is going on within your relationship. It is astonishing how quickly parents may find themselves enjoying punishing their child and children may find themselves enjoying being punished. We can think of punishment as a way of not empathizing. Parents may feel once they have punished the feelings are dealt with.

'But if I don't punish, how is he going to learn right from wrong?' asked the father of an eight-year-old boy. When we talk about teaching children right from wrong we are talking about helping them to understand the consequences of their behaviour. For example, this boy was consistently found watching television in his bedroom instead of doing his homework. The consequence for him was that he was then trying to do his homework later in the evening when he was too tired. If his father wanted a punishment that had a chance of working it had to be one that the boy could understand was a legitimate consequence of his behaviour, such as insisting that he stayed downstairs until he had done his homework.

The child who is too good

'We don't really understand why we are here . . . he is such a good kid, we've never had a day's trouble with him.' Zac's parents were bewildered by his class teacher's referral to me. Their level of puzzlement only increased when I asked, *'Do you ever think he is too good?'* Parents rarely think of their child's behaviour as too good; they are more likely to see it as them being cooperative and a pleasure to have around. But Zac's teachers were concerned; they felt he was just *'too eager to please . . . it's not natural in an eight-year-old boy.'*

The risk of being too good as a child is that we may never learn to assert ourselves or become our true selves. Children who are too good often sense what their parents expect of them, i.e., what behaviour will make their parents happy, and may unconsciously sacrifice their own personalities in favour of being their parents' antidepressant. Zac's mother was both highly strung and prone to depression. His father had adopted an attitude of not rocking the boat to keep the peace with her. Zac sensed the dissatisfactions on both sides in his parents' marriage and grew into the frame of mind that, *'I'm the only person who can make*

Mummy happy.' He thought he could do this with total compliance and by *'not arguing or fighting with her'.*

What does 'being fair' mean?

Alice, aged twelve, was incandescent with rage when she discovered her ten-year-old sister was being allowed to wear eye make-up to the school disco. Alice herself had been made to wait until she was eleven and her cries of, *'It's so not fair'* echoed throughout the house.

Alice's parents tried to help her to understand that her sister and she were different people. They had different needs and abilities and so 'being fair' was not so much about treating them the same but more about making sure they both had what they needed to make their lives happy and successful.

Treating children in the family differently may leave parents with an uneasy sense that they are being inconsistent. This is, of course, not true. You are not contradicting yourself so much as recognizing the different needs and changes in family life. Alice was very angry that the rules had changed in her family but she had to accept that however much she protested her parents had the right to change their minds.

To smack or not to smack

We thought in the introduction about how a smack will certainly show a child how far they can go, but it may do little for developing mutual respect. In my experience, smacking a child simply makes the child angry and eventually that anger will be played out in one way or another.

> Whether or not you smack your child is going to depend very much on how you feel about it.

Of course, many parents smack because they feel angry and helpless. The parent who complains, *'Nothing else works'*, is really saying they long for a more positive response from their child but they don't know how to elicit it. Smacking may shock and subdue a child, but it is unlikely to make the parent and child feel close to each other (although we need to remember that smacking is a very intimate act). Five-year-old Terry was constantly pinching and biting his baby sister. His parents decided the best way to manage his behaviour was *'to give him a taste of his own medicine'*, and they smacked him, pinched him and even gently bit him as punishment. *'Now he knows how it feels,'* they declared. Maybe Terry did, but what he also felt was that no one understood how he felt about this new baby. And what he learned, paradoxically, was that smacking, biting and pinching are an appropriate way to express rage because that is what his parents did.

What smacking means to a child

The problem with smacking is what do you do after you've smacked? Sometimes a tap so quickly becomes a smack, a smack so quickly becomes a thump and a thump so quickly becomes a beating. The risk is not only of things going too far. How does the smacked child learn to recognize when they are being abused? Small children cannot distinguish the difference between being hit as part of a disciplinary procedure and being hit as part of abuse. Even more worryingly, they are likely to link violence and love together in their minds. In the short term, this may encourage them to repeat the unwanted behaviour in the hope of being smacked as a way of being physically close to their parent. In the long term, it can lead them into destructive, abusive adult relationships.

Smacking makes a child feel ashamed and guilty. If you are a pro-smacking parent you may feel this is a good thing and the child will be deterred from repeating the behaviour. But the other side of shame is helplessness and your child can be left feeling a helpless victim.

Constant smacking can lead to your child feeling that there is something bad about them, rather than about their behaviour. Such children find themselves in a dilemma. Deep inside they know their parents should not be treating them like this, but what can they do about it? How can they protect themselves? They are likely to do so in two ways. The first is to protect themselves from 'bad' parents by shifting the 'badness' from their parents onto themselves. They may feel safer in the world by thinking of themselves rather than their parents as bad. Or they may learn to respond to violence by being violent.

My parents smacked me and it never did me any harm

The problem with the simple 'it was good enough for me' attitude towards smacking is that parents who think this way are suffering from amnesia. In times of stress or not knowing we all tend to fall back on being loyal to our parents' way of doing things. But the parent who says smacking didn't do them any harm may be forgetting or denying how they felt as a child when they were smacked. We can think of this approach as a way of both trying to justify their parents' behaviour and of trying to avoid being angry with their parents for the way they were treated by them.

On being consistent

Of course, we are all aware of the importance of parents being consistent in their setting of rules and boundaries. Children have to be able to rely on the fact that what is not permissible today will not be permissible tomorrow. At the same time, they have to be able to rely on the fact that their parents will listen to them and will be flexible if necessary. That said, you are likely to find yourself being inconsistent with your child because children set out to make parents be inconsistent . . . and, of course, unconsciously, we are all inconsistent, so try not to set too high a standard.

When one parent undermines the other

You are almost bound to undermine each other even if you are making a conscious effort to support each other. As an occasional event, undermining each other's authority will be an ordinary part of family life. When it does happen, you, as parents, will need to talk the issue through away from the children. It may be that one parent was manipulated by the child or simply did not agree with the other parent's stance but felt unable to say so openly. However, if you find yourself constantly undermining each other's authority with the children then you need to be thinking about your relationship and what you are trying to communicate to each other through this behaviour.

Summary

- Naughtiness is very much a matter of the way a child's behaviour is construed by adults.
- Naughtiness is a descriptive word. Why do we so often use it instead of, for example, spitefulness, mischievous?
- Children need to be told what to do.
- We always give children two messages: a conscious message and an unconscious message, which may be about what we really feel but do not want to feel.
- A little defiance is no bad thing! Children need to push and pull their own world in order to develop their independent personalities, but they need to do so within the security of firm boundaries.
- Saying no can make us feel we are being aggressive, spoiling a child's fun, withholding something from a child. We also know that saying no creates distance between people.
- Saying no helps children to learn who we can say no to, when we can say no, why to say no and when we can stop saying no.
- When you are setting a rule ask yourself exactly what you hope the rule will achieve.
- Discipline helps to keep us safe from the dangers of other people and the dangers of ourselves.
- Boundaries show us how to respect ourselves and other people and help us to develop a sense of independence with responsibility.
- What matters is not so much what behaviour you choose to discipline, as how you choose to discipline it.
- If you are very rigid about discipline it may be because you feel anxious about losing control or of your child being out of control.
- If you are lax about discipline it may be a solution to being afraid of being too punitive.
- If you are anxious about being over-aggressive with your child you may parent by being a martyr.
- Believing that children will learn from their own mistakes all the time ignores the fact that children are still learning to make the right choices.
- When you shout all the time it may be a response to feeling

frustrated and unable to find appropriate ways in which to manage your child.

- The idea that a baby can be spoiled is rooted in the thought that if babies always receive attention when they cry they will continue to seek attention. This notion not only completely misunderstands what it is to be a baby, it also gives an extraordinary picture of childcare, as though children should not want to seek their parents' attention and parents should not want to give their children attention.
- We can say that it is possible to spoil a baby by not helping them to develop the skills to meet their own needs.
- Babies and young toddlers cannot understand your anger.
- Above all, toddlers want to explore their parents' love.
- Toddlers need time in, not time out, when they are having a tantrum.
- In the middle years of childhood, pleasing you is going to begin to take second place to your child pleasing themselves and their peers.
- In the middle years children respond well to being given choices.
- Punishing children often doesn't work because it ignores what a child really needs.
- The risk of being too good as a child is that we may never learn to assert ourselves or become our true selves.
- Treating children equally does not necessarily mean treating them the same.
- Smacking children is likely to make them angry.
- We are all aware of the importance of parents being consistent in their setting of rules and boundaries. At the same time, children have to be able to rely on the fact that their parents will listen to them and will be flexible if necessary.
- You are almost bound to undermine each other as parents even if you are making a conscious effort to support each other. But if you find yourselves constantly undermining each other's authority then you need to be thinking about your relationship.

CHAPTER 5
Bedwetting, Bottoms and Bad Language
– Worrying Behaviour –

'Pooh bottoms to you! Pooh bottoms to you . . . (pause) . . . I said
pooh bottoms to you, and that is very rude!'
(Four-year-old to his mother as he collapsed into giggles)

We can't grow up if we don't take some risks and practise going to extremes. Neither can you parent successfully without taking risks and sometimes going to extremes. Your 'extremes' will have an impact on your child, be it yelling too loud or inappropriately, over-reacting with a harsh punishment or even being goaded into giving a sudden smack. How long-lasting an impact this has on your child will depend very much on how often you are extreme and how you manage it afterwards (see Chapter 4).

Things are always two-way in parenting, and your child's extreme behaviour will worry and upset you. As I discussed earlier, naughtiness is very much a matter of how a child's behaviour is construed. In some families, yelling and shouting at each other are part of everyday life. In others, to raise your voice or 'answer back' would be thought of as rude and unacceptable. And, of course, much depends on the age of your child. The five-year-old who steals sweets from the cupboard may be less worrying to you than the twelve-year-old who shoplifts. But nothing will make you feel you are 'getting it wrong' as a parent more than when your child flirts with delinquent behaviour. In this chapter we are going to think about some ordinary extremes of childhood behaviour and when to recognize the behaviour has become 'extra ordinary' and you need to seek help.

Bedwetting

'I can do a big pooh on the lavatory now,' announced one three-year-old as her grandmother opened the door to greet her.

> Children are very preoccupied with their bodies, especially with what goes into them and what comes out of them! Parents are also very preoccupied with children's bodies, mainly in trying to help children to manage their own bodies independently.

Both parents and child may feel it is a huge achievement on both sides when a child is able to use the lavatory appropriately . . . and in time. And this is interesting because control of the bowels and the bladder is a developmental stage all children, with the exception of some with special needs, will reach naturally before they join school. While many children are dry day and night by three years old, many will continue to wet the bed occasionally until they are five years old and it is not uncommon at seven, especially for boys. And yet bedwetting can be a real worry for parents, almost to the point of panic: *'I thought we were through all this,'* said one mother. *'It's a symptom he's going backwards.'* What this mother was forgetting is that there is no such thing as a symptom-free child, nor should there be; children have a repertoire of ways of coping with life and bedwetting is one of them. While we need to take seriously any child who regularly wets the bed having previously been dry, only you can decide how much this is 'problem behaviour' for you as parents. Once you see behaviour as a problem you are adding 'stress' to parenting and stress makes it difficult for us to think as creatively about behaviour as a communication. In one sense there is nothing wrong with finding a behaviour a problem, but it may be worth trying to work out why it has such a powerful effect on you.

Consider this:
- What does it say about you if your child wets the bed?
- What would your parents say about your child wetting the bed?

Some reasons why bedwetting worries parents

I was once asked to see a five-year-old boy who was a persistent bed-wetter. He had run the gamut of his parents' and health visitor's skills and when he had also exhausted mine I asked him suddenly one day:

'Jamie, do you like sleeping in a wet bed?'

'Oh, yes,' he replied cheerily.

Jamie's bedwetting was never a pleasure for his parents. His mother complained about the washing and could hardly hide her anger. *'Is he ever going to get over it?'* she demanded. This was an interesting question for how could Jamie 'not get over it'? He was not going to be dependent on her for the rest of his life. But as a parent it is easy to panic and fear that any loss of bodily control on your child's part means you have failed as a parent or there is something wrong with your child and that this temporary lapse may become permanent. Of course bedwetting is a problem because it causes, amongst other things, a lot of work in the night and additional washing. How intensely you feel bedwetting is a problem is going to be dependent on your own history and your own fears of continence and incontinence. For some reason, 'wetting ourselves' seems to be a very human worry. And of course, when your child bedwets it raises anxieties about their dependency on you. This can be particularly true where a child has been dry and then reverts to bedwetting. Parents may be left fearing, consciously or unconsciously, that the child is *never* going to be independent.

Bedwetting as a communication

Winnicott highlights the fact that babies can pee anywhere at any time. A child who persistently wets the bed is reverting to being a baby. They are, in fact, saying, *'Look, I can pee where and when I want!'* Now as the success of toilet training is highly dependent on your toddler wanting to please you, we have to think where this need to express independence and power might be coming from; has something happened which could be making your child anxious and feeling out of control in their life – a new baby, a house move, a bereavement, for example? Or could they be feeling angry about something, almost outraged by a sense that they cannot control events in their lives? Children know that parents attend to their bodies and so when they have a worry they can't put into words they may use other orifices than their mouth to communicate.

An older child who is bedwetting may have a secret worry that they are struggling to contain and that metaphorically 'leaks out' at night. A twelve-year-old girl began to wet the bed when she transferred to the secondary school some distance from her home. It emerged that she was being bullied on the bus to school each day but was afraid to tell anyone for several months. Her self-esteem plummeted not only because of the shame and misery of being bullied, but also because of her feelings of shame and disgust at wetting the bed at her age. We can see how important it was that her parents did not get angry with her for doing so.

Managing bedwetting

- First and foremost keep a sense of proportion. Young children may have isolated patches of bedwetting and so too may an older child under stress. Children need a repertoire of symptoms to communicate with adults. For some children bedwetting may become 'their thing' that they revert to when they are worried. Once bedwetting becomes a regular occurrence then your child is trying to communicate anxiety or distress.
- Try to stay calm and remember this is a temporary phase and try to treat the bedwetting in a matter-of-fact way. It is best to resist the temptation to praise your child for a dry bed as there is a risk that they may construe that there is something wrong or bad about having a wet bed. This can be very worrying because, of course, wetting the bed is beyond their control.

Soiling and smearing

However much bedwetting may worry a parent, the child who soils and/or smears faeces is going to be seen as a much bigger problem. And indeed it is, in that soiling and smearing of faeces is a much more dramatic and aggressive communication and quite complex to manage. Child psychoanalyst Melanie Klein has described soiling and smearing as an intrusive and powerful communication from a child. So the first thing to think about if your child is soiling/smearing is what is the culture around faeces in the home? Is pooh never mentioned or is it a source of humour, something to be joked about? Or is it regarded as an everyday part of life that is just taken for granted, like food, for example? Small children are both proud and interested in the faeces that come out of their bodies. Sometimes parents cannot hide their disgust and will be just a bit too hasty in flushing them away; to the child this may feel as though a possession of theirs, if not indeed a body part, has been rejected by their parent. Unconsciously, the child may then get into a power struggle in which they will refuse to use the potty or the lavatory but then pooh secretly in a place that they have chosen, almost as though they are trying to hide their faeces to protect them from being stolen.

Soiling in the under-fives
Four-year-old Natalie was referred to me by her nursery school teacher because she was soiling inappropriately in school. She seemed to have settled well in this her first term, although her teacher had noticed she was rather quiet and withdrawn. She had responded particularly well to the gentle encouragement of her nursery nurse, Ella, who had unfortunately had to take extended sick leave after Natalie had been in school about six weeks. Natalie had asked for her frequently, but otherwise there had been no obvious change in her behaviour. However, it soon became clear Natalie was 'deliberately' soiling in school, sometimes on the floor beside the lavatory but more recently in a corner of the classroom. This had enraged Ella's successor who felt that Natalie's behaviour was like that of 'a little animal'. When the teacher spoke to Natalie's mother, she discovered that Natalie had been soiling at home for several weeks and then trying to hide her faeces by covering it with lavatory paper or even pushing it down the plughole of the washbasin.

When I met with the family, a complex and interesting story

emerged. Natalie's parents had been married for fifteen years before they adopted her aged ten months. By that age Natalie had already had, for a number of reasons, three foster carers. She had been a *'good baby'* in her mother's words, but had become *'difficult and stroppy'* at around twenty months old. It was about this time that Natalie's father had been promoted, which involved him travelling more with his work and sometimes being away from home several nights a week. Natalie's mother volunteered she found parenting much more stressful than she had ever imagined. She missed the freedom of her child-free lifestyle and also felt that as Natalie became more difficult to manage and her husband was less able to share her care as much, *'I was pretty firm with her . . . I could see otherwise she could rule the roost.'*

Family life seemed to settle down with a new routine but when Natalie was just over three years old her mother was rushed into hospital with appendicitis. Natalie was sent to stay with her grandmother, whom she knew well, for a couple of weeks and it was on her return that the soiling began.

We can think about Natalie in several ways. She was a child who had experienced a number of breaks and losses before she was a year old. We wondered if her father's absences not only made her sad and angry because she was missing him but also because at a deep level, they were evocative of her early experience of 'losing' her carers one after the other. When her mother became ill and they were separated she was not only sad and angry but also fearful that she might lose *this* mother. Natalie's mother seemed to have controlled her behaviour, but perhaps not her feelings, by firm management but when she lost her favourite nursery nurse it seemed as though she was overwhelmed with her anger and was unable to express it except by poohing in inappropriate places.

It is very easy in parent/child relationships for communications to be quickly generalized and so the initial power struggles between Natalie and her mother were expressed by Natalie in bodily behaviour. In thinking about Natalie it was important for us to consider why she had chosen this particular symptom of soiling to communicate with her mother.

Soiling in older children

Soiling and smearing in older children is a serious communication that a youngster is in a complex muddle and conflict; it may be a way of dealing with strong feelings about power and control and anger. Such a child is likely to need professional help and in the first instance you should contact your health visitor or doctor.

Managing soiling and smearing

- It is unfair to be angry with the child who soils. That said, you need to bear in mind that soiling is a child's attempt to make you angry! Remember that however deliberate it appears, soiling is not a deliberate act. Consciously, the child has no control over this method of communication. For the child, soiling is about a loss of control and doing something forbidden. As parents, it is most important to think about what it is in the child's life that might be making them feel out of control and powerless.

- You may very well feel angry and disgusted with your child's behaviour. This is partly because it makes you feel that somehow you have failed as a parent, but it is also because you are picking up maybe how your child feels about themselves. The best way to help a child who is soiling is to take the pressure off them in almost every area of their life and to give them lots of special time and reassurance.

Children have many ways of communicating their feelings around issues of power and control. In addition to bedwetting and soiling, they may often use what seems like meaningless or irrational fears.

Fears and phobias

Fear is an ordinary and necessary part of human development. Fear keeps us safe and helps us not to take foolhardy risks – or at least not to take them too often!

There is nothing wrong with being frightened unless, of course, the fear prevents us from enjoying life to the full by making it difficult for us to do things we want to do or in children when fear is not age appropriate. As adults we sometimes forget how scary it can be to be a new person in the world. The two-year-old who is terrified he will fall down the lavatory and be flushed away is telling us how it feels to be unsure of how the world works and how powerless and out of control that uncertainty leaves a child; but a twelve-year-old expressing a fear of falling down the lavatory is saying something very different. He knows it is not possible to be flushed away and so we have to think about the internal meaning of this fear for him. By this I mean, what does falling down the lavatory represent for him? In other words, why does he not feel his environment is safe?

Children live on the cusp of their imagination and are consequently very aware of the 'what ifs' of life. And the 'what ifs' of life are always idiosyncratic. If we think of two twelve-year-olds afraid of falling down the lavatory the root cause of this fear is unlikely to be the same. For this reason, children's fears can seem bizarre to adults and while a small child's fear tends to elicit our sympathy, adults can be embarrassed and irritated by seemingly irrational fears in older children. An irate father returned fuming from a swimming trip with his nine-year-old son who had sat crying on the edge of the pool, *'too scared to jump in'*. Maybe our irritation with such fears is because older children's fears resonate with our own. At a very deep level, they remind us of the precariousness of life and how little control we really have over life events.

We need our fears

It is interesting that almost invariably fear in both older children and adults is seen at best as negative and at worst immature. We could argue that at the moment it is an entirely appropriate reaction for Londoners to feel fear following the 7/7 bombings and yet they are being exhorted, for very good reasons, not in the least the maintenance of daily life, to be unafraid.

Fears in the under-fives

Even the newest of babies will let their parents know when they feel frightened or at risk. When they feel you may let go of them, drop them, or that you are handling them in an unexpectedly careless way, their arms will jerk towards yours while their legs curve up instinctively like a little monkey searching for something or someone to clasp themselves around. This so-called 'Moro response' is likely to be even more violent if you mis-time removing the security of your hands as you lay the baby in the cot or on the changing mat before they can feel the security of the mattress beneath them. At such times, the baby will even cry out in fear.

Older babies may be frightened by ordinary, everyday objects like a vacuum cleaner, hairdryer or having their hair washed. Others will play happily in the bath but be terrified of water gurgling down the plug-hole as the bath is emptied. Parents may be bewildered, even irritated, by these irrational fears, but are unlikely to expect a baby to cope with them alone. You are more likely to take them seriously and comfort and reassure your baby. So it is interesting that as babies grow up there is a real risk of adults dismissing their fears as *'silly'*.

Fear as a communication

Fears are a child's way of communicating to adults that there are things in their life that feel overwhelming, inexplicable or mysterious – you may well find yourself saying, *'Welcome to the human world!'* Sometimes their fears seem quite irrational, such as the two-year-old who is terrified of feathers, and it is not uncommon for small children to be afraid of characteristics and aspects of people such as beards or even spectacles. Such fears are often a toddler's way of getting to know strange and unfamiliar things in their world. They are a kind of self-protection, so the toddler is saying to the feather, if you like, *'You show me that you're harmless and then I'll accept you – until then I'll fear you.'*

These fears are very different from those based on an experience where the child has realized that life can be risky and unexpected things can happen. An eight-year-old began to scream with terror when a leaking pipe caused a small cascade of water to flood down his classroom wall. He remembered the day when he was a toddler that his mother had left the bath running while she answered the phone. The water had poured down the staircase leaving him extremely frightened.

His fear was based on reality in that he had learned there was a risk of something happening which was not only threatening but also beyond his control. What he was not taking into account was that he was now six years older and so not nearly as helpless in the face of the unexpected.

Fears about unlikely events

Some children can become excessively afraid about unlikely events such as the house catching fire or their parents dying. In Chapter 3, we thought about seven-year-old David and his fear that something bad would happen to his sister. Such fears are nearly always symbolic of an underlying fear that the child cannot locate or feels he has to hide. There is always a risk in taking children's fears too literally as their fears are often displaced and so not as the child describes them. The skill seems to be in doing both; we need to take children's fears literally, but also to reassure them their fear may be unrealistic.

Ten-year-old Serge was referred to me because of his excessive fear that his house would burn down. This fear had gradually grown since he was about seven years old and his parents were now finding it unmanageable. He would stand beside his mother when she was cooking at the gas stove to make sure that 'nothing catches fire' and would repeatedly go back into the kitchen to ensure that she had turned the gas off. He refused to stay in the room with an electric fire burning, even when it was extremely cold. He found it difficult to sleep until he had been downstairs to check that his parents had 'turned everything off' before they had gone up to bed. He would then go round the kitchen unplugging all the appliances in case of an electrical explosion.

During our first family meeting I asked Serge what else, apart from electricity, might be explosive in the house. It emerged that Serge's parents had a volatile marriage and there were frequent violent rows. He eventually volunteered that he was afraid the house would burn down because his parents 'would explode it' in one of their frequent rows.

Fear or anxiety

Ten-year-old Mera had a glorious singing voice and usually sang solo in concerts. She had initially been delighted when her teacher entered her for an inter-school competition for a place in the local Youth Music Festival. She was even more delighted when she won both a place and a solo part.

As rehearsals began she became more and more anxious, eventually declaring she didn't want to be in the concert at all. She said she was afraid: *'I'll mess up and everyone will laugh.'* She began to have night-mares which always began with her walking on stage confidently in a *'well cool dress'* and then something dreadful happening such as her opening her mouth and no sound coming out or her completely for-getting the song. She became anxious about going to bed because she didn't want to have the nightmares and was increasingly tearful as the day of the next rehearsal approached. Trying to encourage her, her mother reminded her how much her friend, Sally, enjoyed singing a duet with her and how she would miss her if she dropped out. *'Oh, there's plenty of better singers than me there,'* snapped Mera. *'Sally can sing with one of them.'*

Mera had got into a muddle. She had been used to being the star singer in her own school. When she arrived at the rehearsal she had dis-covered that there were lots of good singers from lots of schools. She had enjoyed being 'the best singer', and deep down was now beginning to worry that if she was not the best then she might not be as much liked and admired.

In his book *Terrors and Experts*, Adam Phillips talks about how often the thing we fear is paradoxically the very thing we want. Mera and I thought about how maybe deep down inside her she felt very angry with the other good singers who seemed to be putting her in the shade. She was anxious about her own performance, of course, but at an unconscious level she was secretly hoping that the other singers might 'mess up' so she could continue to be the star of the show.

Mera shows us clearly the difference between fear and an anxiety. A fear is focused on an identifiable object and is realistic. For example, a child may be appropriately afraid of a barking dog which has the potential to bite. Anxiety is the same as a fear but when the object has become obscured and the fear is unrealistic, it is an anxiety fear. In Mera's case, she was saying she was afraid she may not sing well when really she was afraid of losing her star status. As is so often the case with children, what Mera named as her fear was actually concealing an underlying anxiety. To stay with the example of the barking dog, we would think a realistic fear had grown into an anxiety if an older child continued to be afraid of a barking dog when they were well able to take steps to avoid the dog. In such a child, the barking dog has come to have an internal meaning for them; by this I mean, the barking dog they see may remind them of a 'barking dog' bit of themselves, i.e., their own aggression.

Sometimes we have to do a great deal of work with a child to uncover the disguise. This takes time and patience. By their very nature, fears are difficult for children to talk about. In Mera's case she needed to be allowed to cook a conversation slowly with me and her parents around the 'what ifs' of her fears.

Phobias

Children (and adults!) experience a large category of feelings which we call fears. Many children's fears are a realistic anxiety; it is realistic to be afraid of a barking dog. We all know dogs can be unpredictable and also that they can bite. Given the intensity of children's fears, especially toddlers' fears, it is interesting how easily they often fade away. A small child may be terrified of spiders for several weeks and then it seems as though they forget that they are scared of spiders and carry on with their life. However, sometimes fears do not go away but rather become more intense. Once a fear has begun to dominate a child's life we would think of it as the more serious condition of a phobia. From the age of three Millie would scream at a picture of a spider in a story book and at the outset of any outing would anxiously ask her mother, *'Will there be spiders there?'* This is very different from the three-year-old who is only afraid of a spider when they actually see one. A phobia is an imaginary fear. Everyone can see the dog a child fears but a phobia is only real to the child. As Millie's mother said, *'I can't see why spiders are so frightening.'* We all accept a dog may bite but spiders have never hurt anyone. For a child like Millie the crucial question is, what does a spider mean to Millie? What we needed to explore was what the spider was representing in Millie's mind.

I met Millie when she was eight years old. Her mother brought her to see me because of her phobia about the dark. About a year previously, she had seen the film of *Snow White*. Even though she was familiar with the story, she had become distraught after the '*kind old lady with the apples*' had suddenly turned into a witch and poisoned Snow White. For several weeks Millie had suffered terrifying nightmares and eventually began to refuse to go to bed at night. This fear of going to bed had gradually grown into a phobia about the dark. She was not only terrified of the dark, but would frequently check during the day to see if it was *'getting dimsy outside'*. Whenever she was going out, she would be hysterical with worry that it might get dark, *'while I'm away from home'*.

Of course Millie could not explain why she was frightened of the dark, but she could explain when I asked her *'what dark meant'*. She explained that dark meant: *'Blackness . . . I can't see who people and things really are . . . dark comes very suddenly . . . it comes scurrying.'* I was struck by an eight-year-old's use of the word 'scurrying', and it reminded me of her earlier fear of spiders which are, of course, black and scurrying.

The phobic child is projecting something about themselves that they dislike or are afraid others will dislike onto something else, in Millie's case 'the dark'. Millie's teachers and parents had both described her as a *'sweet and gentle child'*. And indeed she was but what also emerged was that Millie was a very angry and worried child. Her younger brother had arrived when she was two-and-a-half years old. Millie's mother described how she had seemed delighted with the baby, but how she had also been aggressively affectionate towards him. Her hugs were sometimes just a little too hard and her kisses had tended to quickly become little bites. Her mother was quick to add that on the whole Millie was *'very good'* and the two children had always played well together. We began to wonder if to three-year-old Millie the black scurrying spider represented her aggression towards her sibling, which she was afraid might come scurrying out with deadly consequences. This early phobia had abated with the health visitor's help but a few months before the trip to *Snow White*, Millie's father had left the family home so her mother's new boyfriend could move in.

Although clearly distressed and angry at this dramatic change in her life, Millie had made relatively little fuss. Ostensibly she seemed very fond of her step-father and was both demanding of his attention and attentive to him. At one point, her mother described her behaviour towards her step-father as *'ingratiating'*. We came to an understanding of Millie as a child who feared that her strong, aggressive feelings were too destructive to show to others. She was striving very hard to keep up her image of 'sweet and gentle'. Perhaps she was so rattled by the kind old lady who turned out to be a witch because it reminded her of herself. At a very deep level she was terrified that the witch in her might suddenly burst out and be recognized. She made herself feel safe and also other people safe from her, by projecting her aggression onto the dark, i.e., it was the dark that was aggressive and frightening, not her.

Managing fears and phobias

- Fears and phobias are difficult to manage because they are so real to the child. They can't be dismissed by reassurance, but neither do you want to risk enlivening them by being overprotective of the child. The skill seems to be in trying to be as matter of fact as possible and also in not labelling children's behaviour too readily. Babies of nine months or thereabouts may become distressed when other people approach them with their mothers. Sometimes this is referred to as 'stranger anxiety'. The assumption here is that the baby is afraid of strangers, but maybe it is not so much that they are afraid of strangers, but they prefer to be with their mother. This would seem to be a perfectly normal and natural desire for a nine-month-old baby!

- Toddlers' fears are often equally normal and natural. They tend to be based on self-protection and an anxiety about strange places or people. It may not be that the toddler is afraid of the new experience or person so much as they are showing appropriate caution asking themselves is this a safe place or a nice person? Sometimes they may be surprised by their own independence. A three-year-old on a train with her mother was excitedly holding the tickets, waiting for the ticket collector to come along the train. When he appeared, she began to run excitedly down the carriage only to suddenly stop in her tracks and turn back to her mother. One could almost see her thinking, *'Am I being too bold?'* Many toddlers' fears are simply their way of keeping themselves safe. Her mother encouraged her gently to stay where she was until the ticket collector reached her.

• There is a real art to coping with fears in early childhood. If we take a five-year-old afraid there is a monster under the bed, how should parents handle it? You can look under the bed with the child and reassure them that there is no monster there but don't go hunting! Sometimes the child will try and get the parents to search the room and this can only exacerbate a fear, i.e., there is a monster but it is somewhere you haven't looked. It may be much better to just say firmly but kindly, *'No, there is no monster.'* You can then go to acknowledge that you do understand that the child is afraid and worried about something.

• Fears and anxieties in older children are often associated with anxieties about growing up and an overprotective parent creates a fearful child. A ten-year-old boy refused to go to sleepovers on the basis that he was *'frightened'*. His mother was indulgently understanding and made no attempt to encourage him to go but said, *'Well, maybe you'll be able to go to sleepovers when you're older.'* As time went by, it became clear that this mother really did not want to let go of her son and that he was fast developing the idea that he had to look after her. Older children need to know that you understand their anxiety, but they also need firm and gentle encouragement to take steps into the wider world and conquer their fears. If we stick with the example of the sleepover, it may help to explore with your child what they need in order to reduce their fear and anxiety, for example would they like you to text them or do they want to take a special object from home?

Explicit sex talk

A constant theme of this book is that it is impossible to parent without to some extent reliving your own childhood. In the previous chapter we thought about how your feelings as a child when you were disciplined will inevitably colour how you enforce rules and boundaries with your own children. How much more is this true when it comes to managing issues around your child's body and later their emerging sexuality! You will constantly remember how your parents made you feel about your body. And this varies enormously from family to family. Some parents are relaxed and unembarrassed and will walk around naked in front of their children as much as they would walk around clothed. Others may be more embarrassed and even ashamed of their bodies, feeling that 'private parts' must very much be kept private.

Children are endlessly fascinated about their bodies and as they grow up most children will go through a stage of using explicit sex talk. The reasons why they do so and whether or not you should be concerned will depend very much on your child's age.

Explicit talk from the under-fives – 'poohs, wees and bottoms'

Somewhere between the ages of two and five years, most children go through a period of 'lavatory' talk. At this age they are fascinated with two things: their own bodies and how they work and making an impact on adults. We are all familiar with the way they will announce words like 'stinky pooh' at any opportunity, often repeating them over and over again before they collapse into helpless giggles. Sometimes you can actually see them gauging the adults' reaction, so appearing outraged or laughing heartily will goad them equally into more extreme utterances.

This is perfectly normal behaviour in young children, but how you manage it will form part of the platform and colour your relationship with your child about body matters in the years to come. Shakespeare said, *'There is no right or wrong, but only thinking makes it so . . .'* Equally, words cannot be 'rude'. The parenting task here is to help your child to understand the difference between private and public use of language. From a child's point of view, if it is 'rude' to say *'bottoms'* in public, then *'bottoms'* must also be rude in private.

Managing lavatory talk

- Try not to suggest that such talk is either rude or naughty. At the same time, you can hold in mind how would we sustain excitement if nothing was rude or naughty?
- Try to give a natural and measured response as you would to any other language. This may not be easy in front of a critical mother-in-law, but hold in mind that any extreme reaction from you will provoke even more extreme language from them! Saying something like, *'Yes, and silly billys to you'* may help them to understand that you understand that this is playing with words. If they persist you could point out firmly but gently, *'We've said bottoms a lot now, let's find something else to say.'*
- Children can be enormously relieved when they are stopped from going on in the lavatory talk vein. Unconsciously, what you are doing is stopping them from entering the adult world, which can only be a relief. You will also have to accept that you are not always going to give a natural and measured response, sometimes you are going to react. This is inevitable because in using lavatory talk children are trying to find out how grown-ups will respond.
- Most children outgrow lavatory talk by their first year at school. And so we have a reason to be concerned about a child who carries such language on into the school years.

Explicit sex talk in the early years: 'I want to sex my teacher'

Six-year-old Alfie's teacher was worried by his explicit sex talk. Following the Christmas holiday he was referring to almost anything as *'sexy'* and at almost any opportunity. He was inappropriately commenting on characteristics such as *'big breasts'* and going up to other children, giggling, and asking them about their *'willies'* and *'mins'.* When she overheard him telling another child, *'I'd like to sex my teacher'*, she decided to seek help.

Consider this:

- How would you understand Alfie's behaviour?
- How would you manage Alfie's behaviour?

Of course, our immediate cause for concern with such a child is whether or not they are at risk of sexual abuse or are being sexually abused. While this is always something to hold in mind, it should not be our only understanding of explicit sex talk from children of this age. Children today are exposed to a plethora of sexualized messages in the media and to explicit sexual scenes on television. We could think of Alfie as talking about something he has either seen, heard or experienced from another child or an adult.

Talking about it may be his way of trying to understand it. So if we think of explicit sex talk in a child of this age as being more of an enquiry, then we are more likely to find constructive ways of managing it. Alfie's teacher met with his mother who shared her concerns about Alfie, but had been too worried and too embarrassed to raise them with the teacher.

> But we do not need to take sex talk at this age too literally; children will also use it as a way of communicating other needs which they cannot name or understand.

It emerged that Alfie's father had recently had a long spell of unemployment and was eventually forced into taking a job a considerable distance from home, which meant he was only home every other weekend. Alfie's mother was open in saying how much she and her husband missed each other and how it was difficult for Alfie because on the weekends his father wasn't home he was the sole focus of his mother's attention but, of course, on the weekends that his father was home, both his parents couldn't help but feel that Alfie was rather in the way at times!

Alfie seemed to be using 'sex talk' as a way of telling the adults that he felt left out and short of affection. His age-appropriate curiosity about sex and bodies in general had been increased by his unconscious understanding that Mummy and Daddy were close in a physical way.

We also need to remember that by Year 3 or 4, some children are beginning to find being a child rather frustrating; they may express this as life being *'so boring'.* To such children, 'being older' seems so much more attractive and this can lead them into trying to sound grown-up, an easy task with all the media 'models'. As I have said before, one of the tasks of parenting is for parents to encourage children to enjoy all the exciting things they are able to do at their age while they are waiting to grow up.

Managing explicit sex talk in 5–8-year-olds
Make sure you monitor what your child sees on television, DVDs and even in your daily newspaper.

- Remember children want you to be shocked by what they are saying so try to keep a humorous response. Think about whether your child could be asking for information about how the body works. Make time to listen and talk in simple, age-appropriate terms.
- Could there be any reason why your child might not be feeling as close to you as they usually do? Try giving them some special time and attention.
- Hold in mind the possibility of sexual abuse and if the explicit sex talk continues or becomes more exaggerated, then seek professional help. In such conversations you will need to follow your child's lead by saying something like, *'You seem a bit confused about bodies.'*

Explicit sex talk in older children . . . the age of dirty jokes
A five-year-old boy was brimming with glee as he announced he had a joke to tell me. He hopped from foot to foot as he spluttered:

'Knock! Knock.'

'Who's there?' I obligingly enquired.

'Nicholas'

'Nicholas who?'

'Knickerless girls shouldn't climb trees,' he announced, collapsing into giggles.

Small children's 'rude jokes' are rarely funny to anyone but the teller. They can be mildly embarrassing and often seem pointless, but they do have a point. We can think of this boy as gradually becoming aware of the difficult differences between boys and girls and the reasons why they are different. He is both curious and embarrassed. Telling me the joke could have been his way of asking me for information about 'knickerless girls' and informing me that this was a cause of concern for him.

In late childhood, as adolescence dawns, children may again turn to jokes, especially 'dirty jokes', as a way of communicating with adults. *'We only laugh,'* said Freud, *'when a joke comes to our help'*

Humour is a big part of life for the older child, especially, it seems, for boys who will relate to each other with much good-natured teasing and banter. As they become more aware of their sexuality they will tell rude jokes both to each other and to you. Sometimes they are simply repeating what they have heard. A nine-year-old girl approached her father saying,

'Have you heard this one? To the woods, to the woods . . .'

'No, no, I'll tell the vicar.'

'I am the vicar.'

Her father, somewhat taken aback, replied, *'Well, what does it mean?'* to which his daughter replied honestly, *'I don't know but it's funny.'*

This story highlights how it is the shock effect of older children's jokes which is important rather than the content. This father was riveted suddenly into paying attention to his daughter. He was shocked at her joke, not so much at its relatively benign content, but that it was his daughter who was telling it to him.

Older children may use 'dirty jokes' to bridge the gap between home and the outside world. We could think of this girl using this joke to say to her father, *'I've heard this outside of home and I don't understand it but I am curious about it.'*

Managing explicit sex talk

- Accept you may be shocked by your older child's crude jokes and remember that trying to shock you may be a way of both trying to get your attention and to get you to explain something to them.
- Try to respond to the communication rather than to the joke. You can think about whether or not it's possible that your child could feel you have been distracted from them more than usually of late. If that could be true you could respond to the joke casually by saying you realize you haven't been giving them much attention lately.
- Think about the content of the joke. Could they be asking you for more information on a sexual or bodily matter?

Summary

- In one sense there is nothing wrong with finding your child's behaviour a problem, but it may be worth trying to work out why it has such a powerful effect on you.
- Children know that parents attend to their bodies and so when they have a worry they can't put into words, they may use other orifices than their mouth to communicate.
- In young children, bedwetting is an attempt to revert to being a baby as a way of coping with anxiety.
- In older children, bedwetting may be a way of communicating that the child has a secret worry.
- Soiling in small children can be a way of trying to cope with over-whelming anger.
- Soiling and smearing in older children is a serious communication that a youngster is in a complex muddle and conflict; these may be strong feelings about power and control and anger. Such a child is likely to need professional help.
- Fears are a child's way of communicating to adults that there are things in their life that they feel overwhelming, inexplicable or mysterious.
- Psychotherapist Adam Phillips has written about how often the thing we fear is paradoxically the very thing we want!

- A fear is focused on an identifiable object and is realistic. Anxiety is the same as a fear but the object has become obscured and the fear is unrealistic, it is an anxiety fear.
- Once a fear has begun to dominate a child's life we would think of it as the more serious condition of a phobia.
- The phobic child is projecting something about themselves that they dislike, or are afraid others will dislike, onto something else.
- Children aged 2–5 are fascinated with two things: their own bodies and how they work, and making an impact on adults. Lavatory talk illustrates both these preoccupations.
- In older children, explicit sex talk does not necessarily have to be taken too literally; children will also use sex talk as a way of communicating other needs which they cannot name or understand.
- Telling crude or sexual jokes may be a way of your child trying to get you to listen to them.

CHAPTER 6

When Things Seem To Be Going Wrong

– Lying, Stealing, Bullying and Bad Company –

'Much delinquent behaviour can be understood as people trying to get close to each other.'

(John Bowlby)

Lying

'How can she do it, how can she look me in the eye and lie?'
(Parent of ten-year-old)

'There's something wrong [with our relationship] *. . . I mean, why can't she tell me? If she trusted me she'd tell the truth.'*
(Parent of eight-year-old)

Lying is one of the most difficult behaviours for parents to understand as a communication. When you discover your child is lying to you, you are not only shocked, you are also likely to feel angry, hurt, puzzled and let down.

Nine-year-old Shelly J and her mother were in the middle of their second visit to me. Mrs J was enraged and was reporting how Shelly had lied to her twice since our last meeting. After the first lie her mother had removed her television from her bedroom for a week as a punishment. But two days later Shelly had lied about why she was late home from school.

Shelly had been gradually sinking shamefacedly into her chair but suddenly she bolted upright and shouted, *'Well, I think that was so not fair to take my telly 'cos I ate the cake.'*

Her mother retaliated in an equally loud voice, *'I didn't take the telly because you ate the cake. I punished you because you lied about it; it's the lying I can't stand.'*

Shelly was unrepentant and now in full flood.

'Well, you lie,' she protested. *'I know you lie, grown-ups do lie.'*

And of course Shelly was right. It is not only politicians who spin. We are all, to some extent, putting a spin on our lives, whether it is making up an excuse not to do something we don't want to do or living beyond our income to impress others. D. H. Lawrence said we need to lie like we need to wear trousers. Maybe one of the reasons adults find children's lying so difficult is because it mirrors for us our need to deceive.

Why do children lie?
- When did you lie as a child?
- Can you remember why you lied, and how you were feeling at the time?
- How are you lying at the moment?

Just as adults deceive in different ways, so do children, and different lies at different ages can be communicating very different messages. However, what all children's lying has in common is that it tests their environment, i.e., it asks *'Are the adults really listening to me?'*

Lies typical of children
- Lying over trivial matters.
- Boasting lies – lying about experiences and achievements.
- Lies to establish independence.
- Dissociated lies.

Lying over trivial matters

The first seven years
'Did you clean your teeth?'

'*Yes*'. . . but the toothbrush is dry and the cap of the toothpaste is not thrown into the hand basin as usual!

You are more likely to be irritated than worried when your child lies over trivial matters. You are probably infuriated at the futility of such lies: *'She knows she'll be found out, it's obvious, it's so easy to check on and yet she goes on doing it,'* cried one frustrated parent. Trivial lying is usually at its height between the ages of four and seven years. At this age, such lying can be understood as a developmental stage for the child. Until such an age, your child perceived you as knowing all about them and their world, almost magically being able to sense and meet their needs before they voiced them. This gave them a tremendous sense of security. However, part of your child's quest for independence is to begin to desire a secret life away from you. Freud said that a child's first successful lie to their parents is their first moment of independence; as I said earlier, it proves to the child that their parents can't read their mind.

If your child continues to tell excessive trivial lies after the age of seven, it is likely that the lying is less a stage of development and more a communication about how they are feeling. Children cannot move onto the next stage of development until they feel they have completed the one they are in; is your child simply telling you that they feel they have not quite completed this stage of growing up? On the other hand, they may be telling you that they feel intruded on by you. It may be a way of telling you that they feel you know too much about them and in this case it is worth asking yourself how much age-appropriate freedom does your child need? Are there some areas you should be 'letting go' now your child is seven years old?

Lies in the middle years
Let us return to nine-year-old Shelly. What was worrying her mother most was that Shelly's lies were linked to a change in her behaviour. She

had always been strong-willed and argumentative but Mrs J reported, *'I had a firm grip on her. She knew I meant what I said.'* Now she felt Shelly was becoming 'furtive' in that she would lie about where she was going and which friend she might be going to see. The last straw had been when Shelly had failed to turn up at Gym Club and she and her friend had been found in the local park, chatting to some Year 6 boys.

One of the problems with children's lying is that parents may often see it as one of the first steps towards delinquency. Of course, it could be that Shelly was in danger of going off the rails. However, we need to bear in mind the developmental tasks of older children. They are in the process of separating from you and trying to establish an independent and private life. And having a private life means having secrets.

> Older children may use lies as an important way of estab-
> lishing their independence. They need to have secrets from
> you.

Consider this:
- How do you feel when your child lies?
- What does it make you fear about a) your child, b) you as a parent?

Managing trivial lies and older children's lies
How you respond to your child lying and having secrets is going to be very much coloured by the way your parents responded to your lying and keeping secrets. It is worth reflecting on both how your parents reacted to your lying and also how you felt about the way they managed it.

- You do need to accept that your child will lie to you from time to time. Try also to remember that there is a difference between taking lying seriously and taking it personally. There will be lies that you can turn a blind eye to and others that you will need to confront. Each family will have to decide for themselves what they consider to be an important lie.

- Try to remember that the point of children's lying is to wrong-foot adults. Lying often comes out of the blue and takes you by surprise. While it is important to try to have a general policy on how you are going to manage lying in your child, it is important to accept that in the heat of the moment you may do something that you wish you had rather not done. A general rule of thumb is that encouragements and incentives can be more useful than punishment (see Chapter 4).

- There are ways of letting a child know that you know they have lied, even if you decide not to confront the lie. E.g., *I'm pretty sure you haven't cleaned your teeth and I hope it won't happen again.*

- You can understand that an older child may need to lie to you from time to time but this does not mean you should take a *laissez faire* attitude towards it. This is a time when you need to consider seriously which lies are important.

Boasting lies

Lying about experiences and achievements

Nine-year-old Jean had caused a rumpus at school by inviting several children to her birthday party, and her description of the conjurers, etc., who to attend, caused much excitement. When no written invitation appeared, most parents telephoned her mother to verify the event. However, two girls turned up and of course there was no party organized. Jean's parents were horrified. Why would Jean lie in such a way? A party for her birthday had not even been discussed.

Jean was seen by other children as something of an 'oddball', an outsider, who was rarely invited to other children's parties. She was hurt and bewildered by her unpopularity and tried to 'buy' friendship with good things to offer, such as her party. For a few days it seemed to work; she was the centre of attention with her description of the event to come, for a while she felt 'good enough', liked and valued by her peers.

Colin, aged eight, would often boast about his lavish Christmas and birthday presents. Other children would gasp with envy as he described his exciting latest holiday adventures, etc. *'I felt stupid, when the others said what they'd got* [for Christmas] *. . . so I said we'd be going to Disney. I knew it was a lie, but then everyone was listening.'* In reality the presents didn't exist and the holiday, if it happened, was much more ordinary than Colin described. However, he felt he could gain popularity by causing envy. Somewhere inside he did not feel 'good enough' to be loved and admired for himself. He had to 'put a gloss' on his personality.

Daisy's parents had a terrible shock at the latest school parents' evening. Eleven-year-old Daisy had been reporting excellent test results to her parents, telling them that she had finally been placed second in her class. The reality was that Daisy's performance was more or less average academically. She had sought to impress her parents with spectacular results in an attempt to gain their love, praise and recognition. She felt these were conditional on her good achievements, rather than freely available simply because she lives!

> From birth, the two things children are most commonly praised for are their looks – *'what a beautiful baby'* – and their achievements – *'she was walking at eleven months . . . talking by eighteen months . . . reading before she went to school.'* Sometimes children get into a muddle. They come to believe that they can *only* be praised and loved for such progress. Such children live in a precarious world, putting themselves under extreme pressure to succeed for fearing of losing love and approval.

When success is a burden

A very bright ten-year-old appeared for his session with me distressed and irritable following a school award ceremony, where he had carried off most of the class prizes. *'Now I've always got to do it,'* he sobbed. *'I've always got to get an A in everything.'* His success had begun to be a burden instead of a motivation. He saw a direct equation between the amount of his success and the amount his parents were able to love him. Of course, his parents had never intended to give a message that failure academically meant failure to be loved, but the boy felt under intense pressure once he had an A to always get an A. It was not that this boy had only been praised for academic success but we need to remember parents always give more than one message. These parents highly valued academic achievements and their child misconstrued this as academic achievements were *all* that mattered, or at least what mattered most, to the parents. On the whole, children want to please their parents; the problem arises when they feel they can only please their parents in a certain way by following a set script.

Consider this:

- How much do you think you only praise your children when they are following your script?
- How much do you surprise your children with rewards, emotional or material, for no obvious reason?
- How do you celebrate your children because of who they are, and not for what they may or may not achieve?

Tolerating our own incompetence

> *'To live a creative life we must lose our fear of being wrong.'*
> *(Joseph Chiltern Pearse)*

Part of growing up is accepting that we cannot be good at everything. It is interesting to wonder why children feel they should be good at everything. Perhaps for a child being good at everything means being exclusively what their parents wanted them to be. Every child growing up has to accept that to some extent, be it very minor, they are a disappointment to their parents. Children may find it very hard to come to terms with their own incompetence which is not surprising because most people around them, older siblings, adults, will be much more able in every area than they. Children (and adults) will sometimes lie to cover up their incompetence. One sees this very clearly around the age of two or when a child drops something or falls over and responds, *'I meant to, I wanted to . . .'* even sometimes doing it again to prove a point! The classic example must be the three-year-old running into Mummy crying, *'Mummy, some little girl wet my knickers!'* It is likely that your child may be envious of the skills and abilities of older people and this envy can lead to impatience about growing up. Your child's envy and longing to grow up gives you an important task. You have to enable your child to tolerate being the age they are and help them to look forward to being older. You have to help them not to lose the fun and excitement of being the age they are – and not to regard 'NOW' merely as a time of waiting to be competent.

Telling boasting lies can be a child's way of communicating that they fear rejection if their achievements are less than perfect. And they are also communicating how they see the adults around them perceive their own incompetence. Think about the culture around incompetence in your home. Is one sex allowed to be incompetent and not another, e.g., is it alright for Mummy not to be able to reverse the car but appalling if Daddy dents the number plate? Do you react to your own mistakes with: *'I was so stupid . . . I was really dumb . . . I felt such a fool . . . I didn't want to look a fool . . . I didn't like to say I didn't know . . .'?* Or by anger: *'How was I to know . . . I should have been told.'?* Such responses may communicate to your child that there is something wrong with making a mistake.

> What children need is the idea that while one endeavours to do one's best in life, incompetence is part of being a human being.

Managing boasting lies

- Reassure your child that it is alright not to know, that even parents and teachers were once small and unknowing and had to struggle to learn and master skills.
- Tell your child stories from your childhood that illustrate your struggles to come to terms with your incompetence.
- Tell your child stories of your incompetence as an adult. Explain how you feel about your incompetence.

Lies that explain how I feel

Ellie was seven years old when she and I met. Her teachers had been concerned about her for some time, but her referral to me had been precipitated by a rather dramatic incident in the classroom. One Monday morning she had arrived at school very distressed telling her teacher her hamster had died and that her mother had put it in the dustbin. She had been given the hamster for her birthday by her father shortly before he had left the family home. The teacher took Ellie's distress seriously and at 'news time' the class had a little goodbye ceremony for the hamster. Ellie continued to be upset for several days, by which time the teacher raised the matter with her mother. It emerged that Ellie did not have, and never had had, a hamster, let alone one recently deceased!

Sometimes children will tell a story – a complete fantasy – as a way of explaining unhappiness or experiences they do not understand. Ellie knew she was unhappy, she knew she felt bereft, but she couldn't put her experience into words. She made up a story that made sense to her. It was an explanation of her feelings linked to an experience to which she could relate. So often adults will use metaphors to explain how they feel about an event, e.g., *'I felt as if I'd been run over by a steam roller.'* Ellie was doing the same but, because she was a child she was omitting the words 'as if' – to her it felt as though this event had happened.

Managing lies that explain how I feel

- It is important not to punish your children for telling lies to explain how they feel.
- Explain to your children that they are expressing how they feel. For example, in Ellie's case, as if a beloved pet had died, and no one cared or understood her pain.

Dissociated lies – 'It wasn't me!' – The good guys vs. the bad

Perhaps even more difficult for parents are 'dissociated lies'. Sometimes children under extreme stress, feeling very unhappy, will appear to cope very well with life. However, they can often be described as having one irritating and perplexing flaw. They will lie and maintain a lie, even after they have been found out. They have a gift for keeping up a plausible and a convincing lie under questioning. If they can be persuaded to admit to a lie, they may apologize, but may very quickly commit the same offence and lie about it again. So what is such a child trying to communicate?

It is important to realize that such a child *believes* he is telling the truth. You may well have had the experience of a small child with an imaginary friend, such as Christopher Robin's 'Binker'. Your child may have used the imaginary friend as a scapegoat for his own misdemeanours. In a similar way, under extreme stress, an older child may split off part of himself, almost as though it is another person. The part that gets split off is likely to be the part that the child construes as 'the naughty part', the unlovable part of himself. The idea in the child's mind is that if he disowns the unlovable part of himself, then his parents will only be aware of the lovable in him. Such a child, asked if he is lying, replies quite honestly, *'No'*, because he has separated off the person who did commit the offence.

Earlier in the chapter I talked about how the child who lies may have a sense that there is something 'wrong' with them, something unlovable that has to be redeemed and rectified if they are to maintain their parents' love and affection. I was asked to see a twelve-year-old girl, Amy, who had always attended the same school. As she moved through the school, each class teacher had suspicions that she was stealing. Each time Amy was questioned she would be cooperative, charming, open, and deny guilt, steadfastly looking the teacher in the eye. Nothing could be proved, and in any case, Amy seemed so plausible. The staff reasoned that it would be impossible for her not to show traces of anxiety in lying about such serious offences.

A few months before her referral to me, Amy had been caught. Initially she denied stealing, but when presented with the evidence admitted it and offered a direct apology, although her teachers had commented that they didn't believe she meant it.

Amy was referred to me not for stealing, but because she seemed depressed. And she was, for Amy was beginning to realize that it was indeed her who had been stealing. There were not two Amys, a bad one who stole and a good one who didn't. Previously she had believed there were and had dissociated herself from the Amy who stole. She appeared plausible in her lying because she actually believed she was telling the truth.

Managing dissociated lying

- Dissociated lying is the rarest form of lying in childhood. It is important to remember that the child has dissociated themselves from their lying and whilst they may seem to be 'trying to get away with it' they themselves may actually be unaware that they are lying.
- Dissociated lying is a serious communication from the child that they are very troubled. Adults need to take dissociated lying seriously and seek professional help for the child.

Stealing

You may be very frightened if your child is found stealing, particularly if it happens on a regular basis. You may be frightened you have done something wrong as parents. You are also likely to be frightened about your child's future – will they become a delinquent, a petty criminal, a train robber? Although most children steal on one or more occasion, be it a forbidden biscuit or sweet, or something larger, continual or persistent stealing may be a desperate communication.

What does stealing mean?

'*I needed something so I steal it.*'
   '*What did you need?*'
   '*Dunno, it's not the stuff . . . like I nicked . . . it's like inside.*'
   Nine-year-old Amos struggled to explain his persistent stealing. He knew the important point about his stealing was not what he had stolen but his feelings that had motivated him to steal. On the whole, children steal for one of two reasons:

- Children steal in an attempt to retrieve emotional experiences they feel they have 'lost'. Amos's mother had died two or three years before he began to steal. What worried people was, as is so often the

152   When Harry Hit Sally

case, he was stealing utterly worthless objects such as bits of string, rubber bands, the odd piece of chalk, etc. Such a child is trying to tell you how he feels about himself. When a child loses something important emotionally, he is likely to blame himself for the loss. What did I do to lose the person I loved, or to lose the affection I once had? Am I not worthy of being loved? Am I a useless bit of string, rubber band, odd piece of chalk, etc.?

- Children will steal objects in an attempt to try and fill an emotional vacuum. We need to remember children will nearly always use behaviour to tell us what they need.
- Winnicott says stealing can be understood as 'a sign of hope'. It can be argued that the greater the value of the things you steal, the more hope there is for you in the future. The child who steals is likely to have some hope that they deserve good things, that they have a right to love, affection, time, admiration. Such a child is fighting for their place in the world. A similar child in the same position who doesn't steal could be understood as feeling they are worthless and have no rights on other people. As Bowlby says, a lot of delinquent behaviour comes down to people trying to get close to each other.
- Children steal to find out if someone is keeping an eye on them. When a child gets away with stealing, it can be a terrifying experience because to the child it proves that there is no adult in charge.

Managing stealing
- There is a difference between the child who steals on impulse and the child who is making a habit of stealing. Try to explain that you understand that stealing is their way of telling you they have a secret worry or unhappiness.
- If your child is stealing, shower them with spontaneous affection, kindness and treats. This may seem a shocking solution, but it makes sense if you hold in mind that when your child steals they are saying, *'I need love and affection.'* Spoiling can give the message, *'You are valuable, you are lovable, you are worthy, because you are you.'*

Spoiling your child can be a way of saying, *'At the moment you are a version of yourself that we love anyway, we love you whatever you are like.'* Such a message indicates to a child that their behaviour is part of them, and that they are loved just the same. This is different from saying, *'I like you, but not your behaviour,'* as children are often likely to hear you saying, *'I don't like you.'* Set a firm boundary on your child's stealing by explaining to them that stealing isn't working for them in that it isn't getting them what they need. Explain to them that they steal because they feel bad inside, but when they are caught stealing, they feel even worse about themselves.

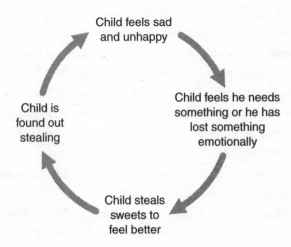

- Seek professional help if, regardless of your child's age, they are stealing regularly and over a sustained period.

An extraordinary problem

However much you know that most children steal at some time in their lives, you are going to be worried when you discover your child stealing. The time to become most concerned is if you feel your child simply cannot help stealing, they seem in some way compelled to steal regardless of the consequences or punishment. Compulsive stealing is a child's way of telling the adults that he no longer believes or trusts that they will meet his needs. The only way that he can get his needs met is by stealing. Such a child requires professional help.

A different kind of stealing

I was recently asked to see a university student who was one of seven children. Her mother was a single parent and worked long hours to give the family a reasonable standard of living, often returning home mid-evening, understandably tired, and often with further work to do. Stephanie described how difficult it was for any of the children, but particularly the older ones like her, to have any quality time or conversation with their mother. Weekends were a hurly-burly of housework and individual activities.

She recalled being taken as a child to the local fair by her mother on a Bank Holiday Monday. The other children were all occupied for various reasons. She described her pleasure in having her mother's undivided attention and then, how as they walked home she began to feel uneasy and unhappy. On arriving at the house, she hid the two little plaster rabbits she had won in the bottom of a drawer.

We came to understand that Stephanie feared that she, and perhaps her siblings, could only have quality time, affection, understanding, and conversation with their mother, at the expense of each other. She was left with a sense that all gratification was stealing. She had little sense of adults wanting to give to her spontaneously. As she walked home from her splendid afternoon at the fair, she felt like a criminal who had stolen something, not only from her deprived siblings, but also from her busy mother. She had robbed her mother of being at work.

Not surprisingly Stephanie was finding it very hard to enjoy successful relationships as a young woman. As soon as she became close to someone, she felt overwhelmed with guilt that she was stealing the relationship from someone else.

Stealing because I'm envious of Mummy

When your child was a baby, all good things – food, comfort, etc. – came from you. Part of growing up is realizing that other people than

Mummy and Daddy can give us good things. Ultimately, we learn that we can satisfy our own needs. However, Melanie Klein has written about the muddle that can arise for some children who do not successfully negotiate this stage of development.

'All good things I have come from Mummy.'

'Mummy has all the good things in
the world. She possesses them.'

'Therefore, I can only get good things from Mummy.
I cannot own them myself.'

'I am envious of Mummy.'

'I feel resentful.'

Envy and resentment

I have already talked of feelings hunting in pairs. The other side of envy is aggrieved deprivation. An envious child is living in a state of 'not entitledness' and will find it difficult to negotiate the necessary stages of being dependent on adults. Adults know it is difficult to feel close and trusting of someone they resent. Such children are afraid of being dependent and may adopt an 'I care for nobody, no not I' attitude to relationships. They may show little concern for other people and lack respect for other people and their possessions. This bravado may lead the child to stealing, i.e., simply taking what he wants without asking for it. Such a child may be communicating real distress, a feeling of being deprived because others have so much.

Managing stealing rooted in envy
- This is a serious muddle, and if you feel this applies to your child then seek professional help. Such a child may be communicating that they somehow feel abused by other people. The risk is that their stealing may lead to even more worrying abusive behaviour towards other people.

Bullying
'I am rough and tough,' said nine-year-old Gemma, raising both arms in the air in a gesture both menacing and defiant. *'I am rough and tough.'*

'You're rough and tough,' I affirmed.

'Yep.' Another dramatic gesture, this time nearer my face.

'And if you weren't rough and tough, what would you be?'

Tears sprang into Gemma's eyes, her cheeks flushed: *'Well,'* she said rubbing both her hands over her face, *'I used to like people, but nobody liked me, so now I'm rough and tough.'*

'Do people like you rough and tough?'

'No, but I don't cry anymore.'

No one likes to see a child being bullied, and parents are usually horrified if their child is accused of bullying. And yet it can be argued that as human beings we have a basic need to bully. There are all sorts of ways in which we try to make other people do what we want them to do; in families we call it discipline. We may pressurize people sweetly with charm or more strongly with coercion. Most adults would maintain that they feel a duty to protect the more vulnerable members of society and, indeed, in many ways this also seems to be a human instinct. But at the same time who can say that they have never felt like bullying someone even if they have never acted on that wish?

Few parents can tolerate the idea of their child being a bully; even fewer can bear the thought of their child being bullied. Adults are often filled with a sense of dread, hopelessness and rage about bullying, be their child the victim or the bully. Perhaps these feelings are linked to our own relationship to the two key feelings at the heart of the bullying relationship – domination and fear.

Understanding the bully

- Do you remember bullying anyone as a child? How did it feel?
- Did you ever watch someone else being bullied? How did you feel?
- Were you bullied as a child? Why? Who did you tell?
- Have you been bullied as an adult, e.g., in the workplace, in a relationship? Did it feel different to being bullied as a child? If so, how?

A ten-year-old boy was referred to me because of his constant bullying of his seven-year-old brother. Paul had never seemed to accept the arrival of Ian and took every opportunity to make his life a misery. He was also almost consistently rude and aggressive to his parents, having frequent dramatic outbursts of temper. The family had struggled for several years with this behaviour, but sought my help as the school was now reporting complaints of Paul bullying other children.

In our first family meeting Paul presented as an articulate child with a mature vocabulary. I noticed that whenever he made a point to his parents, he would do so emphatically. When they disagreed, paused to respond, or if Paul just felt he hadn't been heard and taken seriously in the general melee of conversation, he would reiterate his point more firmly. On some occasions, he would stamp his feet, bang his fists and almost cry.

When I asked what was making him so angry he said, *'No one listens to me, I'm not important.'*

'And do you think people listen to you more when you shout?' I asked.

We can think of bullying as being an extreme and inappropriate way of persuading someone to your viewpoint. In the session, Paul had begun to bully at the moment he felt hopeless about being heard. We began to think of his problem so much as, *'No one listens to me'*, but that he felt bullied by his parents when they produced his sibling. He felt they had never heard his overwhelming sense of being usurped by his brother. His life had become an attempt to bully his parents into understanding how he felt. He felt helpless and vulnerable in the face of both his parents' power – and outrageous behaviour. He tried to overcome these feelings by being a strong and powerful bully. The vulnerable and frightened Paul had become the vicious, powerful Paul.

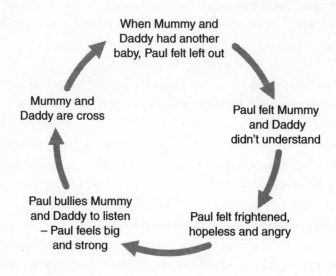

Bullying to pass on the pain

Children who are bullies have themselves often been victims in some way. The child who feels afraid and anxious may look for another child to carry that feeling for him. In this sense there is a good deal of passion in the bully/victim relationship.

> Be in no doubt, the bully wants to be the friend of the victim. Bullies and victims are caught up in a complex connection with each other. They want to be friends but they can't find a way of being friends.

Kevin was seven when his father finally left home for good. Until then he was frequently missing for weeks at a time and Kevin's mother had long since chosen not to question him about his absences rather than risk *'a God almighty row'*. Following the separation Kevin had frequently been let down on visiting days, waiting excitedly for his father, who never turned up.

During that year he changed from being a rather quiet and submissive child to being a rather sadistic and vicious bully, picking on his victims for no apparent reason. After a particular vicious attack he was asked what he'd gained by making his victim so unhappy.

"Cos I feel bad . . . he's bad now,' replied Kevin.

Kevin wanted his victim to feel as bad as he felt. He was articulating the power/domination relationship at the heart of bullying. He felt afraid, alone, isolated and he thought that by making another child feel the same, he would feel better. Of course, for a while he did, he felt powerful, but it was a hollow victory. As his fear returned, he became hungry for more victims.

Bullying as a mirror of family relationships

Bullying has a number of faces. I have already referred to the fact that children who bully have often been victims themselves. This seems obvious where a child has directly suffered verbal or physical abuse. Less obvious is the impact on children of how the adults around them treat each other.

> Children's relationships with friends are likely to be a copy of how they see their parents' relationship. Whenever parents complain to me about siblings fighting and bullying each other, one of my first lines of enquiry is how much fighting goes on between the parents. Consciously or unconsciously your child will notice even subtle changes or disruptions in you and your partner's relationship. Sometimes they act out how they see you treating each other.

Of course it is normal for there to be discord in parental relationships. What matters is the balance between discord and harmony. Children are constantly witnessing shifts in the balances of power between their parents, often demonstrated by their readiness to play parents off against each other, e.g., *'Dad, can I have my pocket money?'* when Mum has already said no.

Children may be both intrigued by the way adults negotiate the balances of power in relationships – and puzzled by it.

> It is not so much the balance of discord and harmony in your relationship that matters. What matters is how it is presented to the children. Parents should communicate to children that in relationships the balance of power is fluid. The aim is not so much balance as fluidity.

If one parent constantly moans about the power of the other parent, then the children are not going to understand this sense of fluidity in relationships. So there is a sense in which bullying may be an ordinary problem of childhood. Children will experiment with both being in charge and being submissive.

Playing as a way of understanding

Children use behaviour to try and work out and understand situations that perplex them. By re-enacting seemingly unfathomable adult behaviour children can come to understand it. Matthew, aged twelve, was referred to me because of his rude and aggressive behaviour towards his mother and his female teachers. His mother broke down at the first meeting saying, *'He's so rude, so aggressive . . . I just feel bullied by him.'* When I enquired who else in the family might be considered a bully, it emerged that Matthew's father was a caring and concerned man who found it difficult to express feelings of tenderness and kindness. For example, if the mother were ill, the father would express his concern for her by saying in an irritable and angry voice, *'Oh, go on, go to bed, go on. I'll see to things here, go to bed at once.'*

Matthew was growing up with the notion that *'men bully women'*. When he spoke roughly to his female teachers and classmates, his behaviour was construed as bullying. Matthew was confused by this understanding of his behaviour. As far as he was concerned, he was practising how to be a man, not how to be a bully.

In a similar way a girl who consistently sees her mother bullied may grow up with the notion that women sacrifice their needs to men. In later life she may display behaviour that would give people the idea that she felt self-sacrifice was something wonderful and special. Nothing could be further from her thoughts; she is simply experimenting with being a woman.

When parents feel like bullies

At our first meeting, nine-year-old Jennifer drew a picture of a face with terrifying teeth.

'It's a scary face,' she said, *'my mum's scary face.'*

'Your mum has a scary face?'

'Sometimes. My mum's scary face is really scary. My mum's scary face takes out my soul.'

Jennifer seemed totally unable to make friends. Other children avoided her because of her bossy behaviour, which would quickly turn into both verbal and physical bullying. Family sessions revealed a mother desperately doing her best but who was unwittingly bullying her children. Her own mother had been a cold, authoritarian figure. She was determined to have a closer and warmer relationship with her own children, which she did. However, at times, under stress or acute anxiety to 'get it right' she would remain loyal to her mother and either lose her temper or demand (i.e., bully) her children to share their troubles with her. Needless to say at such times they were reluctant to do so.

The feeling in the family was that 'Mum has a terrible temper'. At times the children were terrified of her and Jennifer's father was forever trying to smooth things over but at the same time he was desperately upset and helpless in the face of his wife's outbursts. Jennifer didn't see herself as a bully; she was simply modelling on her mother's behaviour to try and get people to do what she wanted.

In ordinary family life a lot of bullying goes on, but it is not called bullying. Children bully parents, and parents bully children. Parents often call their 'bullying' discipline and control. Children's bullying may be regarded as constant demands, nagging and defiant behaviour.

Parents can seem and feel enormously powerful to children as they are growing up. One of the tasks of childhood is to find solutions to the power of the parent and some children may think that bullying the parent into submitting to their wills is an appropriate solution. The common task of both parents and children in a family is to try and be heard properly, to feel recognized, to feel present and to have their needs recognized, if not always met. Both parents and children will realize that there is a lot of frustration intrinsically built into this process and as there is no such thing as a perfect parent (or indeed a perfect child) bullying is almost bound to happen. Some family members will try to insist other people do things, to force on other people what they want. Others will not. What differentiates a forceful person from the bullying person is the way in which the other person responds. The parent, or indeed the child, who stands firm against a bullying demand prevents the other person from becoming a bully. So we can think of bullying as a relationship between a forceful demand and an appropriate response.

Defiance is important because in early childhood your child has a mission of trying to get their needs met. Children aged between three and eight years old will try very hard to bend their parents' will to theirs. If you always do what your child wants then you, of necessity, make your child into a bully. It is important you meet the demands of your children that you want to, that you think are appropriate, and stand firm but kind over other demands. If your child feels secure and confident that you will hear their needs, and respond appropriately, they are not as likely to have to fall back on bullying tactics as the child who feels unheard.

Why are some children more bullied than others?

Why do some children seem to invite bullying? As one teacher described, *'He lies down and shows the others his belly, of course they bully him!'* And adults can be very irritated by the child who just seems not able to help annoying other children.

Donald Winnicott talks of the 'nuisance value of symptoms'. Children who invite bullying are making themselves a nuisance to somebody else and that may be a very important communication for them. We need to remember again that the behaviour adults may regard as a problem so often is felt by the child to be a solution. Difficult and worrying behaviour can be a child's toolkit for helping them to cope with life. As one twelve-year-old said to me recently, *'When they bully me they know I've got a life, I'm not a no one.'*

Children who constantly try to get under other people's skin may be experiencing a real dread – perhaps all our true dread – of being unnoticed and ignored. This twelve-year-old felt intensely isolated, and preferred the satisfaction of feeling that his peers hated him to the anxiety of not being sure whether they noticed him. It may sound tough but no child has to be a victim if they don't want to be one. For him, it felt better to be actively disliked than to be on the fringes of the group.

A victim may prefer to feel hated by their peers than to feel ignored by them, but neither experience makes them happy. However, not all victims invite bullying. Children who are different in any way, be it their skin colour or wearing spectacles, can be picked on simply because they are different. Such victims may be left with the idea that to be different is not only alienating, it is, as one child said, *'Spineless . . . they think 'cos I'm fat I'm weak.'*

If your child is a victim

No child should feel ashamed of being bullied. Encourage your child to talk about what is happening to them. You will need to reassure them that it is not their fault they are being bullied and no one deserves to be bullied. Your child will need help to try and understand their part in this bully/victim relationship. This is a delicate matter because a victim will be very sensitive to feeling blame. Ask if they know what it is about them that makes other children want to bully them. Eight-year-old Joss's parents were moved when they asked him this question. *'Well, I'm a bit fumbly . . . and then I get mad and walk off,'* he replied. They had not realized how frustrated their uncoordinated son had felt when he was in a group of children. It was easy to see how his clumsiness followed by a temper tantrum was going to make him a target for bullying. They were able to help him to find other ways of managing his frustration as well as helping him to improve his game skills.

It is the responsibility of adults to ensure no bullying takes place at either home or school. If your child reports bullying, then tell a responsible adult as quickly as possible. Your child may initially protest, but they will also be relieved that the adults are in charge.

Do toddlers bully?

So many children socialize easily that we can presume it is instinctive, forgetting that they have to learn how to make friends with other children. It is an extraordinary transition from being someone special in the family to being one of many in a group. Making friends is as much a developmental stage as learning to walk and talk. Children master the skills in their own time and at their own pace. Some will always be more content with their own company – nothing wrong with that – but by eight years old, most will have made some form of friendship, so the child who is unable to relate to other children needs to be taken seriously. Enjoying your own company is different from being isolated.

Most parents want their child to be seen as sociable and friendly if for no other reason than it shows you have done a good job as a parent. So three-year-old Harry's mother was appalled when his nursery teacher complained about his bullying behaviour towards other children. He was biting, scratching, grabbing other children's toys and recently had been seen kicking a child who had tried to stand up to him. She became more and more distressed as she described how Harry had always had difficulty in relating to other children. When he had first attended playgroup he had been seen on several occasions rushing over to another child and pushing them over. He had been firmly reprimanded, frequently, for his behaviour and told to *play nicely*.

Now 'nicely' is a good game and children are always being encouraged to play it! However, for children like Harry it completely misses the point. At eighteen months old children have very few ways of making their desires known. They may very well not have the necessary language. So it is not uncommon for an eighteen-month-old to see a child they like and push them over as a way of making contact. So we can think of bullying as a friendship that can't find a way of making itself work. It can be an inappropriate way of trying to become closer to someone.

We began to understand Harry as a child who missed out on a stage of learning. He had quickly learnt that pushing other children over was 'naughty' but he hadn't grasped a more appropriate way of approaching other children as he grew up. There had also been a series of stresses in the family over the past eighteen months: a house move because the father had lost his job, and his grandmother had died. We came to understand some of his 'bullying' of other children as his way of taking out his stresses on his peers. His parents had been understandably stressed and depressed over the past eighteen months and maybe Harry felt they were less available to him and less attentive to him than he would have liked.

It is interesting the way bullying is contagious. You are likely to want to respond to your child's bullying by trying to bully them into behaving differently. No child should ever be allowed to bully another. As adults, we may not be able to prevent bullying, but it is our responsibility to create an environment in which bullying is not encouraged and not tolerated. However, we should always be as worried about the bully as the victim. The child who is bullying is asking adults to take them seriously and is drawing attention to their unhappiness. A bully is always relieved when they are prevented from bullying.

Managing the bully

- Try to avoid being either angry or punitive as this will only make a bully feel guilty.
- Try to help your child to talk about their victim. What might the victim have they would like? Is there anything they have that their victim might like? In this way you are helping them to think about their relationship with the victim.
- Could your child's bullying be related to what is happening in your relationship as parents?
- Children who bully always feel confused and powerless. If you feel talking isn't helping or if your child can't talk to either you, a relative or a family friend, then it is probably advisable to seek professional help.

What do you do when you don't like your child's friends?

Eight-year-old Zen's parents were very worried about his friendship with a boy in the same class. Zen had always been a well-behaved child, both at home and at school, but since he had palled up with Boyd, he had become increasingly truculent and, as his father described, *'His language is beginning to be very fruity. We feel Boyd is leading him astray.'*

Twelve-year-old Agnes's parents had a similar problem. They had been pleased, and relieved, that Agnes had remained relatively unsophisticated and to some extent still more of a child than a teenager. When she began secondary school she developed a close friendship with Elaine, who came from a very different kind of home and who quickly released Agnes's latent interest in cosmetics, pop magazines and boys. Neither girl had been in any kind of trouble or indeed taken any great risks but Agnes's parents were worried. *'We just don't like the girl,'* said her father. *'Where is it going to end? Drink? Drugs?'*

We have been thinking of children as learning to become choice-makers, and friends represent one of their first major choices outside home. In the early years children do not really choose their friends – they tend to be friends of your friends, or at least of the adults you know. This may continue through their early years at school but by Year 4 your child will be beginning to choose friends independent of your circle. So in a sense, choosing their own friends is symbolic of a child's first steps to independence.

What do friends mean to children?

For children, friends are not only companions along the way. It is through friends that children learn there are many ways of behaving, many kinds of interests, many cultures in which people live and that there are many ways of being a child.

Children will often mimic their friends' behaviour. We can understand both Zen and Agnes's parents' fear that they were taking their first steps to delinquency but it is much more likely in Zen's case in particular that he was simply curious about how it felt to be Boyd. We can think of Boyd as Zen's chosen sibling. To Zen it seemed that Boyd could behave outrageously and get away with it and he wondered what that was like.

> We need to remember that friends are chosen siblings. Children will often choose a friend to help them work out a relationship with a sibling or help them to understand what it would have been like to have had a sibling or a different kind of sibling.

Zen had a bossy and intolerant older brother who was much more defiant in the home than Zen. In his friendship with Boyd, we could think of him as practising being an extreme form of his brother, i.e., what does it feel like to be my brother?

Zen's parents were worried about who was now teaching him to speak and behave. But Agnes's parents had real fears she was being 'led astray' by Elaine. Friends are symbolic of a number of issues for an older child. They may choose a similar kind of child as a friend who will help them to develop their mutual interests outside home. Equally, they may choose a very different kind of child who can give them a vicarious experience of being someone different to their family.

Agnes may have been attracted to Elaine because she saw in her the girl she thought she would like to be; Elaine gave her the confidence to experiment with being someone her parents would not expect her to be. Agnes knew she was worrying her parents. She knew also that Elaine was generally considered to be 'bad company' by her teachers and peers. So we can think about what else she was trying to communicate with this friendship.

Agnes was typical of a child her age. She wanted to develop her own interests and privacy. However, she also wanted her parents to be interested in her world. We have already thought about how worrying your parents can be a way of making sure they are involved with and thinking about you. Maybe the friendship with Elaine was a way of getting her parents to focus on her. It had misfired, in that her parents were so preoccupied with this friendship that they were not taking enough interest in the rest of Agnes's world, which was what she really wanted.

- Maybe you would rather blame bad company for your child's behaviour than accept that they may have a side to them you dislike or don't approve of and you say you can't control.
- Bad company may be an older child's way of disowning versions of themselves that are unacceptable to parents.
- There is a fine line between monitoring their friendships and choosing their friendships for them. Of course, the more you moan about a friend, the more attractive that friend becomes to your older child.

Managing not liking their friends

- Don't presume the undesirable friend is *only* bad company. Children can often recognize the good in each other much more quickly than adults. You may not be able to understand the friendship but that doesn't necessarily mean it is all bad for your child.
- With younger children like Zen you can make it clear that they can behave like their friends outside the home but there is still behaviour you will not tolerate inside the home. With older children you may need to foster conversations in that you can encourage the child to think about the consequences of their behaviour. In Agnes's case, her mother talked to her about both the advantages and the

disadvantages of dressing and making up so you looked much older than your chronological age.

- Try not to be overanxious. Hold onto the fact that so far you have probably helped your child to make good choices and there is no reason why that should not continue. If you are overanxious your child will sense it and become anxious and worried themselves. Try to trust your child and also try to trust yourself that if they do get into trouble through friends you will be able to help them back on track.

Summary

- Most people will admit, even if only at times, of trying to create a false impression in part of their lives, i.e., lying on a daily basis.
- The child who lies over trivial matters is on a quest for independence. Freud said that a child's first successful lie to their parents is their first moment of independence; it proves to the child that their parents can't read their mind.
- Older children may use lying as a way of having a private life.
- Sometimes children get into a muddle. They come to believe that they are only praised and loved for their achievements. Such children live in a precarious world, putting themselves under extreme pressure to succeed and may tell boasting lies about their experiences and achievements.
- Boasting lies may also be a child's way of coping with their incompetence.
- Sometimes children will tell a story, a complete fantasy, as a way of explaining unhappiness or experiences they do not understand.
- Dissociated lying is the rarest form of lying in childhood and is a serious communication from a child that they are very troubled. Adults need to take dissociated lying seriously and seek professional help for the child.
- Children steal because they feel they had something important emotionally and they have lost it and are trying to get it back.
- Children steal because they feel they need something emotionally that they haven't got.

- Children steal to find out if someone is keeping an eye on them.
- Stealing may be regarded as an ordinary problem of childhood until it becomes compulsive.
- Bullying is an inappropriate and extreme way of trying to persuade someone to your point of view.
- Children who are bullies have often been victims in some way themselves. The child who feels afraid and anxious may look for another child to carry that feeling for them.
- Be in no doubt, the bully wants to be the friend of the victim.
- There is a sense in which bullying may be an ordinary problem of childhood. Children will experiment with both being in charge and being submissive.
- In ordinary family life a lot of bullying goes on, but it is not called bullying. Children bully parents and parents bully children. Parents often call their bullying discipline and control. Children's bullying may be regarded as a constant demanding, nagging and defiant behaviour.
- Children who invite bullying are making themselves a nuisance to somebody else and that may be a very important communication for them.
- Sometimes children will choose a friend who allows them to experiment with being a different version of themselves.
- We need to remember that friends are chosen siblings. Children will often choose a friend to help them work out a relationship with a sibling or help them to understand what it would have been like to have a sibling or a different kind of sibling.
- There is often more to children's friendships than adults can see or understand.

CHAPTER 7

Parent and Teacher Associations
– Understanding Issues at School –

'School is such an ordinary and routine part of a child's life that it is easy for adults to forget or to underestimate what a powerful experience it is for children.'

(Andrea Clifford-Poston)

'Growing up is not all honey for the child, and for the mother it can be bitter aloes.'

(Donald Winnicott)

Work is a customary part of any adult's daily life, but that does not prevent it from being enjoyable, boring, stressful, frustrating, demanding, interesting, and so on. School is children's 'work'. It is also your child's first major encounter with the outside world and a step for which you will have been preparing them all their life. You will also have been preparing yourself; at the very least you will have thought now and then about what life will be like when your child goes to school, and you may have been actively making plans for that time.

Yet it seems many parents feel ambivalent about their child's first weeks at school. To begin with, the first day seems to dawn surprisingly quickly. I have a vivid memory from my early days as a young teacher in charge of a reception class. On the Monday of the second week in the autumn term, I heard a loud altercation between four-

and-a-half-year-old Peter, who had been at school a week, and his mother who was collecting him. On going to investigate I discovered a furious and scarlet Peter refusing point blank to sit in his pushchair. His mother looked bewildered, explaining how she usually had the greatest difficulty in getting him to walk anywhere. Starting school can prove a confusing and anxious time for parents, as Peter's mother soon discovered. The four-and-a-half-year-old toddler who had been more than happy to be pushed around the shops in August, quickly turned into an independent and stroppy schoolboy within a week in September.

Parent teacher associations

When your child started school you were probably anxious about handing them over to the care of an unfamiliar adult, wondering will the teacher understand them, will she be able to read their little signals in the same way as you do? Will she know your child is special and different from all other children, because they are yours? Will she protect them adequately, taking their upsets and joys seriously?

The answer to most of these questions is no. Your child's teacher will not have the same emotional bond or the same sensitivity to your child as you as parents. That is not her job. Her role is to provide a warm and trusting environment in which your child is able to develop confidence and skills, to explore the world and to also realize that good things can come from other people as well as from parents.

The class teacher is often the child's first significant adult in the outside world and they may experience the same love and hate for her as they do for you, their parents. While you may be delighted if your child settles well into school, it is also natural to feel some envy and rivalry towards this other adult who is seemingly as important, if not more important than you, for a significant number of hours a day.

'Miss James says, Miss James says . . . that's all we hear nowadays.'
(Parent of reception class child)

Paradoxically, you will feel anxious and disappointed if your child does-n't like their teacher. But you will feel outraged if the teacher doesn't seem to like your child. How you feel about your child's teacher and the manner in which you approach them will be highly coloured by your own experience of school.

In Shakespeare's *The Tempest* Miranda describes to her father how she has told Ferdinand, her new-found love, of her childhood experi-ence of being cast away at sea, adding, *'and I not knowing how I cried out then, will cry it o'er again.'*

> Do you remember your first day at school? When your child starts school, you re-live starting school. Your child goes to school, you the parents go back to school.

School is a potent symbol for adults and we cannot underestimate its resonance. It is not unusual for a highly successful, articulate parent to blanch at the suggestion that their child's difficulties in school should be discussed directly with the head teacher. Many will admit to feeling quite scared: *'The problem is, she* [the head teacher] *thinks she's talking to an adult, but inside I'm a quaking six-year-old.'*

Starting school

A group of mothers asked to share their main anxiety about their child starting school gave a predictably wide range of answers: *'Will he cope with the demands?', 'Will he have friends?', 'Will he be bullied?'* etc. When asked then to recount one outstanding memory of their own school days, all gave stories illustrating their experience of their main worry for their child. That said, there are also universal childhood problems around schooling and we are going to focus on these in the remainder of this chapter. Again, how you react to and manage these problems may depend very much on your own childhood experiences and the advantage is that your experiences will sensitize you to the things your child might suffer from at school.

Your early school experiences may be indelible. What can be
guaranteed is your worst experience will become your crusade at your child's school gates, e.g., if you were bullied at
school, then you will crusade against bullying at your child's
school.

Should we send him to nursery school?

I remember as a student teacher being highly amused by a tutor whose
mantra was a phrase along the lines of, *'Children are all very individual
and must be treated as such.'* Now I realize never was a truer word
spoken! Children develop at radically different rates and so it is very
difficult to give prescriptions for a whole age range, such as 'under
fives'. It is also true that we have a diverse range of playgroups and
nursery schools in Britain, which differ widely in their approach to
education in the pre-school years.

Consider this:
- What do you want nursery school to do for your child?
- In choosing a nursery you may want to focus on what the nursery
  considers to be 'attainments'. What does this nursery value? Play
  and social activities? Academic achievements? A mixture of both?
  Or what?

Hold in mind that for you, as parents, going to nursery may be
necessary and make sense, but for your child it is a powerful
transition.

It is a huge step to move from being the focus of your parents' attention at home to having to learn to share one or two adults with a large
number of classmates. We need to remember that from the child's
point of view the classroom is, in effect, full of siblings.

Learning to share

One of the advantages of your child attending a pre-school group is that it will help them consolidate sharing. But in order to share we have to be sure that we already have enough for ourselves. So the emotionally vulnerable or immature toddler may not be ready for this experience in a large group. They may be helped to develop more healthily by being introduced slowly to more and more experiences of sharing within the home.

Learning to play

Donald Winnicott has written about how developmentally toddlers are moving from a stage of solitary play, i.e., playing alone in the presence of an adult, to mutual play with their peers. By mutual play he means learning to give and take, sharing not only toys and equipment but also ideas and imagination. Mutual play is how toddlers learn about relationships with other people. Nursery school can be a valuable resource for children to develop these skills.

Learning about adults

Small children experience their parents as the source of all good things, and they have an almost magical belief in their parents' skills, abilities and knowledge. At pre-school, toddlers may learn that good things can come from other adults as well as their parents. They will realize that their teachers know new and different things from their parents, which can be enormously reassuring to a child about to encounter the wider world. For as your child approaches their fifth birthday, they have to take the major step of starting 'big school'.

The child who has difficulty settling in school

Given it is such a huge and powerful experience, it is surprising that for most children the transition from home to school goes relatively smoothly. Most will experience inevitable conflicts in moving from one world to another, ranging from different values, and different expectations to a different routine. For example, it may be acceptable at home to eat your lunch on a tray in front of the television, but this will not be acceptable at school. Alternatively, crisps may be emptied from the bag into a bowl at home, but may be eaten from the bag in the playground. However, on the whole, give or take the odd wet bed, the odd temper tantrum, the mild refusing to eat, the over-tiredness, for many children this transition will go smoothly.

Coping with like and unlike

Other children experience a real difficulty in settling. Of course much will depend on the similarity of the two worlds: for example, it is not surprising when a five-year-old Asian child, who has recently arrived in the country, experiences difficulty in starting school in a class where everyone speaks English.

> In this book we are very much thinking about children's behaviour as a communication, and the inherent difficulty of working out what is being communicated and to whom it is addressed. Equally important is what the child is hoping to receive back from the adults and how they are going to cope with what they expect to receive? For example, the five-year-old who has extreme temper tantrums each morning, refusing to go to school, in the hope that he may never have to go to school, is bound to be disappointed!

Control and communication

The teacher's responsibility is primarily to the class as a whole and for this reason children's behaviour in school has to be regarded as something to be controlled. This does not mean that teachers do not try to understand children's behaviour as a communication – indeed they do – but they may also feel under a degree of pressure to prevent the child from disrupting the group and/or distressing other children. When five-year-old Sally was referred to me, her teacher was as concerned about Sally's impact on the other children as she was about Sally herself.

Sally had been at school for just over a term. Each morning began with tears, tantrums and a long list of physical ailments, which she felt meant she could not go to school. Her parents and teachers were handling the problem firmly but kindly, insisting that Sally did go to school. She would always scream as she was separated from her mother at the classroom door. Often Sally would settle down when her mother left, but then became unreasonably distressed at odd times throughout the day. At times she had been allowed to return home.

Looking after the grown-ups

Sally was the youngest of three children, there being a nine-year gap between her and the next child. Her parents' marriage had been unhappy for a number of years and both parents had pursued busy careers, perhaps as a way of ignoring the difficulties in their relationship. Sally was cared for by a live-in nanny who had left as she had started school, and been replaced by a new au pair.

What emerged was that Sally was worried that Mummy and Daddy would be unhappy while she was at school. Much of her behaviour could be understood as a refusal to grow up and become independent – she was refusing to go on to the next stage of her life. This made sense as we understood Sally's perception of her role in the family. Somewhere she had picked up what the parents had verbalized quite openly: *'We are only staying together for the children.'* Unconsciously, Sally was worried that if she grew up there would be no children at home, and her parents would separate.

Do Mummy and Daddy remember me?

Six-year-old Jeremy's story was rather different. He was a lively, chatty and spontaneous child at home, and had made no protest about going to school. Although he talked little about school at home, his parents had no reason to be worried until the half-term meeting with teachers. At this meeting a class teacher told the parents that Jeremy was withdrawn in class, very quiet, often seen staring into space and did not readily mix with other children. As his teacher described, *'He seems to have a secret worry.'*

Although how Sally and Jeremy behaved was very different, it could be understood as communicating a similar problem. The elder of two children, Jeremy had a particularly close relationship with his father, which had developed over the birth of Jeremy's brother when he was two years old. His mother had been extremely ill and his father had taken over much of Jeremy's care. His father worked locally and until Jeremy went to school, he had regular contact with him both by popping into the home during the day and also on the telephone. What emerged was that when Jeremy went to school, he somehow felt forgotten by his parents. He seemed unsure that his parents had a space in their mind for him and thought about him when he was not present. We began to understand how important the phone calls during the day with his father were to Jeremy. They were usually initiated by Jeremy and seemed to be his unconscious way of checking that he hadn't been forgotten; when he went to school, of course, he lost his dad's phone calls.

Helping children like Jeremy

Children like Jeremy are afraid that as far as their parents are concerned they are 'out of sight, out of mind'. They need constant reassurance that their parents do not forget them when they are absent.

- We looked at why Jeremy felt he might be forgettable. Could he be trying to draw attention to the fact that his parents were unusually preoccupied at this time?
- Jeremy was helped by his parents telling him that they knew he worried about being forgotten, but that didn't make it true!
- In the evening his parents tried to throw into the conversation casual phrases like, *'When I was at work, I was thinking about you and I was thinking about how you liked baked beans.'*
- Some children will find it reassuring to find a little note from their parents or a small surprise gift in their lunch box. This may be a simple, *'I love you'* or *'Thinking about you'* or your child may need something more concrete such as, *'When you are eating your lunch at school, I will be doing so and so.'*

Permission to forget about Mum and Dad

It is interesting how children who settle very well at school may exhibit similar anxieties to Jeremy. I remember being present in a friend's home when her five-and-a-half-year-old came home from school. Sitting having orange juice and a biscuit, she was clearly rather down. Her mother noticed and said:

'You seem a bit glum, Mandy.'

'Yes,' she said, and two tears rolled down her cheeks. *'Sometimes when I'm at school, I'm so happy I forget about Mummy and Daddy.'*

Fortunately Mandy's mother was quick to reassure her that although Mandy might forget about her, the job of mothers is to keep remembering their child. When children forget about their parents because they are enjoying themselves, they can become extremely distressed for two reasons. Firstly, they may be worried that the same may be true of their parents, i.e., their parents may forget about them because they are having such a good time away from them. They may also feel guilty for forgetting about their parents. This is another example of 'magic thinking', where children can become confused that forgetting about a parent is the same as 'getting rid of', or even 'killing off' a parent. So whilst you, as an adult, understand 'forgetting' about your child as being temporarily focused on something else, to your child forgetting about you may feel like an active attack on you.

What does school mean to the under-eights?

The years between five and eight are known developmentally as the latency years. Small children are very preoccupied with and curious about their bodies and their parents' bodies and how they are made, what they can do with them, what goes into them and what comes out of them. This is because the world of bodies is the only world a baby and toddler really knows. This interest in bodies involves sexual curiosity and a preoccupation with where babies come from. In the latency years, sexual curiosity goes underground and school provides children with a focus for their curiosity and an exciting resource for discovery; they can learn about the world from the safety of the classroom. They may throw themselves into school enthusiastically, eager to learn not only about the facts but also about morals, rules, and social and environmental issues.

School also provides the latency child with the opportunity for learning about friendships and discovering influences other than home. They will be starting to form solid friendships and to notice differences in the way their friends lead their lives and the way they lead theirs.

The child who doesn't learn

A child of good enough ability who seems to settle in school and yet seems unable to make progress academically can be of great concern to parents and teachers alike. Such a child may be a real challenge for the parental expectations discussed earlier. Such a child may also be a real challenge to a teacher – if a child does not learn, then there is an unspoken implication that maybe a teacher is not doing her job.

In order to learn, a child needs a secure base from which to venture out into the world and permission to be curious.

A secure base

The term 'secure base' was first used by Mary Ainsworth (1967) to describe how a baby uses the mother 'as a secure base from which to explore'. Most children, she believed, get this secure base from the knowledge of being loved by two people who love each other and who love them. These two people, i.e., the parents, or parent substitutes, may not be living together. Separated parents, who can convey an ongoing respect and warmth for each other, may well provide a secure base. (Where there is overt hostility between separated parents, the situation becomes more complex.) This may seem idealized, but, of course, such an ambience in a child's life does not preclude there being difficulties within the family. Adam Phillips said: '*Being a human being is a messy business and there is nothing guaranteed to make a good life.*' However, despite life's ups and downs, when the relationship between parents is good enough, a child will have an optimum opportunity for learning.

Why a secure base is important

- A secure base gives a child a sense of good self-esteem, i.e., I am lovable and I am capable.
- A secure base encourages a child to achieve: *'When I grow up I will be a daddy'; 'When I grow up I'll be a teacher like Mummy',* etc. The child sees advantages in being grown up and acquiring adult skills such as reading and writing.
- A secure base allows a child not to be preoccupied with what their parents are thinking. They are free to be curious about other things.

> *'I think I am a good bloke, therefore I am a good bloke.'*
>
> *(Graffiti)*

Children are concerned about what is in their parents' minds, because they are dependent upon them. The more secure a child feels that the adults around them recognize and accept them as a person in their own right, with their own unique way of thinking, feeling and expressing themselves, then the more free they are to learn. It is only when a child is heard and appreciated that they are able to learn. What links a child to the world, to life, to shared experiences and meaningful relationships is when what is real to him is real to somebody else.

Permission to be curious

Children need to feel free to be inquisitive – to let their minds roam around the questions of their world. This may seem an extraordinary thing to say and may provoke confusion, but when there is a secret in the family then a child may quickly come to learn not to ask questions about that secret. Eventually it may become impossible for them to question anything, for fear they will discover the thing that mustn't be known.

George was six when he was referred to me. He was thought to be of gifted intelligence, but was making very little headway in school. Something his teachers had noticed, and that his parents confirmed, was that while George was able to absorb information very readily, he rarely asked the questions one might expect of a bright child trying to extend his knowledge.

George's family picture was complex. His parents were separated but continued to share the family home. His father had a mistress with whom he spent Tuesday and Thursday nights. His parents did not want their separation to be made public for family reasons. They explained to George that his father was away from home on Tuesday and Thursday nights because *'Daddy was at work'*. During his pre-school years George had accepted this explanation but when he went to school, and began to learn more about jobs and the nature of the work, it simply didn't make sense.

> Often when a child appears not to be learning, it can be not so much that the child is failing to learn, but that he has a different agenda, a different curriculum to that of the school.

A child like George may wish to study 'Why Dad left home' – this may be the area of his curiosity. His 'maths' may be 'What doesn't add up in my life?'; his 'history' question, 'Why have certain life events happened to me and how much is it my fault?' Psychotherapist Michael Eigen talks of the child's 'official' and 'unofficial' development. Officially a child may be expected to follow the school curriculum; unofficially he will have his own curriculum to study.

Understanding the learning process

Children are sometimes assessed as having a problem in learning, or even a learning difficulty, without due regard being given to the different processes in the stages of learning. The parallels between the process of learning and the process of feeding are well documented. We take something in, we make it our own, and we pass it out in a different form. In thinking about a child not learning, it is important to understand which stage in the process of learning the child is finding difficult. Is it the process of taking in information, the process of processing information, or the process of reproducing information in a meaningful form? If you think of all the times that you cannot eat, then you are likely to identify the times when it is difficult for a child to learn:

- When there is a physical problem, i.e., the child cannot hear or see properly, or has a specific learning difficulty such as dyslexia.
- When the child is in emotional turmoil: for example, if they have a secret worry or are preoccupied and anxious about unhappinesses in their life.
- When the child is simply not 'hungry' – the ability of adults, and other children, to motivate a child to learn cannot be over-emphasized. Nor indeed can the impossibility of 'force-feeding' a child. Sometimes the child may simply not be hungry. If loss of appetite is the child's way of trying to communicate, then it may be almost impossible for adults to motivate him until that communication has been heard.
- When the child is already 'full' – the implications of the school time-table and excessive parental pressure over homework are obvious.
- When the food or the giver of the food is unattractive. When a child has a warm relationship with a stimulating and responsive teacher in an attractive physical environment with clean and well-presented equipment and materials, then you have the optimum situation for learning.
- When food has associations. For example, some people may associate tomato soup as a comforting winter warming dish, while others may associate it with illness, the food that was always offered when they weren't well as a child. A twelve-year-old at her first high tea at boarding school was appalled when the pupil sitting next to her said of the poached eggs on toast *they look like dead eyes*. When a child is asked to read aloud, he is asked to read aloud all his associations with the words and story. A sixteen-year-old, abused and abandoned by her father, described her difficulty in studying *King Lear* for GCSE. Such perceptions are always idiosyncratic and this is what can make it so difficult to understand another person.

The hyperactive child – 'He simply doesn't listen'

'The problem is he just doesn't listen, that's half the problem anyway; you can see he's just not concentrating.' I have almost come to expect that or a similar line to be included in any description of a child referred to me with distracted and distracting behaviour. Requests for a diagnosis of ADHD (Attention-Deficit/Hyperactivity Disorder) are very common nowadays, and while I am not disputing the authenticity of physical and neurological problems, I am discussing here the emotional basis of poor concentration and hyperactivity and what the child might be communicating by these symptoms. The child who can't stay still, either physically tearing round the classroom or scraping his chair when seated, etc., or is restless, jerky or fiddling in class, can be an irritant as well as a cause for concern to both teachers and parents, particularly if the adults have a sense that the child 'won't' rather than 'can't' listen or sit still.

Understanding restlessness

> *'People don't understand about my feet, my feet keep moving because my head is sad.'*
>
> *(Bereaved ten-year-old)*

When asked how they are coping with a trauma or anxiety, adults will quite often say, *'Well, I keep busy. I try not to think about it too much.'* And so it is for children.

Keeping busy, trying not to think about something may be expressed by a child in hyperactivity. Constantly 'on the go', such a child may be avoiding painful and difficult thoughts and feelings as though they feel they can expel them through activity.

Sometimes, the hyperactive child is trying to show teachers and other adults what life is like at home. Learning becomes practically impossible because most of the child's energy is going into being active. They can't concentrate because they are working very hard not to concentrate on something!

The hopefully depressed

When you are depressed it is likely to be obvious to those around you – you are likely to be listless, lethargic and unmotivated. Children's depression is different from adults, – the depressed child may be tense, alert and constantly on the go. Why? The depressed child is hoping that someone may hear and understand; the depressed adult often feels hopeless that no one can hear and understand.

> Children's depression is different from adults, in that it is frequently mixed with a persistent hope of recovery.

The depressed child's activity can mislead adults because the communication may not be clear. The child may be dismissed as 'attention seeking' when in fact he may be 'attachment seeking' (Williams).

Hyperactivity can be understood as a failure to attach, i.e., a failure to establish the 'internal' secure base talked of earlier in this chapter. In the words of a nine-year-old, *'I go out in space. I mean like I'm on the moon. I mean like I'm heavy but I want to be weighted.'*

This hyperactive boy felt he was dangling, not securely attached to an adult, and therefore unable to explore his environment in a meaningful way – the moon walk was the fun, not the study, part of space travel.

Watch the quiet ones

However, the hyperactive child may be much more hopeful about his predicament than the depressed child who sits silent and withdrawn at the back of the class. Such a child may not so readily seek to attract the teacher's understanding because he has lost his hope of recovery and ceased to look for helpful adults.

The child who doesn't listen

Eight-year-old Nora drove both parents and teachers to distraction with her failure to listen. When asked to do something, she would appear to take notice and nod, but the task would rarely be completed. My first question about any such child is, *'Who listens to her?'*

Nora's parents were appalled to realize how little they listened to her. Both Nora's siblings were in their late teens and at mealtimes the four adults in the family tended to talk around the table together, directing the odd kind word towards Nora and paying lip-service to anything she had to say.

> We learn to listen by having the experience of being listened to by others.

When anxiety is helpful

The child who fails to learn should be understood to be communicating a problem of childhood, and be taken seriously. Understanding 'not learning' as a communication can help to depathologize a child in the sense that we can talk to them along the lines, *'There is nothing wrong with you, there's nothing wrong with your brain, but you are trying to tell the adults something.'* I have already talked about how children cannot help but be curious about what goes on in their parents' minds. There is a difference between an anxious, preoccupying curiosity and a relatively easy and relaxed curiosity. It could be argued that we only think about our parents when there is a problem, so the happy child is free to learn about other things.

Trying new food – just a taste! – preparing children for starting school

> *'Tom has an interview at secondary school tomorrow . . . it's traumatic!'*
> *'Why is it traumatic?'*
> *'He's never been interviewed before.'*
> *'But why is it traumatic?'*
> *(Two mothers overheard on a bus)*

Parenting is a paradox. From the moment of birth you are bonding with your child in order that he will feel safe and secure and close to you.

Consider this:
- How were you prepared for school?
- What would have made your first days at school happier?

> From the moment of birth, you are helping your child to separate from you and to go out into the world to lead his own life. Starting school is a tangible mark of the end of your child's babyhood.

The likelihood is that you are ambivalent about your child starting school and they sense your ambivalence. This gives you the task of trying to provide a balance between letting your child know that they will be missed, i.e., your day will be different without them, and encouraging them to go out and tackle this new adventure with enjoyment and confidence. Letting your child know that they will be missed and that you will be thinking about them while they are at school is a very different matter from conveying you don't know how you are going to cope without them. If, as the mother on the bus, who was quoted above, seems to be conveying, every step outside the home is regarded as potentially fraught or even traumatic, then it is not surprising if the child is very anxious and less likely to cope. On the other hand, if you present your child with clear boundaries, empathy and a good liaison with the child's school, then the optimum conditions are likely for your child to thrive.

'It's strange, you want them to go, you are pleased for them, it's a big step . . . but you don't want them to go . . . I know I'm losing control of him.'

(Mother of eleven-year-old)

Clear boundaries

- Remember, your child does not choose to go to school. School is imposed upon them by the adults. It may be necessary to explain to your child that they have to go to school and that they will have to go every day until they are sixteen years old. One five-year-old, woken on the second Monday morning of term by her mother with: *'Come on, Sophie, time to get up to go to school,'* stared in blank amazement at her mother and said: *'I've been to school.'*
- You may need to state and restate the obvious; remind your child that they will come home at the end of every day.
- Tell them that you will be thinking about them during the day. Explain how you hope they will be getting on happily at school while you are getting on happily at home, looking forward to seeing them in the evening.

Empathy

- It is likely that your child is both excited and anxious about going to school. Accept both as ordinary phenomena of childhood. If they seem particularly anxious, explain to them how new beginnings are always both exciting and anxiety provoking. Talk to them about how you felt on your first day at school. Tell them what you will be doing during the day so that they can have a mental picture of your day.
- Some children can feel comforted by carrying a tiny toy from home in their pocket or school bag. Equally, a little note from you slipped into their lunch box or school bag can be helpful.

Liaison

- Find out as much as possible about your child's school and teacher beforehand. If possible, talk to a parent who already has a child at that school.
- Visit the school, initially without your child. If possible, observe a class or assembly in action. Talk to the head teacher and to the teachers. Does this school 'taste good'?
- Children feel secure when they can anticipate what is going to happen next. It is usual nowadays for children to have a preliminary

visit when starting school. Show your child where to hang their coat, where the toilets are, and help them to understand the classroom routine.

How do you feel about your child's teacher?

Your child will quickly pick up how you feel about their teacher. I remember in my first teaching post, coming into conflict with a five-year-old boy who eventually burst out: *'Well, anyway, my dad says you're only a chit of a girl.'*

It is important to present the class teacher as a caring and approachable person. Explain to your child that if they have a problem at school they can tell the teacher and she will try and help them in the same way as Mummy does at home.

Home time

- When your child comes home from school, listen to their day, but try to avoid asking direct questions. Asking children questions can often lead to monosyllabic answers or the answer the child thinks you want, for example: *'Did you have a good time in the playground?'* Your child may feel that they have to say *'Yes'* because they should have had a good time in the playground, or give a monosyllabic reply because that answers the question. Phrasing such as: *'How was playtime?'* may be more of an invitation to conversation.
- Remember children can settle into school initially very well, and then a few weeks into the term experience difficulties. It is ordinary for children to begin to have doubts about an experience which they realize is now a reality. It may be fun and exciting to attend school for a few weeks; it may become more of an anxiety when they realize the length of the sentence!

Moving up to secondary school

'It's going to be good 'cos you do all sorts of new stuff and they've got really good sports equipment . . . but I've heard your stuff gets nicked and you can't tell anyone . . .'

It's a landmark in family life when a child goes to secondary school. Everyone knows something important is happening and yet no one understands fully the enormity of the event. In Brian's last term in his primary school he talked endlessly about going to the senior school in September. He was excited: *'Well, this school has got boring now and there you do lots of good stuff like clubs and foreign languages . . .'*

Halfway through the long summer holiday he was finding it difficult to sleep. He was restless during the day and was irritable with his siblings. When his mother suggested shopping for his new school uniform his anxieties welled over. What if he missed the bus? What if he couldn't find the right room? He had heard there was *'mega homework'* and *'you get detention if you don't do it'*. The work might be too hard and he wondered if he would be able to cope with it. His list of worries seemed endless and his parents were equally endlessly reassuring.

It was clear, however, that during the first few weeks of term Brian was struggling to cope until he came home distressed over what seemed like a minor incident. In spite of meticulous planning he had left one gym sock at home. He was afraid to tell the gym teacher and had taken another boy's sock from his bag. Of course, he had been discovered and given a detention to be served later in the week.

Brian's mother was furious with the teacher. She felt he had overreacted to a worried new boy and couldn't wait to telephone the school the next day to say so. She pointed out that they lived some distance from the school and so a detention was a serious punishment in that it meant Brian arriving home later in the dark. You can imagine her shock when she was told that this was one in a series of mild bullying incidents in which Brian had been involved.

When I met with Brian and his parents several interesting understandings emerged. Brian recounted how he had been trying to find a tutor room and had got lost. He had asked a group of older boys who passed him on the corridor to direct him and they had sent him to the wrong room. It became clear just how small and helpless Brian felt in this large comprehensive school as opposed to have been one of the older and more responsible children in his primary school. We came to understand his 'bullying' as not so much bullying but more him

Parent and Teacher Associations 191

desperately trying to protect himself in a situation in which he felt vulnerable. We could see his confusion at having to move from classroom to classroom as opposed to the security of one classroom and one teacher in primary school.

But it was not only Brian who was struggling; his mother was quick to acknowledge that she had *gone over the top* in her phone call to the school and now felt embarrassed by her behaviour: *'I was a real raging lioness and it really wasn't necessary.'* She acknowledged that she was worried about Brian going to secondary school because she knew she would have less control over his life. *'Half the time I just won't know what he's doing or who his friends are,'* she said sadly.

Helping your child with the transition to secondary school

Children know the transition from primary to secondary school is an enormous event in their lives. But don't presume they understand what is happening to them because it can be a powerful experience.

- Try to ensure that your child has as many facts as possible about their first day and week at school. They will have heard lots of myths which may make them both excited and anxious.
- Share with them how you felt about going to secondary school. Hearing about what worried you and what you enjoyed and how you coped will help them to feel less isolated. Allow for fluctuations in their behaviour. They may be world weary, nothing in their world seems right and they may assume a constant air of martyrdom. This is as much a way of coping with bewilderment, stress and anxiety as is reverting to immature behaviour. Remember, at an unconscious level they are aware that their next big transition will be leaving home.
- How well you cope with your child going to secondary school is going to depend on your feelings about them establishing an independent life in general. Now would be a good time for you to start planning how you are going to live your life when your children grow up.

Issues with homework

If I had been writing this book twenty years ago we might not have thought it necessary to include a section on homework. For homework used to be an issue of the secondary school years but now children may be set homework from Year 3 onwards. Indeed, I heard lately of a pre-school child being asked to find three autumn leaves and draw them as homework.

Today's children are more tested and assessed than any other generation. We can understand the pressures on teachers to encourage homework. However, we need to remember that, paradoxically, homework is really school work. I have already talked in this chapter of children holding the world of school and home in their minds together. A child may feel confused when the world of school enters the world of home via homework. Then there is the physical crossing of boundaries as in the room used to do the homework, be it the kitchen table, the child's bedroom or the dining room table. These rooms are usually associated with home events in the child's mind.

So I am not surprised that parents tell me that homework is a major source of friction between them and their child. Many will report spending half the evening, or even the weekend, trying to get their child to do their homework or helping them with homework. They describe reluctant children, fraught children, anxious children. Homework may be important but when it dominates family life it may seem as though school is more important than what goes on at home.

- You can encourage and support your child with their homework by providing both good facilities and your help if they need it.
- Try not to let the doing of homework develop into a battle between you and your child. You can point out calmly and clearly that you do expect their homework to be done and that you expect it to be done by a certain time.
- If your child consistently refuses to do their homework you could make it clear to them that you are not going to fight with them about homework. Instead, you will send their teacher a note explaining that they haven't done their homework and asking the teacher to deal with the matter.

- Don't be afraid to discuss the amount of homework your child is set with their teachers.

What are you going to do when your child goes to school?

'Freedom comes slowly at first.'

(Brian Keenan)

One of the interesting aspects of having a child is that the child organizes your life for you. Having your life organized for you can lead to a fear of freedom, leading some mothers to describe their separation from their child when he goes to school as 'a rupture'. Your child has gone to school, you are now thrown back on yourself, what do you want to do with the time? Your child now has another occupation and this gives you potential mental freedom.

The cult of parental business

Parents often describe to me how they seem to have no more time once the child has gone to school. The school run, household chores, dog walking, to say nothing of working full time, all seem to fill the time before the final school run of the day. The risk is that as a parent you can spend your day waiting, mentally or physically, for your child to return from school. Of course, there is a sense in which you will always do so. However, it is a shame if child caring time completely fills the hours that your child is not at home. It is important to acknowledge that you and your child are beginning to separate. You now have the mental freedom to begin to think and plan occupations for yourself. Younger children, work outside the home, etc., may give you relatively little physical spare time, but you can begin to think about being other versions of yourself than a parent.

And finally, be aware of Chinese whispers!

When I was teaching, I always ended my welcome to new parents with a promise – *'We won't believe a word they say about you, if you don't believe a word they say about us.'*

Children's reports of what happens at school are often akin to a game of Chinese whispers. If what you hear worries you, try not to overreact, but to enquire gently of the class teacher. It is more constructive to take issues up as they arise rather than let them build up as anxieties in your mind.

Summary

- When your child goes to school, you go back to school. Your attitude to your child's teacher and school will be influenced inevitably by your own school experiences. What can be guaranteed is that your worst experience at school will become your preoccupation at your child's school gates.
- You can help your child's transition from home to school by careful preparation.
- In order to learn, a child needs a) a secure base from which to venture out into the world, and b) permission to be curious.
- Often when a child appears not to be learning, it can be not so much that the child is failing to learn, but that he has a different agenda, a different curriculum to that of the school.
- Sometimes hyperactivity can be understood as a failure to attach.
- Children learn to listen by being listened to.
- Both teachers and parents may find it difficult to recognize when a child is depressed. Children's depression is different from adults' in that it is frequently mixed with a persistent hope of recovery.
- When a child goes to secondary school it is a landmark in family life.
- Your attitude to your youngster's schooling is going to be coloured by how you feel about them growing up and losing some of your influence over them.
- Homework is really school work, and this can be confusing for a child.
- Parents can be supportive in encouraging, but homework should not dominate every evening (and in some homes the whole weekend) of family life.
- How are you going to use your time now that your child is at school?

CHAPTER 8
Believing in Goodness
– The Impact of Divorce –

*'Divorce raises many questions for both children and adults involved;
maybe the most challenging and creative questions for parents is
"How can we help the children to make the best of it? And how can
we not let the divorce spoil everything?"'*
(Andrea Clifford-Poston)

'My mum and dad have cut up . . . (confused shaking of the
head) *. . . I mean, I mean . . . split up.'*
(Six-year-old David)

David stared at me with puzzled satisfaction. At six years old he had
got the phrase right, but the experience remained bewildering and
painful. And not only for him – his parents were just as likely to feel
'cut up' as well as 'split up'. When divorce happens something everybody, but especially the children, took for granted was permanent has
turned out not to be so; both children and parents have to say goodbye
to something that they had believed was solid and predictable. They
have to accept that their lives have changed irrevocably and things are
never going to be the same again.

In Chapter 7 I talked of the child's need for 'a secure base' from
which to explore the world, physically, mentally and emotionally.
Traditionally and, perhaps, idealistically, we have understood a secure

base as two parents who love each other and love the child. The shattering of this 'secure base' by death, illness, separation or divorce can be potentially catastrophic for both adults and children involved. Both may experience a sense of bewilderment and disorientation that feels like living on sand. As I have said before, families nowadays are very variable – single parents, step-parents, couples parenting but not living together, gay couples parenting, grandparents or other relatives parenting, and these relationships are becoming increasingly recognized as equal to the traditional idea of the family in terms of providing the child with 'a secure base'. However, it can be almost unbearable for parents in a painful crisis themselves to think about and tolerate their children's pain.

A mother, whose husband left 'out of the blue' one weekend, described how she found her four-year-old, lying on the floor shouting, *'I want Daddy, I want Daddy'*, and overwhelmed by her own distress, was only able to respond in a disciplinarian way: *'Get up at once, you are just upsetting yourself.'* Such a parent may well find trying to establish another kind of secure base for her children impossibly daunting. However, the relative success of the variety of ways of being a family today gives us optimism and sometimes, perhaps, models for the restructuring of a new strange and yet familiar secure base for the children of divorcing parents.

It is important to remember that marriage does not necessarily equate with 'family' or 'home'. These are three separate ideas which may often overlap and interlink and which may be able to exist independently as well.

A failed relationship?
It can be extremely sad, painful and disappointing when plans made for and within a relationship do not work out. I once asked a young mother who became severely depressed following her divorce, and who felt a keen sense of failure, *'If you weren't feeling a failure, what might you be feeling?'*

'Disappointed,' she sobbed, *'so disappointed.'*

A forty-three-year-old divorced father was reflecting upon his very new current relationship. Married twice, once in his twenties, again in his thirties, he had not had a sexual relationship for six years but was now very attracted to a younger woman in his office, who certainly seemed to reciprocate his feelings. He summed up his anxiety and reluctance 'to get involved':

'I can't face another failed relationship.'

A teenager was discussing her relationship with her first boyfriend, which had clearly now run its course. Asked what was stopping her from finishing it she responded, *'Then I'll have a failed relationship behind me.'*

If problems hunt in pairs, then so do feelings. Divorce seems to be accompanied inevitably by a sense of failure and lack of self-esteem. It may not be possible to avoid painful disappointment in divorce, but there are other ways of thinking about divorce rather than in terms of success and failure.

- It is almost impossible to give parents any support in remaining together as a parental couple, as opposed to a sexual couple, without increasing their guilt and anxiety about their children. Offering help in remaining together as a parental couple can imply implicitly that it was not in the children's best interests for them to split up.
- Relationships do not fail; they begin, evolve and end.
- Marriages do not fail; they begin, usually with high hopes and expectations, they evolve, usually with a fair degree of chaos, and they end, sometimes prematurely and unexpectedly by death or divorce.

It can be argued that the way parents think about their experience of divorce will influence their ability to help their children to 'make the best of it'. There is a great deal of difference in the following two ways of thinking:

'Where did I go wrong? I'm a bad wife, a bad mother. I guess that makes me a bad woman.'

and

*'Divorce is not what we planned, we'd rather it hadn't happened, but
it has, we'll have to make the best of it, no, make something of it . . .
but I guess we both wish it was different.'*

It is important for us to remember that although marriages and
adult relationships may break up and divorce, there is no provision for
divorce in the parent/child relationship (marriages end, parenting does-
n't). You may decide you no longer want to be part of a sexual couple
with your partner, but you can still aim to remain with them as part of
a parenting couple, even though you are now leading separate lives.

Divorce is an adult decision

'It's not their fault; they are just the victims in all this.'
(Divorcing father of three)

We need to remember also that divorce and separation are adult
choices; children do not choose but have to live with the consequences
of their parents' choice. The risk is that just at the time you want and
need to be helping your child with their reactions to your decision, you
are likely to be feeling confused and unhappy yourself. At such a time,
children can relatively easily get lost emotionally in the muddle.

Nine-year-old Dora's parents had separated and divorced when she
was five years old. Both had quickly remarried spouses who had their
own children. Within two years both parents had further children with
their new spouse. By the time Dora and I met she had nine assorted
siblings, step-siblings and half-siblings. Her parents lived in different
parts of the country, and access visits were inevitably difficult to
arrange and chaotic in execution. Juggling the life of this complex
family was a *tour de force* in planning. Dora felt she had somehow 'got
lost' in it all. Visits to her father often had to be cancelled at the last
minute; on one occasion he had failed to arrive at the designated service station meeting point and Dora and her mother had to return

home, having waited over an hour. There was a sound and simple explanation but, understandably, Dora, already insecure of her father's love and attention, felt abandoned and unable to understand the complexity of life for her parents.

Dora was a quiet, reserved child who made little eye contact and seemed suspicious of my attempts to understand her predicament. She had been seeing me for about six months when one week her mother asked to change her next appointment from early morning to lunchtime and I agreed. However, her mother then forgot the rearrangement and turned up with Dora at her usual time to find the consulting room empty and locked. She quickly remembered, explained to Dora, and returned later. Dora told me how disappointed she had been when I was not there when she arrived.

'I thought you'd gone shopping . . . and . . . forgotten me.'

'And how did you feel when Mummy explained?'

'Good, I felt good, 'cos you hadn't [forgotten].*'*

'So how does it feel to have that good feeling that I didn't forget you?'

Dora slowly looked up and stared into my eyes.

'I don't believe in goodness, Mrs Clifford – it doesn't work.'

Does being powerless in the face of a life event, as children are in divorce, necessarily mean being a victim? It can be argued that it is not what happens to us in life that matters, but the choices we make in response to life events.

Divorce raises many questions both for children and the adults involved; maybe the most challenging and creative question for parents is 'How can we help the children to make the best of it?' Paradoxically, as you struggle to help the children make the best of it, you will probably find that you as the adults also manage to make the best of it for yourselves.

As a therapist working with families pre-, post- and during divorce, I am only too aware that it is almost impossible to give parents any support in remaining together as a parental couple, as opposed to a sexual couple, without increasing their guilt and anxiety about the children. Offering help in remaining together as a parental couple can imply implicitly that it is not in the children's interests for them to split up! But it is not the role of the therapist to keep families together, rather, more importantly, it is to help them to find out how they want to be together and ways in which this can be managed.

What shall we tell the children?

Most separating parents will agree: *'The worst bit is telling the children.'* As one father said, *'How do you find a good way of telling someone you are shattering their world?'* Telling the children is a painful and difficult task and maybe that is why adults tend to go to extremes over children's potential reactions. We may tend either to presume that their whole world is going to be completely shattered or that they will be relatively unaffected and 'bounce back'. It can be just as unhelpful to presume that every change in a child's behaviour is due to the divorce as it is to assert boldly that children will be unaffected or even much happier. There are, of course, extremes in children's reactions – some may be traumatized, while others may seem more content because they are no longer living in a domestic war zone. There is also the fact that children process life events at their own pace. Some children will react instantly, while others may appear to take the divorce in their stride for a long time before another incident triggers a crisis.

There are, of course, as many ways of children reacting to their parents' divorce and separation as there are children. You should not jump to conclusions about how your child may react, but you also need to hold in mind that divorce can have a powerful effect on any child.

Why you need to tell the children

You do need to tell the children! In a study from King's College, London, in 2001, a quarter of the children whose parents had separated said no one talked to them about the separation when it happened. Only five per cent said they were given full explanations and the chance to ask questions. Most reported that they were confused and distressed by the separation.

In the same study, over half the children who lived in two households because of separated parents were positive about their 'divided' lives. Those who had an active role in decisions about these arrangements, and those who said they were able to talk to parents about their problems concerning their 'divided' lives, were more likely to have positive feelings about moving between households. The views of children as young as five (obtained using drawings and family 'maps') were similar to the verbal accounts given by older children.

Children need to be told explicitly that their parents are separating because otherwise you are depriving them of some of the reality of their life. They need to know the facts so that they can mobilize their own resources to cope with the change in their life. They need to mourn the death of the family and to acknowledge consciously that their parents are not going to get back together.

However, you will need to hold in mind that whatever plausible reasons you give your children for the separation there is no avoiding the undercurrents in the family around the topic. How you approach telling your children is going to depend on how you, as parents, are managing the issue yourselves. There is all the difference in the world between warring parents who constantly denigrate each other in an attempt to get children to take their side, and the parents who work hard to try to maintain a united front, putting the children's needs first and trying not to over-expose their differences or hostilities to them. Divorces and separations are as unique and idiosyncratic as marriage and relationships but, as a general rule, there are two focus points to bear in mind:

- It is best if you tell your children together that you are going to separate. This will reinforce for them that you may be intending to stay together as 'a parental couple' if not in a sexual relationship.
- At the same time, it is important for you to realize that for your child there may be no acceptable reason for your separation.

Telling the children together

In order to make sense of emotional experiences, children need to be told the facts. That said, in emotional situations like divorce and separation there are no absolute facts. It is important to talk to each other beforehand and agree on what you are going to say. If you can't do this talking face to face, then try to sort it out in writing. This may sound straightforward and obvious but it may not be that easy.

> It is best to keep information as simple as possible and as honest as possible. Children do not need to know all the details of why the adult relationship has broken down.

Children may persist in wanting a reason and it is hard for parents to keep the boundaries. When one parent does not want the divorce they may object to the 'united front' approach. Whilst this may be understandable, it is also a time to put the children's needs first. What are you hoping for if you do not present a united front and, instead, present yourself as the hurt and injured party?

'It's not your fault' . . . adult business

'They rowed and rowed and I used to wish they'd separate. I used to wish my dad would just go, and then they'd stop having rows . . . but I never meant it, I never meant it' – a nine-year-old sobs when she talks of her parents' impending separation.

'I said to them, "I don't know why you two don't just separate. You're always fighting, you'd be better off apart."'

'I didn't think they'd do it. I just couldn't stand it' – a twelve-year-old talks of how, although he longed for his parents' separation at times, for him it 'came out of the blue' when it happened.

Families nowadays are very different from families even a generation ago. The boundaries between parents and children are much more blurred, but this is a time to be aware that in families there is adult business and there is child business.

- Your child needs a clear, direct message – *It's not your fault, it was nothing to do with you, this is adult business.* They may feel powerless and angry at such a message, but they will also feel relieved of the unnecessary burden of feeling it is somehow their fault.

- Your child's pain may not be avoided, but it can be relieved rather than exaggerated. The four-year-old who asks: *'Why doesn't Daddy come to see me?'* is not helped by the desperate and abandoned mother who responds, *'Because he doesn't want to see us. There is nothing I can do.'*

- We need to remember that there is no magic in words. Whatever reassuring messages you give your children, they are unlikely to believe you. You need to hold in mind that telling the children is a long-term project, which will involve you all working through the child's conviction that somehow it is their fault that their parents have separated.

- When talking to the children being honest may mean presenting information not only in an age-appropriate way, but also in a way beset for their emotional health. *'Daddy doesn't love Mummy anymore. He still really likes her, but he's met somebody else he would like to live with now'* may be initially less wounding to a child than a bald statement that one parent simply doesn't love the other one anymore.

Despite parents' mixed and confusing feelings at this time, what your child needs, most of all, is to be reassured that both parents still love them, that both will continue to want to see them and, perhaps most importantly, that they are not going to be asked to choose between their parents.

When a parent leaves suddenly

Goodbye makes us sad and angry

Sometimes a parent leaves suddenly or in hostile circumstances and there may be no opportunity to prepare the children. Your first task as the abandoned parent is to do everything possible to persuade your former partner to contact the children and help with explaining to them what has happened. To say this is ideal is to understate! It is highly likely you will be left feeling hopeless in the task of helping the children with their bewilderment and sadness. In such a situation, it may be more important to focus on how disappointing and painful it is for the child not to see their parent than to focus on facts and reasons why the parent doesn't visit.

'Why shouldn't I criticize my ex to the children?'
A parent is part of a child; if a child feels that one or both of their parents are 'bad', then they run the risk of feeling that part of themselves is also bad. As anyone investigating a child abuse case knows, children will go to enormous lengths to cover up for and defend their parents. You may feel better if your child knows how badly the other parent has behaved, but your child will not.

When you know the other parent won't be in touch
Sometimes you know at the time of the separation that the departing parent is unlikely to have much contact with your child. As the remaining parent you have a formidable task. Children cannot be expected to think rationally when their whole world has been turned upside down. You may well be left to soak up the child's pain, anger, disappointment, and sense of abandonment.

> *'It's not fair . . . it's their mother who's left . . . but I get all the bad behaviour . . . you'd think it was my fault.'*
> *(Divorced father of two)*

Children may be afraid of being angry with the departed parent for fear of keeping them away!

Sometimes it may be most helpful not to offer explanations or excuses for the absent parent, but to simply accept how the child feels, e.g., *'It makes you sad and angry when Daddy isn't in touch.'*

Children's reactions to divorce and separation

We need to hold in mind that divorce is an unpredictable business. You should not presume how your child is going to react to the news, but you are likely to have their shock and bewilderment expressed in two questions: *'What has happened?'* and *'What will happen to me now?'* It is important to tell your children that you know they cannot understand why this is happening and to acknowledge and hold their feelings of both panic and bewilderment.

It just doesn't make sense

Out shopping in a busy high street I came across three girls in a shop doorway. The two older ones, aged possibly nine and eleven years old, were casting anxious looks at a younger one, aged about four years old, who was sobbing bitterly. As I approached the shop door my eyes met the older girls'. I asked what the matter was. They looked embarrassed and awkward, as the younger one sobbed, *'Daddy doesn't love Mummy anymore.'*

'I'm sure he loves you.' I reached to comfort her.

'No,' she sobbed. *'No, he'd stay . . . '*

Tom, aged twelve, was devastated when his parents separated. A rather formal family, his parents led very separate lives with Tom at boarding school, but had maintained a seemingly happy enough home for him during holidays. He had no inkling of the deep unhappiness in their marriage. *'They say they like each other, but they don't love each other. They say they don't like each other enough to live together, so I have to take turns with the holidays. I'll always be only a little of myself now.'*

The two children above had little conscious idea of the impending break-up, and their shock and disbelief is evident. In both cases, their parents had tried to explain simply and honestly that they no longer wished to live together, but that they both continued to love the child. To these children, this simply did not make sense.

If 'Daddy doesn't love Mummy anymore' then the child fears that he doesn't love part of *them* anymore. As a seven-year-old said, *'Maybe I smell. I put my mum's perfume on, but maybe I smell.'*

It is interesting how in families siblings are often referred to by a collective noun, 'the children' or 'the girls' or 'the boys', 'the twins', 'the little ones', or as an overwhelmed father of four used to say 'that lot'. At one level this is understandable, but at another it emphasizes the thought I raised earlier, that in distress it is often hard for adults to recognize how individual children in the family are feeling; adults tend to speak of how 'the children' are reacting.

Consider this:

- There are as many experiences of divorce as there are people experiencing divorce.
- In my clinical experience, while there are common themes for all children, it is also a unique experience. Some children will seem to take the matter in their stride, others may be inconsolable.

'Particular to thee' – the unique experience

Psychotherapist Murray Cox has highlighted the scene in *Hamlet* where the prince is beginning to go mad following his father's death. His mother, Gertrude, tries to comfort him. She points out that many young men of Hamlet's age lose their father and recover without falling apart in the way Hamlet seems to be doing, she adds:

'Why seems this so particular with thee?'

'Nay, madam, I know not seems, it is.'

Perhaps one of the difficult tasks for parents is trying to accommodate this fact in a family. Trying to hold in mind that 'particular' for each child is demanding and stressful at a time when parental resources may be low. It may be easier to think of the reactions of 'the children' in a blanket way.

When one child carries all the sadness

Peter, Philip and Jane came to see me with their father eighteen months after their parents had divorced. Initially the parents had 'shared the care', with the children living with their mother during the week and their father at the weekends. A year later, the mother was offered promotion at work which meant a change of location, and the father decided to remarry. It was thought to be in the children's best interests now to be with their father during term time and spend their holidays with their mother.

Peter and Jane seemed to have coped well with the initial upheaval of the divorce. They were distressed at the break-up of the family home, but they seemed to settle quickly into the new routine. In common with many children, Peter and Jane were greatly helped to settle by the fact that they felt genuinely wanted in both their parents' homes. However, they were anxious and upset when the arrangements changed again and their mother moved away, but again they settled down quickly with a routine of daily phone calls and the odd weekend visit when it could be arranged.

For Philip, aged eight, life had been much more difficult. At the time of the separation he had been distraught. An extrovert child, he had many interests – cubs, gym club, etc., – which he promptly refused to attend, eventually sobbing, *'I don't want people to know my family have split up.'* He became quiet and withdrawn, sleeping and eating poorly and his school work suffered.

As the months went by he seemed to adapt to the initial new regime, but would cling to his mother on Friday evenings when she left and to his father on Sunday evenings when he left. His mother described him as *'going through the motions, not really seeming to enjoy or dislike anything.'*

Eventually Philip began to petty pilfer, first from home, then from school, and eventually from the local shops, precipitating his referral to me. Philip's parents had tried hard to understand and comfort him. They were puzzled why he had been so affected, wondering if it was connected with 'middle child syndrome'. They were relieved the other children had reacted so relatively well and felt a mixture of guilt and frustration over Philip.

'Philip's upset, 'cos he misses his mum'

At the beginning of the family session, Peter and Jane were quick to volunteer they had all come to see me, *''cos of Philip, he's naughty'*, which later became, *'Philip's upset, 'cos he misses Mum.'*

'Is it only Philip who misses Mum?' I asked.

'Yes,' Peter said quickly. *'Well . . . no . . . not really–'* he swallowed hard, *'–but Philip misses Mum.'*

Maybe Peter was giving us a clue! Sometimes one child can carry all the distress, grief and anxiety for the other children. By becoming 'the unhappy one' (or even 'the happy one') in the family, the other children can be freed to get on with their lives. There is a sense in which Philip was free to feel grief. His brother and sister were freed from grief. Peter and Jane didn't need to think about the less satisfactory aspects of their parents' divorce as Philip was doing it for them.

As time went on, the balance was redressed with Peter and Jane feeling a little more sad, freeing Philip from his role of 'the problem' and he began to enjoy life a little more. Peter was able to volunteer that as the eldest child he felt he had to keep his sadness *'a secret – in case the others get more upset,'* and Jane said, *'I'm not sad, 'cos if I think about my mum, I'm sad, so I don't think about it.'*

'So how do you feel when you see Philip sad?'

'Well, 'cos, that's Philip missing his mum . . .'

'His mum?'

'My mum too,' she said quietly and sadly.

At a follow-up appointment eight months later, it was interesting to see how well the family was coping. Now that everybody was *'feeling their own feelings'* as Peter put it, life seemed more manageable and happy for everyone.

A kind of bereavement?

As adults, we know there is a difference between someone dying and someone going to live in another place and being in touch with us, if only infrequently. But in divorce both adults and children may experience an acute sense of loss which is akin to bereavement. And it is true that the existing way of being a family has gone forever. However, to help a child we need to approach the bereavement feelings in divorce differently from the bereavement feelings caused by death.

- When a child loses a parent through death we know that part of the bereavement process is to help the child to accept that they will never see that parent again in this world. We help the child to let go gradually of their grief and move on with their lives. We would try to help the child to understand that although the dead parent will always be part of them, their life with that parent is now in the past.
- It is different for children suffering a sense of loss through divorce. They may feel they have lost their parent, but of course they haven't; what they have lost is their way of living with that parent. They now have to be helped to develop a new way of living with a parent whom they may not see on a daily basis.
- In divorce, the child has to negotiate a different kind of being together with the departed parent. *'Neil lives with Mummy now . . . when I go to stay with Mummy I sleep in the big bed with her. I expect Neil will sleep in the settee.'*

Needless to say, this six-year-old child had much to struggle with when she found Neil was to share the big bed and she herself was *'in the settee'*. In divorce, the sense of loss may feel as acute as if the parent has died. However, your child should not be encouraged to 'let go' of the departed parent, but rather they need to be encouraged to establish a new way of having a relationship with them.

> Your child may feel as though they have lost their parent. It is important to remind them that they still have the same parent. It is the way of living with that parent that is different.

It is also very common for the parent with whom the child does not reside to feel that they have 'lost' their child, particularly if a step-parent is heavily involved in parenting.

The impact of a child's developmental stage

Children's reactions to divorce will depend not only on their personality and family relationships, but also on their developmental age.

Three years old and under – the importance of attachment

For children under three years the most important developmental task is that of consolidating a sense of being attached to a 'good enough' parent; in other words, toddlers are establishing their notion of a 'secure base'. They are age-appropriately anxious and insecure when separated from their parents – a three-year-old on a family outing may revel in the company of a doting aunt, but will often *'just go back and see my mummy'* – a sort of quick check that their anchor and reference point has not disappeared. This is very different from four-year-old Jane who, a year after her parents' separation, became highly anxious and insecure whenever she left the security of the family home. Visits to someone as familiar as her grandmother always began with her being dragged screaming from the car, and then trying hysterically to get out of the house, sobbing, *'I want to go home, I want to go home.'* She calmed down unusually quickly one day when a visitor commented quietly, *'You can go home, Jane, you can go home, when we've all had tea.'*

This child's security seemed to have been shattered to such a degree that she only felt safe when she was with her mother in their own four walls. The 'secure base' was very much a physical one. As I have already discussed, often the hardest part of divorce for children is that something they had taken as permanent and for granted turned out not to be so. Their capacity to deal with the unexpected may be temporarily, but not necessarily permanently, limited and fragile.

Like all children her age, at the time of the separation, Jane needed her mother to reinforce her sense of belonging, not only by her reassuring presence, but by keeping her in a regular routine. In this way Jane began to build up a sense of security by being able to sequence and predict her life, e.g., *'After lunch, we'll go to the park, and then we'll come home for tea.'* Telling the child the story of their life may also help. Children love to hear their 'own story', how they were born, named, etc. A sense of history will help the child to feel anchored in the present and able to venture into the future.

Four–eight years old – a child blames himself

'I wouldn't do my homework and I kept having argues with my sister and that . . . I expect that's why.' Ian was a belligerent and unhappy eight-year-old, described by his teachers as 'always at the centre of trouble'. His father had found it hard to sole-parent Ian and his sister, and was puzzled by Ian's troublesome behaviour: *'He knows he can't get away with it, he knows he'll get caught.'*

When I asked Ian why he thought his mother had left home, he thought for a while and said, *'I didn't behave . . . like I was noisy.'*

At the time of the separation, Ian had been given the reasons for his mother's departure. However, to him it seemed inexplicable and in spite of being given the facts, he had formulated his own reasons. In previous chapters I have talked of how children at certain ages tend to see themselves as the centre of their world, and to presume they are the cause or the effect of all their life events. Ian's difficult behaviours could be understood as his asking the adults a question: *'Was this why she left? Is this what I did? Is this what happened?'* The more he was punished, the more 'bad' he felt. Ian's father had to work hard at reiterating the clear message: *'It was not your fault, it was nothing to do with you, this was adult business.'*

The importance of comparisons

Eight–eleven years old – 'I just want my old family back'

Carol, aged ten, was angry. Her anger spilled into every part of her life – doors were kicked open and slammed, shoes were hurled into cupboards, food was gobbled at high speed. The slightest frustration was met with violent outbursts of temper. Her mother described her as having *'a permanent discontented look'*. Carol's parents separated when she was seven. Her father's job had taken him increasingly away from home and the parents 'lost track of each other', and both developed new relationships. Carol deeply resented both new partners and her mother's boyfriend had eventually moved out of the home six months prior to our meeting. She spent the weekends with her father who lavished her with expensive gifts and outings, but she was no less angry in his home than in that of her much less wealthy mother.

Initially her parents thought she would settle down as time went by. However, as her behaviour continued to cause concern over a year after the separation, her mother sought professional help. Carol's mother was clearly feeling helpless and inadequate in my first meeting with them. She listed anxiously all she had tried to do for Carol. She described the father's indulgence of her, and finished rather lamely, *'We can't do anything right, we don't know what she wants.'* Carol, who up until now had sat glowering in her chair, interrupted angrily: *'I just want my old family back – I just want a mum and dad living together like everyone else.'*

'It's not fair, it's not fair, I don't want people to know my home is split up, it's not fair,' cried one nine-year-old. Children of this age may be preoccupied with comparisons, who has what, and where they fit into

the pecking order. Often the impact of divorce is reflected in such children's preoccupation. While they may experience their share of guilt and sadness, it can be that the impact of the divorce will predominantly be a sense of rage and injustice. Even in an age where divorce is such a relatively common event, such children may feel that they have been singled out for a raw deal.

Children of this age need time, space and permission to be angry but they also need help in keeping their anger focused. For example, when Carol flew into a rage over being given fish fingers rather than sausages for tea, her mother would calmly and firmly say: *'Carol, you're angry that Daddy and I don't live together, not that you're having sausages rather than fish fingers for tea.'* This seemed to provide Carol with an opportunity to vent her rage about the divorce to her mother and it provided her mother an opportunity to remind Carol that her being angry constantly would not bring her father back.

Retail therapy

Nine-year-old Beth's parents had separated some six months before her father consulted me about her worrying behaviour. Beth's mother had left home suddenly and unexpectedly to go and live with a new boyfriend in Spain. She was in regular telephone contact with Beth but they had only met once since then when Beth had gone to Spain for a holiday. Her father described how Beth seemed to be in a 'permanent sulk'. He volunteered that in the early days and weeks he had tried to cheer Beth up by indulging her with new clothes and toys. *'But now,'* he said, *'she wants more. She never seems satisfied. She seems to think she deserves to be bought anything she wants these days.'*

When he bought Beth to see me an argument developed in the consulting room about his refusal to buy her the latest Bratz doll.

'It's so not fair,' yelled Beth, *'everyone else has one.'*

'Well, who else has one?' asked her father.

'Well, Tamsin and Soph have one and their parents are not even split up.'

We began to understand that Beth had got into a muddle. Like

Carol she believed it was grossly unfair that her mother had left home. She had misunderstood her father lavishing gifts on her. She believed now that she was entitled to more than other children because she had lost her mother and also that enough material goods would eventually fill up the emotional space her mother's departure had left inside her.

Twelve–plus years – grief and loss

Children process distress in their own particular way and in their own time, but by twelve years old many children are able to tell you how they feel about their life events.

> *'I feel really sad about you splitting up. I'm sad for me but it's worse for the little ones, they won't have my happy childhood.'*
> *(Eldest of four children to her mother)*

> *'It's so not fair about you splitting up. We're never going to have proper Christmases and things again.'*
> *(Eight-year-old boy)*

> *'It's really cool having two homes. It's better now you and Mum are much happier, I don't have to worry about you anymore.'*
> *(Twelve-year-old boy to his father)*

However, you need to remember that in times of stress and unhappiness older children (and adults!) may revert to using behaviour to communicate their feelings. You may find your twelve-year-old behaving in an unusually difficult and more child-like way on occasions.

Social and political factors

'But it's not just sad and angry, it's about not having things . . . it's about the other kids.' This ten-year-old boy raged week after week to me about his father's departure. I thought it most important to let him vent this rage and help him to connect it with his equally deep-felt sadness. He had been describing a row with his mother on return from a weekend

visit to his father. It seemed obvious to me that the mother had been the butt of his misplaced anger towards his father. I reflected, *'Goodbye makes us sad and angry.'*

He was quick to remind me that it was not only feelings that he had to negotiate. He had swapped a certain and stable emotional life for a more precarious one. He now felt out of control and had divided loyalties with his parents. He also had swapped a financially secure and generous lifestyle for a much more meagre one. The family home – the only home he had known – had been sold and he and his mother had moved to a much smaller house in a less affluent area. He understood well the link between his loss of social status and his increasing loss of self-esteem. He saw himself as 'different' from his other friends, and 'less good' than them, because of his lack of expensive games and designer clothes. He had suddenly become a member of a 'one-parent family'.

He was having to deal not only with 'the particular' of that for him, but also with how such a family is construed in society. His mother was in the habit of listening to Radio 4 in the mornings. One day, at breakfast, he suddenly asked, *'Mum, is a lone-parent family like a single-parent family? Are we one of these?'* He was beginning to fear that he and his family were cast in a group, portrayed less than sympathetically by the media.

How parents can help

> *'I know I'm doing the right thing, we can't go on suffocating each other like this, but the kids . . . they're devastated . . . we're wrecking their lives.'*
>
> *(Divorcing mother)*

Most parents going through divorce are likely to express, at some time or other, that they have been, or would have liked to, stay together for the sake of the children. Sometimes parents seeking help with their relationship will state that as the reason they are still together. I am always suspicious when that reason is given.

> Couples find all sorts of reasons for staying together and sep-
> arating. Couples do not stay together for the children, the
> children in such cases are invariably a mask for other reasons
> the couple are together. 'Staying together because of the chil-
> dren' can be a way of not thinking about other reasons a
> couple want to be together.

The other side of divorce is that, however willing both parties might be
to try, sometimes relationships do not work. Being a human being is a
messy business and cannot be ordered or controlled always by an act of
will. In my clinical experience, parents seeking help with divorce tend
to fall into two ways of thinking:

- They are over-anxious about the effect on the children.
- They are dismissive of the effect on the children.

The difficult balancing act for you, as parents, lies in being able to
acknowledge that your actions have had an impact on the child, but
also knowing that beating yourself up on this matter will not help you
to bear the child's confusion and pain. In such crisis times, thinking in
terms of right and wrong may be less productive than thinking in
terms of behaviour and consequences. If you divorce there will be one
set of consequences for the children; if you stay together, there will be
another set of consequences for them.

Nobody chooses their parents; we take what we get and make the
best of it. So how can parents help children to make the best of their
parents' separation? This is a difficult task when you may also be wondering how you yourself are going to make the best of it. You will also
be anxious not to say or do anything that will encourage your child to
believe that you are going to get back together.

This is a time when you may be feeling hopeless and deskilled as a
parent. However, if you can manage to convey to your child that you
understand how difficult this is for them but that it will still be possible

for them to have good times then you are well on the road to helping them to make the best of it. The risk of feeling over-guilty and anxious because your child is miserable is that you may convey to them that life can only be terrible now.

Children should never carry responsibility for their parents, but they can be helped to envisage a happier time ahead if they are involved in age-appropriate pieces of planning about how the family is going to manage life in these new circumstances. A child may feel less out of control and bewildered if they have a sense of the family sharing the project of how to deal with this new crisis. There are no magic fixes for managing divorce and separation in a family, but there are three aims which may help for a good enough situation:

- Try not to draw the children into your adult hostility.
- Try not to mix facts and feelings.
- Be reliable and consistent over contact arrangements.

'I feel like a Christmas cracker' – on not drawing children into parents' hostilities

I have already mentioned the paradoxical importance of children not being drawn into adult conflicts. Of course there is a sense in which they always are, but parents can take conscious steps to limit the extent.

Tom, aged eleven, was about to spend Easter with his father and step-family. Half an hour before he was due to leave he announced he had to go to the shops to buy an Easter present for his father. Knowing there was insufficient time for this, Tom's mother was immediately put in a dilemma; if she agreed the father would be kept waiting at the meeting point with two small step-children. She tried to persuade Tom this wasn't essential and that his dad would be just as pleased to see him but to no avail.

In recounting the episode, she said, *'Of course, I realized I was really fed up because he hadn't bought me an Easter present, so why should his dad get one!'* A rather poignant ending to this story was that Tom had chosen a *Beano* book for his father and was overwhelmed with joy on

Easter morning when he found his dad had bought him the same one. *'He bought me the very same, Mum, he bought me the very same, we are dead alike.'*

It can be very difficult for the parent who has custody to tolerate the seeming idealization of the other parent – as one child described it: *'Santa Claus Daddy'.* At such times, it is essential that parents hold on to the fact, as this mother did, that the child is likely to feel less secure of the parent he visits and he may be afraid of being angry or disruptive with that parent for fear of driving them further away. As a ten-year-old said, *'I try hard at Dad's. I don't want to let him down. I don't want him to be disappointed 'cos . . . 'cos . . . I have to be his best son.'*

When it's alright to be unhappy

Crucial in this process is a parent's understanding of the child's behaviour prior to and following visits. When Tom was five, access visits always ended with Tom having nightmares the last night at his father's and the first night back at his mother's. His father construed this as his being happier with him and not wanting to return to his mother. The mother construed it as the access visits were upsetting Tom and needed to be curtailed. Fortunately, both resisted the temptation to blame each other and were helped to understand that the problem was Tom's struggle to cope with the transition from one parent to another. He needed to be reassured by both parents that they were pleased to see him and would hold him in mind in his absence.

Keeping Mum and Dad together in my mind

'On Saturday I went to Cub's party and Mummy went out with her friend, and on Sunday I played football with James, and Mummy went shopping for a party dress for next week.' Tom's mother was describing her frustration at her loss of a private life. Her children telephoned their father every day and would recount not only their activities but also hers in great detail. When they stayed with their father, they did the same about his life.

'I know it would be disastrous for me to tell him not to tell his father

what I am doing, but I'm fed up with it,' said the mother. She was able to appreciate that what Tom was trying to do was to keep his parents together as a couple in his mind, even if they were separated physically. To ask him to limit what he said to either parent would be to draw him into their hostility and run the risk of him feeling more of a 'Christmas cracker'. Fortunately for Tom, his divorced parents had learned a crucial lesson early on in their attempts to remain together as a 'parental couple'.

Try not to mix facts and feelings

'I don't know what happened, I just phoned to discuss which weekends he [Tom's father] *wanted the children next term, he kept saying, "Well, I'm away that weekend" or "We've got theatre tickets that weekend" and we ended up having a blazing row. I pointed out I wished that I was free to make social arrangements.'*

It may seem obvious, and rather artificial, to suggest parents try to keep the making of formal arrangements for the children, money, etc., separate from conversations about feelings. Conversations over practical matters are potentially emotionally highly charged, with a covert agenda of anger, resentment and guilt. It could be argued that it is almost impossible to have a conversation to arrange for a child to see one of his parents, without both parents feeling guilty and upset that they have created this situation for the child.

- Some parents find it more straightforward to make arrangements in writing. When feelings are flying high, it is easy to mishear or misconstrue not only words, but tone of voice; writing it down can help to avoid misunderstanding and confusion.
- Letters to be delivered by the child need to be handed over with a pleasant and constructive, *'Would you give this to Daddy, it's about your next visit',* rather than a somewhat angrier, *'Give this to your father',* which may consolidate the child's anxiety about having parents who dislike each other enough not to be able to speak to each other.

The importance of reliability and consistency

'My dad's taking me skiing at Christmas, it'll be really good, my dad's going to teach me to ski.'

'Has he said that?'

'Yes.'

'Recently?'

'Yes, my dad's taking me skiing.'

'Sometimes Dad has good ideas but then he can't always do it.'

'If he doesn't do this then I'll kill him. This'll be his last chance, I'll kill him.'

This conversation between a nine-year-old and her mother was painful to witness. The mother knew it was highly likely the father would renege on his promise and was struggling both to let the child down gently and also to persuade the father to tell her sooner rather than later.

- As a parent, you will probably struggle to keep a balance between your guilt and your genuine concern that your child feels they remain the centre of your lives. Generally speaking, giving priority to an arrangement with your child may be one way that this message can be conveyed. That said, children are not running the show and all the adults will also need to lead their own lives.
- If for any reason a visit has to be cancelled, the child will need not only a careful explanation and reassurance of the parent's disappointment, but also an opportunity to express their feelings – sadness, disappointment, anger, resentment, rejection, etc., to both parents.
- A factual argument, *'I had to work, I'm really sorry'*, may be essential at the outset, but what the child also needs is a message that the parent understands how they feel, not just a justification of what has happened.
- Remember: to the child there may be no explanation good enough for a cancelled access visit.

> While consistency and reliability are always essential ele-
> ments of parenting, they become of prime importance
> following a divorce. Parents need to keep reminding children
> that they want to see them and to be scrupulous in keeping
> arrangements.

Nine-year-old Morag lived with her mother in Scotland. Her father
and his new family had moved to London when she was four years old.
Money was limited and, for various reasons, access visits difficult to
arrange, but every summer Morag spent two weeks with her father. For
three years this had been the only time she had seen him, though he
kept in touch by phone and letter. One summer he was unable to have
her for a variety of complicated matters in his current family. He was
as distraught as Morag about the matter, but attempts to console her
on the phone turned into rows and tantrums as he persisted with factual information, feeling increasingly guilty and defensive in the face of
her distress. *'Daddy doesn't love me,' she sobbed, 'he doesn't, or he'd come
and see me. I only go once a year, he'd let me go if he wanted to see me.'*

Morag's father was encouraged to absorb her pain and anger and
not to defend against it by explaining it away with the facts of the situation. She was able to have more sense of being held in mind by him
and feel more connected to him, and her rage gave way to sadness. It
was a harrowing experience for her parents, but they were both able to
help her make the best of it by accepting and sharing her feelings. Her
mother arranged other enjoyable treats for the holiday without trying
to pretend they were the same or as good as visiting Daddy.

Fun together or a waste of time?

For a child, the most worrying feeling can be that parents regard being
with them as a waste of time, and children will quickly construe cancelled arrangements as the parent having something better to do. Dora,
with whom this chapter opened, frequently overheard her mother
refusing invitations on the basis of *'Well, I've got the children.'* Dora

slowly built up a picture of a mother who would rather be accepting social invitations, but was constrained to spend time with her children. A vulnerable child may be quick to construe, *'I have to go to work'* as *' I don't want to be with you'*.

Go to sports day!

Parents' interest in their child's life outside home leads to a sense of pride, achievement and validation. In the general run of things, children can withstand parents not always being able to attend events such as sports day or prize-givings. However, after a divorce, a concrete way of showing children they are still the centre of the parent's life is to place extra emphasis on such attendances. The highlight of Dora's young life was when her father flew from a business meeting in Leeds to Bournemouth to hear her play the recorder in a school concert.

The less you had the more you need

Millie's mother was an air hostess who was frequently away from home, leaving Millie to be cared for by her father, who worked regular hours, and an au pair. When Millie was four, her parents separated and Millie remained living with her father. Her mother was an inconsistent and unreliable visitor, but her father felt unconcerned about this as, *'Millie's not used to seeing much of her mother, nothing has really changed for her in that respect.'*

It may sound paradoxical but the less Millie saw of her mother before the divorce, the more she needed to see her after the family split up. Children who have a warm, close and consistent contact with their parents absorb an internal picture of the parent and their relationship with them – *'Mummy in my heart and I can ask her questions'* – as one child described it. When a parent and child are separated, the child has the potential to enjoy a life independent of the parents, because there is a sense in which they carry the parent with them inside, giving a sense of support and security. Where there has been a less good relationship, the child may have a fragile sense of a 'Mummy in my heart'. They may feel they don't really know the parent enough to hold onto them in times of absence and need frequent contact to strengthen the relationship.

> The advantage of reliability is that when children are not pre-occupied with anxieties about when they may see the other parent, they seem to be able to live in the present and to adapt to their new situation.

When Daddy doesn't visit

'My daddy doesn't come to see us anymore, my daddy's forgotten all about us now.'

(Four-year-old)

Sometimes divorce will mean that children have to negotiate the fact that a parent may choose not to see them. This may be for a myriad of reasons. It may be that the relationship between the parents is just too difficult or hostile for one or both of them to cope with the contact. It may be that the parent cannot bear what they feel when they are in the presence of the child they have left. There may be complications with new partners and/or there may be a general feeling of confusion and bewilderment with one parent genuinely not knowing how to handle things. Sometimes a parent may mistakenly, but genuinely, feel that the child is better off not seeing them rather than struggling to keep the relationship going with both parents. And as one father said, *'I don't see them because it just gives their mother fuel to convince them even more that I'm the bad one.'*

If you can manage to make the new living and access arrangements for the children both tolerable and reliable, then your children are likely to cope. Things become more complicated when there is overt hostility between the parents.

The child as a weapon

Mr and Mrs A had decided to separate after nine years of marriage because of the husband's 'serial adultery'. Mrs A had frequently given him 'another chance', but had come to understand her husband's affairs as a symbol of his general reluctance to take on the responsibilities of family life. She felt he took less than his fair share of the tasks of home and childcare. Commuting to work, he frequently entertained clients in the city after work, arriving home in the early hours of the morning somewhat intoxicated. Sometimes he wouldn't come home, spending ill-afforded money on hotel bills.

Following the separation, he would often not visit the mother and two children from one weekend to the next. At the time the parents sought my help, the husband was about to move in with his current girlfriend, the family home was to be sold, and the mother and children were moving into a smaller property.

Both parents were anxious to handle the telling of the children in as constructive a manner as possible. In a discussion on access arrangements, the mother insisted she would not allow the children to meet her husband's girlfriend or to go to their shared home. As we unravelled this objection, she was appalled to realize that it was partly a way of getting back at her husband. She knew he had little idea how to entertain the children. By limiting access to treat days out and no overnight stays, she was restricting their relationship with their father. She quickly admitted her wish to punish him for his behaviour, but had not realized that she was asking her children to pay the price.

However, even in the best-regulated divorced households, children have to process overt or covert bitterness in the adults' relationship. It can be very difficult for a mother, who is receiving inadequate basic maintenance, not to communicate resentment as her children gleefully recount the extravagant expensive treats they have had with their father at the weekend. Most poignant is the single mother who has saved hard to buy her child a much coveted toy for Christmas, only to have the child return from a pre-Christmas visit to her father clutching the same!

As with every other situation, how children react will be age dependent as well as personality and family role dependent.

Sharing the care – coping with two homes

'I live with my mum from Monday to Thursday and then I go to my
dad. It's okay, I just have to remember where I am.'
'Remember where you are?'
'Yep, it's okay, I see both my parents but, like, my mum likes every-
thing tidy, and my dad doesn't care, so I have to remember to clear
my stuff up at my mum's.'
(Ten-year-old boy)

'During the week I live with my mum and then at the weekend I live
with my dad and that's alright but sometimes I forget to take things.'
(Seven-year-old girl)

'I want to go on holiday with my dad but my mummy's having a big
birthday party and she says it's okay I can choose what I do but I
can't choose, 'cos I don't want to let my mum or my dad down.'
(Eleven-year-old boy)

By encouraging the children to move between two separate families, parents can help to diminish any sense of loss which may accompany divorce. Shared custody is usually a result of both parents actively wanting the children in their homes. Going to Daddy because it is 'his turn' or 'to give Mummy a rest' is quite a different feeling to, *'My dad gets excited because I'm coming, and my mum always stays in Sunday nights 'cos I'm home again.'* However, even in the most well-managed households shared-custody children may need help with the potentially disturbing feelings of being perpetually on the move.

• Children can be helped to trust both environments by having their own room or special place in both homes.
• Ideally, possessions should be left in both bases, so the child has the minimum sense of, *'Being like my bag, I'm carried from place to place.'* Children may be confused at first at what should be kept where and may initially do a lot of chopping and changing. It can

be complicated for the parents, but what is important is that the child has an evolving sense of what goes where in his life.

• A ten-year-old found packing a suitcase every weekend almost intolerable in its symbolism of her split life. A very different experience from the child who says, '. . . *and then when I go into my bedroom, and I see my duvet and stuff, I know that I've been away but everything is still the same here.*' Such a child is likely to feel more in control of their life.

> There are many advantages of shared custody. Children are encouraged to have maximum involvement and contact with both parents and the parents may endeavour to continue a joint upbringing of the child and to be flexible in times of one parent's difficulty or illness.

Playing parents off against each other

At some time or another, all children will attempt to play one parent against the other, to their own advantage. Shared custody provides a potential minefield in this area. Children will try to manipulate parents for their own ends, *'Mummy says I can'* or *'Daddy lets me'*. They may also learn very quickly that one way of looking after their parents is to tell them what they want to hear about the other parent.

Dora's mother was extremely jealous of Dora's step-mother, feeling that the father provided much better materially for this wife than he had done for her. In times of stress, she would ply Dora on return from visits with questions about her step-mother's possessions. Dora quickly learnt that if she said that Joan had a new dress, her mother would be distressed, and so she began to think of more acceptable answers, such as, *'Daddy and Joan had a row 'cos Joan wanted a new dress.'* While this response decreased her mother's distress, it fuelled her mother's ever present rage against her father and made Dora feel both powerful and frightened in her relationship with her parents.

There may very well be different rules and expectations in the two homes, especially if there are step-parents involved. In life children are adapting all the time to different authorities – home, school, youth club, etc. Whilst children may seek to exploit the two different regimes, it can provide parents with a superb opportunity to show children that there is more than one way of doing things: *'But Daddy lets me have supper in front of the TV.'*

'Well, that's fine. Daddy lets you but I won't. It doesn't mean he's right and I'm wrong, or I'm right and he's wrong. It just means we're different.'

Remarriage

> *'Daddy's going to marry Clare, it's the pits, it's the absolute pits, that's the end . . . they'll never get back together now . . . that's it . . . never . . . never.'*
> *(A tearful nine-year-old whose parents had been separated for four years)*

When a couple remarries it has a huge impact on family and friends. Everyone within their separate and joint worlds is affected for better or worse. The couple themselves are likely to be full of happiness and hope and want everyone else to be happy and hopeful for them. Being in love has been described as a kind of madness and when mad, people very often presume that everybody else is feeling the same as them!

It is important for parents to take on board the significance of their remarriage for their children. Even when parents have been divorced for several years, consciously or unconsciously your child will have been wishing that you will get back together. Your divorce may only become absolute for your child when you tell them that you are going to remarry.

A thirty-four-year-old man described to me how his younger sister was getting married and wanted him to give her away. Their parents had divorced twenty years previously and they had seen little of their father since as he had moved to Spain. Consciously, this man thought the wedding would be a good opportunity for the family to meet up and also that his father should give his daughter away on her wedding day. He eventually persuaded his mother and sister to his point of view, but he arrived unhappy and distressed to his session after the wedding. He told how his mother had been sitting in the first seat of the front pew in church and he was sitting behind her in the second pew. After his father had given his sister away, he went to sit directly behind my patient. *'Hell,'* I thought, *'it's just like it was when I was a kid. I'm stuck in the middle between them.'* He went on to describe how his parents had barely exchanged a word all day. Through tears of sadness he realized that he had, unconsciously, been trying to get his parents together again at a wedding!

- Try to remember that your new partner and your child have, as one nine-year-old put it, *'crashed into each other's lives.'* You have chosen your partner to live with you; your child may well not have any choice in the matter.

- Perhaps the biggest influencing factor is the relationship between the separated parents. If you have managed to remain as a parental couple, as opposed to a sexual couple, and are able to be amicable in front of the children, then the children are likely to be able to have a sense of their parents being 'together' in their minds.

- This may mean the new partner is experienced less as a threat to their parents' relationship and it can help to avoid the common fantasy children may have, i.e., that their parents would have got back together had this new person not come along.

- It may be best to introduce your new partner gradually to the children to give them time and space to think, as well as feel, about what is happening.

- It is important for children to attend, and even take part in, the second marriage ceremony as this can help them to feel that they are going to continue to be a significant part in their parents' future life.

There is, of course, nothing wrong with children hoping their parents will get back together and some may need constant reminders that this is not going to happen. However, such a hope for some children can become almost a purpose for living and that is when the adults need to be concerned.

Reconstituted families

The less disruption a child has the easier it may be for them to settle into this new family. It can make a huge difference to a child whether or not they have to accept your partner and their children into your existing home or if they have to move into someone else's home. A child may adjust to step-family life more easily if they are able to maintain other important areas of their life such as their school and neighbours

Children will have their own unique reaction to becoming part of a reconstituted family. Hold in mind it is a different experience for every child even in the same family.

Reconstituted families and blood families are different

It is not always true that 'blood is thicker than water' but it does seem to be true generally in a reconstituted family. You will have to accept that your partner is unlikely to share your instinctive sense of protection towards your child and this is not only going to feel different to parenting with the other biological parent, it is going to make parenting a more complicated task.

As a step-parent you are likely to be approaching your partner's child with a loving determination to make this new family work. As one step-mother said, '*I was really prepared to bend over backwards to make it a success with the kids and it never crossed my mind that they might be determined that it was not going to work.*'

Surprise at your own reactions seems to be an integral part of parenting. You may find yourself actively disliking your step-child once you are living with them on a daily basis. Or you may find you scape-goat them for difficulties within the family or resent the time and attention your partner devotes to them and you may, of course, find that in spite of all your anxieties, you and your step-child can trans-form each other's lives!

Becoming a successful step-family takes time, patience and unbreakable goodwill on the adults' part. As you weave together the different relationships you will begin to realize that there is no such thing as a smooth path. There are always going to be patches of rough in step-families.

Try not to be too idealistic

'We thought everyone would be happy for us and be happy as well, but they weren't,' said a new step-mother tearfully as she recounted the struggle she was having with her two new step-children. They had had a par-ticularly traumatic few years living with their alcoholic mother and then coping with life with their depressed father after she left home. She had presumed that they would share her feelings of joy and hope in the new marriage as a second chance for a happy life. Such a hope may be unrealistic. Parents may have to find a way of living with the fact that their children may be much more preoccupied with strong and complex feelings which may include a conscious or an unconscious desire to sabotage your new relationship.

> All families have unrealistic expectations of each other at times. This may be even truer of step-families where every-thing is coloured by the joy and hope of a 'second chance'.

From the child's point of view

Children may be dealing with painful and conflicting feelings that they can't put into words. Children are intrinsically loyal to their biological parents and it is common for step-children to feel they are betraying their natural parent if they become fond of a step-parent. So children need time and space to develop relationships within the reconstituted family. Some will find it more difficult to adjust than others and they will show you in many ways but the most usual behaviours to be alert to are:

- Identity – *'Who am I in this new family?'*
- Increasingly needing to win or be first.
- Aggressive outbursts.
- Regressed behaviour.

Identity – *'Who am I in this new family?'*

As a result of divorce, children may have lost daily contact and sometimes all contact with one parent. In remarriage they will find they have to share their remaining parent with step-siblings. Not only that they may change their family position or status. One seven-year-old girl was furious to realize, *'Now I'm not the only girl anymore.'*

Increasingly needing to win or be first

Five-year-old Billy was already emerging as leader among his peers when his mother remarried and he gained two older step-brothers. He seemed happy enough with his new family but he became gradually more and more keen to be the best in everything at school. He would become unnecessarily angry and upset if he lost a game or felt someone else was praised more than him.

Aggressive outbursts

'Mark, I've told you three times . . .' Mark spun round on his astonished teacher: *'You're not my mum, you can't tell me anything,'* he shouted in rage. Sometimes children are so overwhelmed by their strong feelings that they need help to think about them rather than to act them out. Since his father had moved in with his step-mother, Mark had become aggressive and difficult towards both the other children and the staff at school. When his teacher discussed his behaviour with Mark's father she was surprised to hear that they were not experiencing the

aggressive behaviour at home. When I raised this with Mark he said, *'Well, there's no point, is there? Nothing's going to change.'* Mark was displacing his resentment of his step-mother and step-siblings onto children and his teachers. He was acting out his strong family feelings at school. He needed permission to feel what he was feeling – sad, jealous and angry. He needed time and space to understand how he felt. His parents tried to help him by giving him names for his feelings, for example, *'Lots of nine-year-olds have secret feelings about their step-siblings, some feel very jealous.'* They helped him to understand how he was confusing school and home and encouraged him to talk to them about how he felt.

Regressed behaviour

Four-year-old Trinny had begun ballet lessons a few months before her mother's second wedding. She was then hopelessly in love with the whole idea and practised every day. She couldn't wait for classes to begin once she arrived at school where it was held.

In the weeks following her remarriage, Trinny's mother noticed a change in her. She was just as excited about ballet but was reluctant to let go of her mother when she arrived at class. She would cling to her but at the same time would be looking longingly at the other children. Just as her mother thought she was about to join in, Trinny would hesitate, and then step back to her mother.

It can be painful for adults to tolerate the ambiguity and uncertainty involved in change, so it is not surprising that children can find it traumatic. Like Trinny they may act out what they are feeling, often regressing to an earlier stage of development. Trinny had been the baby in her family until her eighteen-month-old step-sister had joined them. I was not surprised to hear that since then she had had episodes of bedwetting.

How parents can help

- One of the tasks of a reconstituted family is to accept that they are not a nuclear family.
- Parenting is going to be interrupted daily by adjustments.

- Family members have to accept that changes are necessary for everyone to live in a healthy and happy way. They have to begin to work together to create new family rules, rituals and boundaries.
- The best way for children to learn how to be flexible, how to compromise and how to understand their own and other people's viewpoints is to have flexibility, compromise and understanding modelled by the adults surrounding them.
- Remind your child that they are special because of who they are, not because of their position in the family.

On being adult

I would like to leave the ending of this chapter to Tom's parents. On one visit they were describing the complexities of sharing the care of their two children. They were explaining how it had been much easier when both children were under six and didn't have their own independent social lives. They were describing how, as the children were growing up, they had painfully, and in some ways resentfully, agreed that the children's social life should take priority over theirs. So if Tom was invited to a birthday party on a Saturday when he was supposed to be visiting his father, then Tom would not be put in the position of having to choose, rather his father would make it his responsibility to get Tom to the party.

Potentially this caused a huge disruption in the parents' lives and a degree of acrimony with their respective new partners. However, as Tom's mother said: *'We have chosen to separate, and we must take the responsibility and help the children to cope with the consequences of our decision. They did not choose for us to separate, and we want to keep their lives going in as regular and normal way as possible. Our childcare arrangements work, but they work because the adults work very hard to make it work.'*

'Above all,' said Tom's father, *'we feel they should never have to choose between us. We try very hard to be cooperative and flexible in making our arrangements, even if sometimes we do it between gritted teeth.'*

It is so easy for parents, maybe stressed and unhappy themselves, to be drawn into childlike confrontations with each
other, particularly around arrangements for the children.
Children always and inevitably bring out the child in their
parents.

Believing in goodness

And so to Dora, whom you will remember opened this chapter with
her lack of belief in goodness. She was a deeply unhappy child who
vowed she would never marry, *"cos I don't want my children to know
about divorce.'* After a prolonged period of help she said one day, *'You
know, when my mum and dad split up it felt all jagged, and I didn't like
anybody . . . now . . . it's getting smooth and liking again.'*

'And why do you think that is?'

"Cos I tell you [how I feel] *. . . and you helped Mummy and Daddy to
understand and I thought they didn't.'*

Summary

- In divorce, the most challenging and creative question for parents is:
  'How can we help the children to make the best they can of it?'
- In divorce, families have to find out how they want to be together,
  and the ways in which this can be managed.
- It may not be possible to avoid painful disappointment during
  divorce, but there are other ways of thinking about divorce aside
  from success or failure.
- Telling the children together will reinforce the idea that parents
  may be intending to stay together as 'a parental couple', if not as
  lovers.
- In trying to explain to children why parents are separating, it is usually best to be as honest as possible and as simple as possible.
- No reason will be good enough in your children's minds for you to
  divorce.
- It is important to tell children that you know they cannot

understand why this is happening, and to acknowledge and hold their feelings of panic and bewilderment.

- Your child's predominant thought will be: 'What will happen to me now?'
- Children should never be asked to choose between their parents.
- Children cannot be expected to think rationally when their whole world has been turned upside down. Sometimes it is most helpful not to offer explanations, but to simply accept how the child feels.
- Surprise at your own strong feelings and reactions is an integral part of a step-parent's daily life.
- Try to keep a realistic perspective on step-family life.
- Reconstituted families are different from blood families.
- Parenting in a reconstituted family is going to be interrupted daily by adjustments.

CHAPTER 9

On Never Winning

– A Word to Working Mothers and Fathers –

*'I know now I'll never win . . . if he has problems it's because
of the childminder. If he does well, it's because of the
childminder.'*
(New mother returning to work)

*'I'm torn in two. I love my kids, I love my job. I can't stay at home,
we need the money, I'd go mad, but I end up feeling I don't do anything properly. I can't win.'*
(Working mother with three children)

*'We share the chores, we've worked it all out. We work it out every
Sunday evening. But when the stress is on, my job comes second
and he opts out of home. It's just presumed it's my job really to
run the home. He's the main breadwinner, so what can I do? I
can't win.'*
(Working mother)

Change and opportunity

'The past is a foreign country: they do things differently there.'
(The Go-Between, *L P Hartley*)

If we believe what we read, it was all so easy in the 1950s. Dad went out to work while Mum stayed at home and looked after the house and children. When Dad came home, Mum cooked a meal and the family sat around the dining room table sharing their day. Then Dad read his paper while Mum washed up. Everyone was happy. Or so we are told. Those of us raised in the 1950s may have other thoughts . . .

A young father was telling me of a row with his own father who was watching him bath his baby son. A conversation had begun about the young man's 'hands-on' involvement in his child's daily care, and as in the way with families, an argument began as the new father complained bitterly about the grandfather's lack of involvement in his life as a child.

'For instance,' he said, *'I don't ever remember you bathing me, you just used to come upstairs to stay goodnight when Mum told you to.'*

'I wasn't allowed to bath you.'

'What?'

'I wasn't allowed, it wasn't done . . . of course I wanted to, but it was your mother's job.'

Maybe parenting was easier in one way when each parent had a prescribed role. But that says nothing of the frustrations and disappointments felt by each partner and, because of the prevalent culture of the time, these frustrations may not even have been thought about, let alone expressed. A lively seventy-eight-year-old grandmother, very much the matriarch of her family, was watching TV coverage of the first woman in space. She caused much amusement in the family by suddenly bursting out: *'Oh, what a time girls have today! If I had had those opportunities . . . oh, what I could have done if I'd been born a young woman today.'* The fact is that fifties' mothers may have felt frustrated by being kept tied to the home. Fifties' fathers may have been frustrated at being kept distant from their children. Both sexes would have found it difficult to complain about their lot without feeling they were 'a bad parent' or running the risk of being construed by others as 'unnatural'.

The impact of choice

As we have already discussed in previous chapters, family life is now far more fluid. There are single parents who go out to work full-time and part-time; both parents may go out to work full-time; one parent may work full-time, one part-time; fathers go out to work while mothers stay at home; mothers go out to work while fathers stay at home; one or both parents may now work from home. Sharing the care of the children and household chores is much more common nowadays. Roles and choices available to both sexes are much more complex. While such choices bring freedom, they also bring complications and tensions. Some parents, particularly mothers, trying 'to have it all', often end up feeling that they have nothing. And this can only be exacerbated by the cult of the notion of the 'superwoman'; the idea that women can not only be lovers, mothers and career women, but they can balance and accomplish these roles perfectly.

> The life cycle of the working parent is conceived in huge changes in our society and it is fertilized by the fantasy that everyone can have it all. In fact we can't; life is a series of choices and making a relationship with the consequences.

Employers may also find themselves in a 'double bind'. On one hand they have become much more 'family friendly'. On the other hand, it sometimes seems as though employers have become more demanding and encourage people to work more than they should. We are now also having reports of a growing resentment of child-free couples that they are having to work longer, or antisocial, hours, to cover for employers' family-friendly policies. There is also resentment that 'family-friendly policies' do not necessarily cover employees who may be caring for elderly parents or an invalid or disabled partner.

Where there is no choice

In my clinical experience, it does sometimes seem as though guilt and parenting go hand in hand, especially for parents working outside the home. Parents can never do enough for their children and so you are always going to be left feeling that you are never doing enough.

How guilty you feel is likely to be dependent on how much choice you had about returning to work. There is a huge difference between a parent wanting to work outside the home and a parent feeling they have to work outside the home to keep finances afloat.

Parents seem to feel most guilty when, as one mother said, *'Well, we could manage financially if I didn't work . . . we could just about do it . . . but we like our lifestyle.'* This is a different kind of guilt from the parent who has no choice about working for financial necessity. They may be the sole provider of the family or may need a second income to raise their standard of living. Parents in such a situation may be pleased to be contributing to the family income, but may also feel frustrated and resentful at not being able to give the children what they feel they really need.

'We were so poor as kids . . . but we were rich, we got so much love and attention. But I can't give mine that. I know I should, but I'm so tired at the end of the day. It is really hard to start another job at 6 o'clock – listening to them and giving them attention – however much I love them.'

Just a housewife – should mothers be paid?
Of course, mothers work all the time; they do not decide 'to return to work' after childbirth; it can be argued that the decision is whether or not to extend your working hours by taking on a job outside the home. Like it or not, we live in a society in which we seem to equate value with financial reward. The more important someone's job in society's eyes, the more they are likely to be paid. And we can wonder what the huge incomes of celebrities, media personnel and City 'fat cats' says to our children today. Many mothers have to work, others choose to work, and others may not be able to feel enough self-worth doing the job of mothering, which is unpaid.

'I'm just a housewife.'
'Oh, I just look after the kids.'

Implicit in comments like these is: *'I'm of no real value.'* If mothers were paid for mothering, would the 'just a mother' feeling go away?

In June 2006 a You-Gov poll of 1,736 mothers in *First* magazine demonstrated how profoundly unhappy many mothers are with living a life torn between home and work. More than half felt guilty about time spent away from their children. Two-thirds thought that mothers should stay at home with their babies and toddlers during the first few years – though throughout Britain, less than half do so. A third wanted to reduce their working hours and more than a third said they would give up work altogether if they could. And forty-one per cent reported that they were not happy or confident with the care their children were receiving while they were at work.

Consider this:
- How do you want your children to describe you as parents when they are your age?
- If you were not working outside the home, how would your life be different? How would you organize your time?

Doing neither well
The quotations at the beginning of this chapter illustrate a common phenomenon among working mothers, i.e., the feeling of 'not winning' so what is the battle that is trying to be won?

Mothers may feel guilty if they enjoy their work and are glad to be out of the home. They may feel guilty if they do not really want to work outside the home, but it is a financial necessity. Maybe what is not being won is the status of 'super parent'. The idea is of a mother who manages to combine work and motherhood serenely and competently. At work she is conscientious and efficient; at home she is calm, warm and sympathetic. Of course, such 'super parents' do exist. However, without a very high income to pay for help of an excellent quality, for most women the struggle to keep all the balls in the air becomes a nightmare.

'I'm not so much a juggler, more a Greek plate smasher.'
(Exhausted working mother)

A good enough mother

So we can think of striving to be a perfect parent as a problem for the parent not for the child. What I mean is that parents seem to be driven by an internal demand to be perfect parents, rather than a demand coming from their child. There is a big difference between being 'good enough' and 'perfect'. Your ability to cope with this discrepancy will depend very much on how you feel about your own competence and disappointment.

> Winnicott has written that no child needs a perfect mother. All a child needs is a 'good enough mother'.

The last thing a busy working mother needs to do is to beat herself up for not being super-efficient. Accept that you are doing your best, that you can't be perfect, and you don't have to be. And, in any case, no child needs a perfect parent – such an experience could be utterly frustrating for the child! We would never learn about the shades of grey in life, about negotiating or about how to ask for what we need. This is a time to focus on the fact that you didn't choose your parents, I didn't choose my parents, we took what we got and we made the best of it and that's what children have to do.

From the child's point of view . . .

Quality time – or a bag of crisps?

We all benefit from individual time during which another person focuses on our needs and interests. The idea of 'quality time' in which parents spend short periods of time focused on their children has grown out of the hurly-burly days in the lives of most working parents. It has, of course, many advantages. Parents may feel relieved of their guilt of 'not doing either thing properly' and the children will thrive on having their parents preoccupied with nothing but them for a spell. Quality time is, of course, a good idea if you, the parent, are good at it. If you really enjoy playing children's games, etc., quality time is rewarding for you, but many parents simply do not like such activities. Also, it is impossible to promote intimacy at will. The idea of quality time is that it is a time for parent and child to be close and intimate, but closeness and intimacy have to be spontaneous.

And is 'quality time' what children really need? Perhaps one of the advantages of the fifties' home was that mother was likely to be available to children 'on demand'. Children would be getting on with their activities, and she would be getting on with household chores. But mother and child had instant access to each other. Perhaps what children most need are parents available to them, to focus on their interests and needs, when they want them to. As one mother said: *'She treats me like a bag of crisps, she dips into me when she feels like it.'* Some working mothers may feel stressed by such a comment, others may feel relieved that they don't always have to be planning quality time.

Of course it may suit children to have mother on demand, but mothers can't have children on demand. Many mothers feel bullied by the constant demands of their children. Children don't mean to bully; they are simply trying to get their needs met in order to survive, but their relentless demands and expectations can be exhausting. The late Dr Hugh Jolly helped mothers to feel less bullied by their children by refusing to use the phrase 'feeding on demand', changing it to 'feeding on request'.

Quality time with a child really does have to be *quality* time. Eight-year-old Candice was referred to me on account of her demanding and attention-seeking behaviour. Her mother was puzzled; she admitted she worked long hours outside the home, but always cleared two hours when Candice came home from school for quality time with her: *'And we don't just do homework, I play board games with her.'*

'Yes,' interrupted Candice sadly, *'but you are always writing things down.'* It seemed clear to Candice that even though her mother was spending time with her, her mind was still focused on her work.

'My mum really likes work'

Children quickly get into a muddle. If you have to spend a lot of time on work, particularly at evenings or weekends when your child is around, then they may draw the conclusion that you would rather work than be with them. Children are not open, on the whole, to reasonable discussions about why parents must have other preoccupations than them. The feeling is likely to be that if Mum and Dad liked me they would want to be with me.

- It is important to explain to your children that you too are disappointed when you are not able to spend much time with them because of work commitments. Give a simple factual explanation of the work situation, but focus on how disappointing it is for you both not to be able to spend time together. Try to give the children something to look forward to – but be realistic. Do not promise to take them to the cinema next Saturday unless you are very sure the work pressures will be over by then. While you are waiting for the treat, throw into the conversation: *'I'm really looking forward to next Saturday when we are going to the pictures together.'*
- You may need to remind both the children and yourself that you do not stop being a parent just because you are at work. Obviously, you will be focused on work but you still have a 'space in your mind' for your children in that, at any given moment, you will be able to conjure up all their needs and abilities. Remembering this from time to time may help you to feel less guilty and throwing comments into the conversation in the evening like, *'While I was at work I was thinking about you'* will help to remind the children also.

The parental child

It is inevitable in most busy households that a responsible child, usually the oldest child, will be relied upon to take on some of the minor household chores. While it is important that all family members take their fair share of responsibility, it is not helpful if a responsible child becomes 'a prop' for the working parents. No childhood is perfect, but children who become substitute parents to younger children can feel robbed of their childhood. Making one child responsible for the others may also upset the balance in a family; the older child may feel burdened and resentful, which may result in bullying of the younger children. In their turn, younger children may feel angry and resentful of the older child because they cannot possibly be a 'good enough parent'. You may need to resist the temptation to leave one child 'in charge'. It may be more helpful to leave all the children with specific tasks and responsibilities.

The parental child may be a necessary and integral part of some families. For many they may be the best childcare available. When a parental child is given special privileges or rewards for their role then they may feel they have a special place in the family. They may feel that there is an advantage in feeling closer to both their parents and their siblings.

The exhausted parent – there's nothing wrong with not coping

Exhaustion seems to be an occupational hazard of parenting! A mother once described herself to me as 'an eternal honey pot'. She felt that she had to go on doling out spoonful after spoonful of sweetness all day every day. We all know that the more spoonfuls you take out of a honey pot, the emptier it becomes, and the fact is the more exhausted you become, the more disenchanted with life you are likely to become. You owe it to your family to look after yourself, but most of all you owe it to yourself.

Parenting may involve self-sacrifice, but it should not equate with it. There is nothing wrong with not coping even if it feels as though there is everything wrong with it.

Everybody gains in a family if the parents look after themselves and perhaps one of the most difficult tasks of being a parent is to remember to parent yourself.

Ask for help

Sometimes feeling you are not coping is a way of sending a message to other members of the family that, *'I need looking after as well.'* The risk is that when parents are feeling overstretched they express it to each other in frustration and accusations. There is all the difference in the world in saying to a partner, *'You never help with bedtime . . .'* and *'I'm really tired, could you help with bedtime tonight?'*

High expectations are all well and good if you can keep to them relatively easily. There is no point in feeling guilty if you can't get it all done, nobody can; there is a limit to what any one person can take on and you will do more some days than others.

An exhausted parent can be a real source of worry to a child. Again, your child is likely to construe your exhaustion as their fault, or they may well misconstrue your exhaustion as a lack of interest in them, or distaste for them. One seven-year-old girl used to hear her mother on the telephone saying that work was sending her 'stir crazy'. Her mother was horrified and realized just how 'tired and snappy' she had been when her daughter asked, *'Am I driving you stir fry crazy?'*

- When you are exhausted, explain to your children that it is not their fault, and that they are not expected to remedy it. When you feel you've got it wrong, explain to them that however it feels to them, they are not the problem or at fault. Explain that you want to give them your time and attention, and are disappointed when you feel tired after work and become irritable with them.

- Explain to them how you are going to cure your tiredness: for example, *'I'm going to have an early night tonight.'* There is a difference between enabling children to feel they can help with your exhaustion, and making them feel they have to cure your exhaustion. Saying, *'I'm worn out, working all day, and looking after you kids'* is very different from saying, *'I know I'm snapping at you. I'm very tired, and what would help us to have a better time together would be if you would help me to load the dishwasher.'*

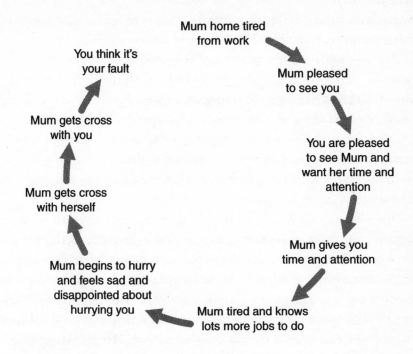

On planning to be a working mother

It is possible that balancing home and work demands is likely to go more smoothly if you plan as much as possible in advance. That said, this is much more of an emotional than a logistical experience and we can't organize feelings out of the way however desirable it may be! There is always going to be the unforeseen to cope with, but making as many safety nets as possible can help to reduce tensions. The secret seems to lie in careful planning, but somehow being able to maintain enough mental flexibility to allow your plans to be disrupted. As one mother said: *'We can cope when plan A doesn't work, we can cope when plan B doesn't work, it's when we get to plan F we start to panic.'*

Before beginning to plan, it is worth considering some of the unconscious reasons colouring any person's decision to work outside the home or not. Some people choose to stay at home and look after the children more as a refuge from work than because they really want to be a full-time parent. Other people may choose to go to work as a refuge from their children! I remember expressing surprise to a friend when she told me she was expecting her third child. Previously she had said she was only going to have two.

'Yes,' she said, 'but it was that or getting a job!'

Emotional advantages of going to work
- We don't have to be so involved with emotional needs.
- We usually understand the task in front of us and we have the possibility of feeling competent at the end of the day.
- Work enables parents to identify themselves as not exclusively a parent.

Emotional risks of staying home to look after the children
- We run a real risk of feeling incompetent in our daily job.
- Parenting is a much more fluid experience; we are constantly involved in emotions and may be asked to do things on a daily basis which we have no previous experience of doing. We may feel that we have removed ourselves from specific competition regarding success, money, status but, whether we like it or not, are entering a new competition as to who is the best parent.

The importance of planning
- If you are working at home, does the fact that you are on the premises mean your family has instant access to you? Both your children and your partner may find it difficult to adjust to the idea that a mother working at home has to maintain strict boundaries around her work. Because she is in the house, it doesn't necessarily mean that she is available to the family. The same can be true of a father who is working at home.
- Who is going to take responsibility for looking after your relationship, ensuring that you make time for each other, have a social life, and enjoy some purely adult activities? This may be particularly important where both parents have full-time jobs. Your priorities will probably be your children and your job, and 'couple time' is likely to become a scarcity unless it is planned.

- Think about your first day back at work. How are you going to feel if you miss the baby? How are you going to feel if you don't miss the baby?
- Single working mothers need to plan where and how they are going to get their adult support and social life.

> Before returning to work, list your priorities as a family. In what order would you place such things as money, time together, expensive treats and holidays, etc.? How are you going to maintain these priorities?

Accept you are going to feel exploited sometimes

Realistically, there are bound to be frustrations and disappointments if you are both working outside the home full-time. Being realistic about that fact can be a great relief. Accept that from time to time one or both of you is going to feel upset and put upon. Balancing parenthood and work is bound to involve compromise and you are going to reach the best compromises by being articulate about your needs. Saying you feel overstretched, put upon or tired out is not a sign of weakness, but try to remember what I said earlier in the chapter about not talking to your partner solely in accusations.

> Try not to involve the children in your resentments. Saying, *'I've worked all day long, but your dad will never load the dish-washer'* is not helpful. Your child will only feel that they have got to take sides or become 'a parent to the parent'. One ten-year-old boy said, *'Mum works so hard for us, I feel sorry for her. I try to help her by keeping the others quiet and things but . . .'*

The twilight and night shifts

Most parents will agree that when it comes to balancing home/work life, two of the most stressful times in the day are the hours around

4.30–6.30p.m., the twilight shift, and the 'night shift' with its constant interruptions to sleep. The twilight shift is when the children arrive home from school, you arrive home from work, supper has to be prepared, homework has to be done, and it is also highly likely that some children will need to be ferried to and from an out-of-school activity. These two focal points in the day need to be planned and arrangements need to be constantly discussed and renewed. You will need to bear in mind that at the twilight shift it is likely to be the same parent on duty every day. What happens when the other parent arrives home? Are you going to hand over the children to them before they can even get their coats off because your head is 'done in'? If so, how does the other parent feel about that and how do you feel about it if they request a breathing space between finishing work and taking up home duties?

The night shift, it seems, can make or break a parental relationship! Parents can have very different relationships with sleep; some people need lots of sleep and others can manage on very little. In parenting, what can be guaranteed is that it is likely, particularly in the early days, that everyone is going to feel very, very tired and that everyone will need time off for sleep.

Advantages of a working mother

A seven-year-old tomboy was struggling with her feelings that *'boys get a better deal than girls'*. With two strong, attractive and clever, much older, brothers, she saw few advantages in being the girl in the family. Her father had a glamorous and exciting job, and she was something of a bully to her somewhat gentle-natured mother. Things began to change when her mother eventually took a job outside the family home. Several months later, on returning from the first family holiday, she drew a picture of her mother in a bikini, holding a briefcase. *'My mum is a lady, she goes to work'* she wrote.

Both parents and children are likely to be ambivalent about mother working outside the home. However, as this little girl discovered, it can provide children with an opportunity to see their mother as an independent person, who can do other things as well as mothering. By providing children with such a role model, it is possible that a working mother may encourage girls, in particular, to grow up and achieve adult skills. Girls are offered a broader spectrum in their future as a woman and may realize very early on that there are many ways of being a woman. Of course, such a thought is more likely to be helpful to a child at say six to seven years old, than at six to seven months old.

Fathers who share the care and fathers who don't

Boys today are also being exposed to a smorgasbord of ways of being a man. Many fathers thoroughly enjoy sharing the care of their children. Others genuinely want to support and validate their offspring by attending such events as school plays and sports days; some enjoy the role of being a full-time father. But we need to remember that shifts in thinking about a father's role are relatively recent. Many fathers trying to share the care will not have had fathers who did so and this is important because men learn how to be a father from their own father. We should not presume that sharing the care is something all men (or women) can do easily or naturally. Like all aspects of parenting, it is something people have to make up as they go along. Nor should we presume that sharing the care is the best or only way of being a father. *'I'm saving this to show my daddy,'* said a five-year-old repeatedly on a day out with her aunt. Children take enormous pleasure in saving up stories and treasures to share with their parents. The father who cannot attend sports days, or doesn't want to, may be just as emotionally involved in the event when he takes a genuine interest in the child's report of it later in the day. Indeed, not attending such events should not necessarily be taken as lack of interest or involvement or indeed a matter of 'wrong priorities'. For many people the working day is long and arduous and taking time off for school events sometimes just places 'family time' under more pressure later on in the week. One father explained ruefully how he had to work two Saturday mornings in a row to make up time for his three children's school plays. Another father desperately wanted to see his son sing his first solo part in the school musical. As he watched for his entrance, he was so preoccupied mentally with the work he had left behind that he missed it and just caught the last few bars of the solo!

There are ways in which it is useful to share the care and ways in which it is not. There is a difference between a father and a mother and children are connected to their mothers and fathers in different ways: for example, they are physically connected to their mother for the first nine months of their lives in ways that they are not connected to their father. What matters to the child is the extent of each parent's emotional involvement in their lives.

Having fun together

When you decided to have children you thought it would be fun. The risk in families is that children have fun, and adults have fun with children. What can get lost is the idea of adults having fun together. In the hurly-burly of family and working life, it seems as though the highest casualty is time alone for you as parents. Part of your planning in returning or continuing to work after the arrival of the children must include the question: 'Who is going to look after our relationship?' Couples have to choose what they are going to look after. How this is arranged will differ from couple to couple. It is simply a question of ensuring that you have time together to do what you genuinely enjoy doing together. It is also a question of having time for solo projects. By one of you taking responsibility for planning your time together, be it arranging a babysitter, or simply noticing what is on at the local cinema, or planning a dinner party or an evening at the pub, time together will be ensured. The paradox is that by one of you taking responsibility for this, the other is somehow freed to also come up with ideas.

And what should adults do with their time alone, and what should they talk about? So often parents will tell me that when they do have time alone, they spend it talking about the children! One young couple were excitedly looking forward to the prospect of their two young children spending their first Saturday night away with grandparents. In the event, they didn't go out for the evening because *'We thought we'd better stay by the phone in case the children rang.'* Of course, it is important to share focused thought and attention on your children, but it is also important to give focused thought and attention to looking after each other, as opposed to the family as a whole.

Single parents

This chapter has been written very much from the viewpoint of mothers within a couple deciding to return to work. Of course, all the points raised are equally applicable to lone mothers – and fathers. One of the most difficult aspects of a single parent's life is finding adult support for themselves and the time, and sometimes the effort, to enjoy adult company. This is a difficult but essential task.

Summary

- Mothers who work outside the home may feel that they do neither mothering nor their paid work properly.
- Mothers who have to work outside the home for financial reasons may feel frustrated and resentful at not being able to give their children the emotional support they feel they could give if they were a full-time mother.
- Would mothering be more valued if it were paid?
- Winnicott has written that no child needs a perfect mother. All a child needs is a 'good enough' mother.
- There is nothing wrong with not coping.
- If you feel you are not coping, explain to your children that it is not their fault, and that you do not expect them to put it right.
- Do children need 'quality time' or do they need parents they can 'dip into' as and when they want – or do they need both?
- If you are preoccupied with work, the children may worry that you enjoy working more than being with them.
- We should not presume that sharing the care is something that all men (or women) can do easily or naturally.
- Many fathers trying to share the care will not have had fathers who did so and this is important because men learn how to be a father from their own fathers.

- We should not presume that sharing the care is the best or only way of being a father.
- Accept that if you are both working outside the home from time to time both of you will feel overstretched and put upon. Try to ask for help rather than hurl accusations about your partner's lack of contribution.
- Parenting may involve self-sacrifice but it should not equate with it; make time for yourself.

References

Ainsworth, N. D. S. & Wittig, B. A., 'Attachment and Exploratory Behaviour of One-Year-Olds in a Strange Situation', in B. W. Foss (ed.), *Determination of Behaviour IV*, Methuen (1969)

Ayolan, O. & Slasher, A. A., *Chain Reaction – Children and Divorce*, Jessica Kingsley (1993)

Bowlby, J., *Attachment & Loss – Volume 2: Separation, Anxiety & Anger*, Hogarth Press (1973)

Bowlby, J., *The Making and Breaking of Affectional Bonds*, Routledge (1994)

Chiltern-Pierce, J., *The Magical Child*, Penguin (March 1992)

Chittenden, M., 'Mothers Boycott Pole Dancing Toy', *Sunday Times*, 4 March 2007

Cox, M., Personal communication with the author

Dasheu, S. & L., *Mariners' Weather Handbook*, Beowulf Inc., Arizona, USA (1998)

Daws, D., *Through the Night: Helping Parents and Sleepless Infants*, Free Association Books (1989)

Dunn, J. & Deater-Deckard, K., *Children's Views of Their Changing Families*, YPS (2001)

Durant, V. M. & Mindell, J. A., 'Behavioural Treatment of Multiple Childhood Sleep Disorders', *Behaviour Modification* (1990: 14: 37–39)

Edgecombe, R., 'The Border Between Therapy and Education' – lecture delivered to The Forum for the Advancement of Educational Therapy, 22 June 1977

Eigen, M., Personal communication to Adam Phillips

Erikson, E. H., *Childhood and Society*, Vintage (1965)

Freud, S., *Jokes and Their Relation to the Unconscious*, Penguin Books (1976)

_____, *Dreams and the Unconscious*, Penguin Books (1976)

Freud, A., *Psycho-Analysis for Teachers and Parents*, Emerson Books Inc. (1977)

Hartley, L. P., *The Go-Between*, Penguin (1953)

Haslam, B., *Stress Free Parenting*, Vermilion (1998)

Hill, A. J. & Franklin, J. A., 'Mothers, Daughters and Dieting: Investigating the Transmission of Weight Control', *British Journal of Clinical Psychology* (1998) 37, 3–13

Hill, A. J., 'Developmental Issues in Attitudes to Food and Diet', in *Proceedings of the Nutrition Society* (2002) 61, 259–266

Hill, A. J. & Pallin, V. V., 'Dieting Awareness and Low Self-Worth: Related Issues in 8-Year-Old Girls', Division of Psychiatry and Behavioural Sciences, School of Medicine, University of Leeds, May 1997

Hobson, R., 'Loneliness', in *Journal of Analytical Psychology*, Volume 19, no.1 (1974)

Keenan, B., *An Evil Cradling*, Vintage (1993)

Klein, M., *Love, Guilt and Reparation and Other Works*, Hogarth Press (1975)

_____, *Envy and Gratitude*, Hogarth Press (1975)

Leach, P., *Your Baby and Child*, Penguin Books (1997)

Lusseyran, J., *What One Sees Without Eyes*, Floris Books (1999)

Luxmoore, N., *Listening to Young People in School, Youth Work and Counselling*, Jessica Kingsley (2000)

Maher, M., 'Bullying – The Lover, The Pimp and The Coward' in *Educational Therapy & Therapeutic Teaching*, Issue no.3, March 1994

Milne, A. A., *Now We are Six*, Methuen (1960)

Phillips, A., Personal communication with the author (1990)

_____, *Terrors & Experts,* Faber & Faber (1996)

_____, *On Kissing, Tickling & Being Bored,* Harvard University Press (1993) and Faber & Faber (1993)

Richman, N. & Lansdown, R., *Problems of Pre-School Children,* John Wiley (1988)

Shakespeare, W., *Henry V*

_____, *Love's Labour's Lost*

_____, *King Lear*

_____, *The Tempest*

Sinason, V., 'Face Values', in *Free Association,* (1985) 2, 75–93

'Little Girl Chic', *Sunday Times,* 6 April 2003

The Concise Oxford Dictionary of Current English, The Clarendon Press

Weldon, F., *Independent on Sunday,* 5 May 1991

Williams, Y., Personal communication with the author (1998)

Wilson, O. H. M., 'Peace at Last: A Model of Sleep Management for Parents', *Health Visitor* 1996; 69, 12: 491–492

Wilson, T., *Working Parents' Companion,* NCT (1999)

Winnicott, D. W., *The Maturational Process and the Facilitating Environment,* Karnac (1990)

_____, *The Child, the Family and the Outside World,* Tavistock (1957)

_____, *Deprivation and Delinquency,* Tavistock, Routledge (1990)

_____, *Playing and Reality',* Tavistock (1982)

_____, *The Family and Individual Development',* Tavistock (1968)

Suggested Further Reading

Books for Parents

Biddulph, S., *The Secret of Happy Children*, Thorsons (1998)

Brasman, A. H., *Can You Help Me? – A Guide for Parents*, Karnac (2004)

Bryant-Waugh, R. & Lask, B., *Eating Disorders: A Parent's Guide*, Penguin (1999)

Clifford-Poston, A., *Tweens: What to expect from – and how to survive – your child's pre-teen years*, Oneworld Publications (2005)

Cowley, S., *Getting Your Little Darlings to Behave*, Continuum (2004)

Haslam, D., *Stress Free Parenting – How to Survive the 0–5s*, Vermilion (1998)

Knox, D. & Leggett, K., *Divorced Dads' Survival Guide: How to Stay Connected with Your Kids*, Perseus Books (2000)

Leach, P., *Getting Positive About Discipline: A Guide for Today's Parents*, Barnardos Booklet (1997)

Lewis, D., *Helping Your Anxious Child*, Cedar (1993)

Parker, J. & Stimpson, J., *Sibling Rivalry, Sibling Love*, Hodder Mobius (2002)

Pearce, J., *Fighting, Teasing and Bullying: Simple and Effective Ways to Help Your Child*, Thorsons (1989)

The Children's Society, 'My Child Still Won't Eat' – booklet containing useful general tips and insights despite being focused on younger children, (2001)

Wilson, T., *Working Parents Companion*, NCT (1999)

Youngminds, 'Keeping in Touch: How to Help Your Child After Separation and Divorce', 'Youngminds' booklet (2003)

General Books

Ayolan, O. & Flasher, A., *Chain Reaction – Children and Divorce*, Jessica Kingsley (1993)

Bowlby, J., *The Making and Breaking of Affectional Bonds*, Routledge (1994)

Erickson, E. H., *Childhood and Society*, Penguin (1969)

Freud, A., *Psycho-Analysis for Teachers and Parents*, Emerson Books Inc. (1977)

Mitchell, J., *Siblings, Sex and Violence*, Polity Press (2003)

Winnicott, D. W., *The Child, the Family and the Outside World*, Penguin Books (1984)

Useful Addresses

National Family & Parenting Institute
Online database for parenting and family support services.
Website: www.nfpi.org.uk

Parentline Plus
Support service for parents.
Website: www.parentlineplus.org.uk
Helpline: 0808 800 2222

Anti-Bullying Campaign (ABC)
Advice and support service with trained counsellors.
Helpline: 020 7378 1446

Babycentre
Website offering the opportunity to make contact with other parents
with children of the same age.
Website: www.babycentre.co.uk

One Parent Families
Advice, support and information for single-parent families.
Website: www.oneparentfamilies.org.uk
Helpline: 0800 018 5026

Kidscape
Charity to help with bullying and child abuse.
Website: www.kidscape.org.uk
Helpline: 08451 205204

Author Biography

Andrea Clifford-Poston M.Ed.
Educational Psychotherapist (UKCP registered)
Diploma in Child Development (London University)
Teacher's Certificate (London University)

Andrea Clifford-Poston is an Educational Psychotherapist (UKCP registered) with over thirty years' experience of working with children and parents in schools, clinics, hospitals and the home. Andrea trained initially as a primary school teacher and taught in various London schools. For sixteen years she was the Teacher in Charge at the Child Development Centre, Charing Cross Hospital, and for many years a visiting lecturer to the Music Therapy Training Course at the Roehampton Institute.

Andrea was a regular guest expert on the *Times* Parent Forum and has contributed to articles in a number of leading childcare magazines, including *Nursery World*, for whom she wrote regular monthly articles for four years. For the past fourteen years she has been in private practice as a Child & Family Mental Health Specialist. She is a member of the Guildford Centre for Psychotherapy. Her book *Tweens: What to Expect From – and How to Survive – Your Child's Pre-Teen Years*, Oneworld Publications, was shortlisted for the IPPY Prize in the USA in May 2006.

Index